D1714691

I'M FROM THE GOVERNMENT

GOVERNMENT

AND

I'M HERE

TO KILL YOU

I'M FROM THE GOVERNMENT

AND

I'M HERE

TO KILL YOU

THE TRUE HUMAN COST
OF OFFICIAL NEGLIGENCE

DAVID T. HARDY

Skyhorse Publishing

CONTENTS

Introduction: "The King Can Do No Wrong"   1

CHAPTER 1 Texas City: A City Leveled, Six Hundred Dead   9

CHAPTER 2 Western United States: Atomic Testing Poisons the
Land and the People   25

CHAPTER 3 Tuskegee, Alabama: Dying "for the Glory of Science"   43

CHAPTER 4 Ruby Ridge, Idaho: FBI Obeys "Shoot on Sight"
Orders   61

CHAPTER 5 Waco, Texas: "It's Showtime!"   87

CHAPTER 6 Looking for Terror in All the Wrong Places   115

CHAPTER 7 Arizona: Operation Fast and Furious Arms the
Drug Cartels   135

CHAPTER 8 The Militarization of Police: Tanks, Bayonets, and
Grenade Launchers   163

CHAPTER 9 The Department of Veterans Affairs Kills Veterans   175

Conclusion: Putting a Leash on the Deadly Bureaucracy   185

Appendix: Proposed Reform of Federal Law   203

Endnotes   207

Acknowledgments   241

Index   243

"THE KING CAN DO NO WRONG"

The United States was established by the Declaration of Independence, a document whose central theme was the official wrongdoing of the King of England and his servants. The leaders of the colonies declared that Americans had rights to "life, liberty, and the pursuit of happiness" and accused King George of "repeated injuries and usurpations" that made him "unfit to be the ruler of a free people." The Declaration itemized King George's "long train of abuses and usurpations," including that he had "sent hither swarms of officers to harass our people and eat out their substance," had "obstructed the administration of justice," and had "plundered our seas, ravaged our Coasts, burnt our towns, and destroyed the lives of our people."

The proposition that a king, a government, *can* do wrong is central to the Declaration, America's foundational document. So how did America get to a situation where government employees, "public servants," can kill by sheer sloppiness and walk away? Where an agency can level a town and kill six hundred citizens and escape all responsibility? Where a federal agency can run guns to Mexican drug cartels, causing hundreds of deaths on both sides of the border, and wash its hands of the matter? Where veterans can die awaiting doctors' appointments, and the hospital administrators can collect their bonuses and walk away?

Answering these questions requires a brief look at legal history. English common law developed the concept of "sovereign immunity," commonly expressed as "the King can do no wrong." But common-law sovereign immunity was actually a narrow concept. A subject could not sue or prosecute the king, but could take legal action against anyone carrying out the king's orders. Americans could better hold their government accountable when they were ruled by George III than they can today!

As the great English jurist William Blackstone expressed the concept two centuries ago, drawing a line between the king and the government:

> The King can do no wrong. Which ancient and fundamental maxim is not to be understood as if everything transacted by the government was of course just and lawful, but means only two things: First, that whatever is exceptionable in the conduct of public affairs is not to be imputed to the King, nor is he answerable for it personally to the people. . . . And secondly, it means that the prerogative of the Crown extends not to do any injury; it is created for the benefit of the people and therefore cannot be exerted to their prejudice . . .[1]

Therefore, in English law, the government and its employees *can* do wrong; it is only the *king* who cannot. Blackstone continued, "The King, moreover, is not only incapable of doing wrong, but even of thinking wrong: he can never mean to do an improper thing." Since the king cannot even *think* of doing wrong, a government official could not plead, "I was just following orders." The courts would not let a royal employee claim that the king gave an illegal or wrongful order, so the full blame must fall upon those lower officials who harmed his subjects. Thus, after the Boston Massacre, the Massachusetts colonists had no trouble prosecuting redcoats for homicide; thus, their English hero, John Wilkes, successfully sued Lord Halifax for illegal arrest—*even though George III had personally ordered Halifax to have Wilkes arrested.* As one American colonist put it, "If the King can do no wrong, his ministers may; and when they do wrong, they should be hanged."[2]

How strongly our ancestors, and their opponents, felt about this can be gauged from their reactions to the prosecutions of soldiers after the Boston Massacre, when Massachusetts charged nine redcoats with murder and convicted two of manslaughter. Even George III and his Parliament did not feel they could go so far as to forbid such local prosecutions. They did pass the Administration of Justice Act, which allowed Massachusetts's colonial governor to transfer a prosecution of a Crown servant to another colony, or to England, if he felt the servant could not get a fair trial in Massachusetts.

A colony could still prosecute royal officials for murder, but the idea that the officials could get a change of venue so outraged the colonists that they labeled this law one of the "Intolerable Acts" and condemned it in the

Declaration of Independence: King George III had protected his soldiers "by a mock Trial, from punishment for any Murders which they should commit on the Inhabitants of these States."

THE AMERICAN EXPERIENCE: OUR OWN COURTS CREATE BROAD SOVEREIGN IMMUNITY

One might have thought the premise "the King can do no wrong" would have no application in a nation with no king, but that is not how things turned out. Indeed, by the time our courts finished, they had immunized government officials high and low from liability for any wrongful injuries they inflicted upon the citizens who paid their salaries.

In the early U.S. courts, the issue of sovereign immunity rarely arose, probably because the main civilian federal functions—running post offices, issuing land grants, and handling military pensions—would seldom generate lawsuits for damages. In an 1834 Supreme Court case, Chief Justice John Marshall noted (with no citation of legal authority) that "the United States are not suable of common right," but allowed the suit since Congress had consented to it.[3] Not until 1868 was sovereign immunity actually used to block a lawsuit, with the Supreme Court stating that "the public service would be hindered, and the public safety endangered," if the government could be sued for injuring its citizens.[4]

Sovereign immunity briefly came under question in 1882, when the Supreme Court allowed the heirs of Robert E. Lee to sue over the wartime confiscation of his Arlington, Virginia, estate, where the Arlington National Cemetery is now located. In *United States v. Lee*[5] the Court, by a narrow 5–4 vote, concluded that governmental immunity had little place in the American system of government: we had no king, and the idea that government would be burdened or inconvenienced by lawsuits was undermined by the fact that the government itself sued its citizens whenever it wanted to. Writing for the majority, Justice Samuel Miller argued, "No man in this country is so high that he is above the law. No officer of the law may set that law at defiance with impunity. All the officers of the government, from the highest to the lowest, are creatures of the law and are bound to obey it."[6]

This understanding did not last. Fourteen years later, the Court's composition had changed: of the five Justices who had ruled for the Lee family, only one was still on the Court. Now the Court had no hesitation proclaiming, as "an axiom of our jurisprudence," that "the government is not liable to suit unless it consents thereto, and its liability in suit cannot be extended beyond the plain language of the statute authorizing it."[7] The ruling in *United States v. Lee* was simply ignored. (The Court would ultimately dispose of *United States v. Lee* by using its favored tool in dealing with undesired precedent: limiting it to its facts and refusing to apply its principles more broadly. The Court held that *United States v. Lee* would only apply where the government had violated the Fifth Amendment by "taking" property without just compensation and not in any other context.)[8]

In parallel with civil immunity, the Supreme Court gave federal officials blanket immunity with regard to criminal matters. In 1890, the Court ruled that California could not prosecute a Deputy U.S. Marshal who, while guarding a Supreme Court Justice, fatally shot an unarmed man. The person shot was attorney David Terry, former Chief Justice of the California Supreme Court. He had been angered by Justice Stephen Field's ruling in a case involving Terry's wife. Both jurists were early pioneers and no strangers to violence; indeed, Field had jailed Terry for contempt, after Terry punched out a Marshal and drew a bowie knife in Field's courtroom. Encountering Field in a train station restaurant, Terry slapped him in the face, and Marshal David Neagle shot Terry down. Neagle claimed that Terry had put his hand into his coat and he feared that Terry was drawing a bowie knife.[9] Terry turned out to be unarmed, and California authorities apparently doubted the Marshal's story. Both Neagle and Justice Field were arrested on murder charges, although Field's prosecution was later quietly dropped.

The Supreme Court (with Justice Terry abstaining, of course) ruled that Neagle could not be prosecuted by state authorities for what he had done in the line of federal duty: "in taking the life of Terry, under the circumstances, he was acting under the authority of the law of the United States, and was justified in so doing; and that he is not liable to answer in the courts of California on account of his part in that transaction."[10]

Both the cases establishing civil sovereign immunity and those creating its criminal law equivalent remain good law to this day (*Neagle* was in fact cited repeatedly in the 2001–2003 "torture papers," which sought to justify use of torture on terrorism suspects in Iraq. If federal employees could kill a citizen, the reasoning went, they surely must be able to waterboard a noncitizen).[11] Except where the government consents, federal employees can neither be sued nor prosecuted for their official actions.

GOVERNMENT KILLS WITH IMMUNITY

Governing without responsibility was convenient for the governing class, if sometimes fatal for the governed.

During the Prohibition Era, it was still permissible to sell denatured alcohol for industrial use. Manufacturers initially denatured grain alcohol by adding chemicals that ruined the taste or emetics that nauseated the drinker. But bootleggers found ways to purify the denatured alcohol and make it drinkable.

The government responded by ordering manufacturers to add poisons to their product—methyl alcohol, which attacks the optic nerve; mercury salts, which damage the brain, kidneys, and lungs; and benzene, which attacks the bone marrow.

In the first two years, New York City alone experienced a thousand deaths from the new brew, with thousands more left blind. Professor Deborah Blum notes, "By the time Prohibition ended in 1933 the federal poisoning program by some estimates had killed at least 10,000 people."[12] New York City's Medical Examiner announced, "The United States government must be charged with the moral responsibility for the deaths that poisoned liquor causes, although it cannot be held legally responsible."[13] Precisely. The national government could not be sued, even when it *intentionally* poisoned its citizens.

Decades later, it became possible to sue the federal government in a *Bivens* suit, named after the 1971 Supreme Court case that established the right to sue.[14] But *Bivens* only applies if (1) the government agents' conduct was intentional, not negligent; (2) their conduct not only harmed a person but also violated his or her constitutional rights; and (3) those rights were already "clearly established," that is, so well established as to be "beyond debate."[15] Further, not every constitutional right qualifies, and some officials, such as prosecutors, have absolute immunity and cannot be sued even if they intentionally violate clearly established rights.

THE FEDERAL TORT CLAIMS ACT

With legal remedies generally nonexistent, the only remedy an injured citizen had was to ask Congress for a "private bill" awarding compensation. To obtain this relief, the injured person had to persuade their Congressman to introduce a bill awarding them a certain amount for their damages, the Committee on Appropriations had to give it a hearing and approve it, the entire House had to pass it, and then the process had to be repeated on the Senate side, following which the President would have to sign it into law. It was a cumbersome process, and many claims were passed over simply because the injured person, or their legislators, lacked political clout.

As the government grew, so did the number of private bills. By the 1940s, more than one thousand private bills were introduced annually, with three to four hundred of them debated and enacted. Congress tired of the process, and where morality had not forced the government to change, tedium and inconvenience did. In 1946, Congress enacted the Federal Tort Claims Act, or FTCA, which *generally* allowed citizens to sue the United States for wrongful acts that harm persons or property. "Generally" merits emphasis because the FTCA also had a long list of exceptions where the United States emphatically did *not* consent to being sued. Prominent among these was what came to be called the "discretionary function exception." The United States refused to be sued for a claim that was "based upon the exercise or performance or the failure to exercise or perform a discretionary function or duty on the part of a federal agency or an employee of the Government, whether or not the discretion involved be abused."[16]

So the United States could not be sued over its officials performing a "discretionary function." But what was a "discretionary function"? Congress gave almost no guidance. Did the phrase cover only matters like promulgating regulations, and not operational decisions in running government programs? Did it cover only high-level policy decisions (for example, creating a National Park), or did it encompass low-level decisions (such as operating the park)? Did it protect only bureaucrats who considered public safety and made bad decisions, or did it also protect bureaucrats who entirely ignored safety considerations?

The discretionary function exception is not the only exception in the FTCA. Congress also refused to consent to lawsuits against the government that arose from assault and battery (unless committed by a law enforcement officer), fraud, libel, slander, or interference with contract rights.[17]

These were not just interesting legal questions to be mulled over with a glass of wine in some law school faculty meeting. They were concrete issues whose resolution would exact a sizeable toll in human life as the government sought to protect itself from liability for negligence and the bad decisions that inevitably come with ever-larger bureaucracies.

Throughout the second half of the twentieth century, the federal courts strongly backed federal agencies and federal officials. The discretionary function exception came to be interpreted so broadly that, unless the agency had imposed clear safety standards that its officials had violated, almost every decision that involved a policy choice (or just *could have* involved a policy choice) was protected against lawsuit. Federal officials have, as we shall see, blown up hundreds of people, spread radioactive waste over enormous areas, and ordered their subordinates to commit murder, all with legal impunity. When the government's misdeeds were challenged in court, attorneys from the U.S. Department of Justice did not hesitate to conduct cover-ups, defraud the courts, and intimidate witnesses—all without worries about disbarment or other discipline. (In this book's concluding chapter, we'll examine how we can deal with these problems.)

When federal civilian employment was small, the risk of being injured by a negligent governmental employee was trifling. Today, there are over two million federal civilian employees, a workforce that dwarfs those of our largest corporations. This enormous workforce has almost complete legal immunity, no matter how lethal its transgressions.

Speaking of lethal transgressions, let us begin with the Texas City explosion . . .

CHAPTER 1

TEXAS CITY: A CITY LEVELED, SIX HUNDRED DEAD

We were taken from the ore-bed and the mine,
We were melted in the furnace and the pit—
We were cast and wrought and hammered to design,
We were cut and filed and tooled and gauged to fit.
. . .
But remember, please, the Law by which we live,
We are not built to comprehend a lie,
We can neither love nor pity nor forgive.
If you make a slip in handling us you die!
     —Rudyard Kipling, "The Secret of the Machines" (1911)

For reasons to be stated later in the report, the committee is of the decided
opinion that the United States Government is wholly responsible for the
explosions and the resulting catastrophe at Texas City; that the disaster was
caused by forces set in motion by the Government, completely controlled or
controllable by it.
     —United States House Judiciary Committee, 1954[1]

ELIZABETH DALEHITE WAS A RELIGIOUS WOMAN, and she had missed her morning prayers. She had spent the day driving her husband, ship's pilot Captain Henry Dalehite, to visit their daughter, then to the Seatrain Shipping headquarters to receive his new orders. As she parked, she noticed a fire on a ship—a common sight in the busy Texas City harbor, where supplies were being rushed to a recovering postwar Europe.

She declined when Captain Dalehite suggested that she accompany him to the headquarters. She was worn out by all the driving and wanted to catch up on her prayers. As he strode away, she took out a prayer card that bore a favorite novena.

A block away, the Texas City Fire Department battled the blaze in the No. 4 hold on the cargo ship *Grandcamp*, where 2,300 tons of powder in paper bags labeled "fertilizer" were destined for France. On the deck, Fire Chief Henry Baumgartner stood directing twenty-seven volunteer firefighters as they towed hoses toward the intense blaze. Seawater boiled away where it touched the ship's hull, and bright white flames jetted through an open hatch, shooting a strange orange smoke high into the air. The nearby docks were already crowded with sightseers, including truant school children rallying to see the spectacle. Shipboard fires were common, but this one seemed special.

It *was* a special fire. The burning "fertilizer" was bomb-grade ammonium nitrate produced by government ordnance plants, using a patented process for creating waterproof explosives. The Fire Department was standing atop a burning *two-thousand-ton bomb.*

Mrs. Dalehite looked up from her novena and saw her husband approaching the Seatrain office. Then the world went blinding white as a shock wave hit, a blow so powerful that it shoved her car into the ditch and blasted her through the window. When she recovered enough to stand, the *Grandcamp* had vanished, as had the Fire Department. The Seatrain headquarters and most of Texas City were leveled. The docks were an abattoir, a slaughterhouse covered with the bodies and body parts of the sightseers. Flaming debris was descending all over the city; oil tanks and refineries were already roaring with flames.

Mrs. Dalehite would never see her Captain again; his mangled body was identified by a friend. Although an exact count was impossible due to fragmentation of bodies, around six hundred men, women, and children died in that instant.[2]

WHY DID IT HAPPEN?

Humans instinctively design systems so one error or omission will not kill people; it usually takes multiple mistakes to yield a fatal result. The path to Texas City—the worst industrial accident in American history—was long.

So long that one begins to question whether the disaster can properly be classed as an accident. At multiple points, the errors were so reckless that private citizens would have been prosecuted for and convicted of homicide—but the individuals making decisions so recklessly were protected by the cloak of the government's immunity.

The chain of events began harmlessly enough. World War II had ended with devastation in much of Europe, as well as in Japan and Korea. Starvation loomed, and it was more efficient to ship fertilizer than food—one pound of fertilizer could produce seven pounds of crops.

At the same time, mothballed government explosive plants were available; these had been producing treated ammonium nitrate, which, when mixed with TNT, made a powerful yet inexpensive filling for aircraft bombs, artillery shells, and torpedo warheads. Ammonium nitrate could also serve as a useful, if hazardous, fertilizer. If the explosive plants were reactivated to produce ammonium nitrate, the government could solve the food problem overseas while providing stateside jobs. To be sure, as any gardener knows, there are many available fertilizers, all more stable than ammonium nitrate. But ammonium nitrate offered the advantage that it could be produced in massive quantities by already existing factories. The substance produced did, however, have certain disadvantages.

KNOWN RISKS

The risks were known. Pure ammonium nitrate is a powerful oxidizer, capable of sustaining violent fires, but unlikely to detonate. Only if mixed with a fuel (Oklahoma City terrorist Timothy McVeigh used fuel oil and nitromethane) does it become an explosive.

In the investigations that followed the Texas City explosion, government representatives evasively described the ammonium nitrate as produced by a "patented process." This was correct but incomplete. Patent No. 2,211,736 is titled "Blasting Explosive." That process involves mixing ammonium nitrate with resin, wax, and petroleum jelly to make an explosive that can be used underwater.

The additives provided the fuel that turned ammonium nitrate from an oxidizer into an explosive, which was precisely why the munitions plants had manufactured it under the patent during the war and used it to fill bombs and artillery shells. The investigations that followed the disaster established that the optimum mix for explosive purposes would contain 0.75–1.5 percent of additives; the ammonium nitrate mix shipped to Texas City had 0.8 percent, so it fell within the right ratio to produce an effective bomb.

The risks were known: in 1944, a munitions plant had blown up during manufacture of the patented explosive. When the government began to consider using the substance as fertilizer, the Army asked the three largest civilian explosive manufacturers for advice. Atlas Powder Company and Hercules Powder Company wrote back to stress the "extreme hazard" posed by such a product; the Dupont Company wrote that the company had stopped manufacture entirely: "As a result of this incident and previous explosions in the ammonium nitrate plant, this company discontinued the coating of ammonium nitrate with any organic compound."[3]

The government chose to proceed anyway and to disregard the risks. Afterward, it would be claimed that decision makers believed that mixing the ammonium nitrate with wax and petroleum jelly would make it better fertilizer, since it would be less likely to absorb moisture from the air and form clumps, which would have to be broken up before it could be spread.[4] But this alleged decision was never attributed to any specific bureaucrat, so the suspicion remains that production of the mixture was a matter of inertia: the factories were already set up to manufacture the mixture, and no one would take the initiative to suggest changing the arrangements.

Still, many understood the risks. When the government hired a civilian firm to make the fertilizer at the former ordnance plants, the firm demanded ironclad legal protection. Its contract with the government provided:

> The Government recognizes that the work herein provided for is of a highly dangerous nature, and that its accomplishment under existing conditions will be attendant with even greater risk of damage to property, injuries to persons, and failures or delays in performance due to uncertain and unexpected causes than would normally exist. The Contractor is unwilling to assume said risk for the consideration herein provided. It is therefore agreed that the Contractor shall not be liable to the Government in any amount whatsoever for failure or delay in performance by it or for any damage to or destruction of property or for any injury to or death of persons arising out of or in connection with the work hereunder . . . [5]

The government had committed to producing a bomb-grade explosive and treating it as if it were harmless fertilizer, despite multiple warnings that it was anything but harmless. So much for the first error in the chain of events that leveled an American city. The chain's second link was simpler.

THE SECOND HUMAN ERROR

The second dangerous decision was to package the explosive in flammable paper bags. To add waterproofing, one of the layers was coated in asphalt, which if heated would melt and soak into the explosive content, adding even more fuel. The melting point of asphalt is fairly high, 175 degrees Fahrenheit for the compound used. At least the bags were unlikely to be exposed to that high a temperature, except that . . .

The process that creates ammonium nitrate must be carried out under great heat and pressure; the resulting chemical comes out searing hot and should be allowed to cool before packaging. But the orders to the ordnance plants were to rush production at all costs. The ammonium nitrate was poured into bags as it left the production machinery and stacked into railroad freight cars to be rushed to Texas City. Tests found that the ammonium nitrate was being bagged at 190 degrees Fahrenheit and above, more than hot enough to melt the asphalt. A Texas City railroad official later recollected that sometimes a boxcar would arrive with bags so hot that men could not handle them. Others observed charred bags and bags that emitted smoke.

THE FINAL LINK IN THE LETHAL CHAIN

In 1947, the government resumed the manufacture of the explosive. During the war, ordnance factories had shipped treated ammonium nitrate packaged in red bags that bore the label DANGEROUS / HIGHLY EXPLOSIVE; but these postwar bags, *containing exactly the same substance*, were labeled simply FERTILIZER / AMMONIUM NITRATE / NITROGEN 32.5%.[6] The railroad industry and the Interstate Commerce Commission required that explosives be shipped with special warning labels and that special written warnings be given to the master of any ship carrying them. By virtue of a new label, shipping would be easier. The explosive was now just fertilizer . . . inert plant food. When the vice president of the railway that transported the material became suspicious because it was coming from an ordnance plant, a spokesman for the plant assured him that the ammonium nitrate was not an explosive.[7] Nothing would be allowed to interfere with its rapid production and shipment.

Ammonium nitrate, converted to bomb-grade material under a patent for explosives, packaged in flammable, asphalt-coated bags at too high a temperature, given labels that gave no clue that the contents were a fire and explosion hazard . . . If any private, profit-seeking firm had done all that and deaths resulted, the only question would have been how many counts were in the resulting indictment, which executives were named, and how long were their prison terms. But this was the government.

ALARM BELLS KEEP SOUNDING

The first warning came from a supervisor at one of the manufacturing sites: "This stuff is overheating and if we ship it out that way we are looking for trouble. What shall I do about it? But if we cut down [the temperature] I have to tell you that we cannot meet these production schedules."

The cabled reply from a "superior officer" was unequivocal: "Production must be met."[8] That attitude held at the highest levels of government. When the Chief Inspector of the Bureau of Explosives warned his superiors that boxcars of the treated ammonium nitrate were bursting into flames, and requested that the material be allowed to cool before loading, he was told that "it is not feasible."[9]

Two weeks later, The Union Bag & Paper Corporation performed tests on the bagging of hot ammonium nitrate and reported to government officials that the bags would break down if the chemical's temperature was higher than 200 degrees. They made a "strong recommendation" that the product be allowed to cool.[10] The company's recommendation was for naught; nothing changed.

In March 1947, Col. Carroll Deitrick of the Division of Ordnance listed railroad fires involving the modified ammonium nitrate. Deitrick noted, "This office suspects that the fires may have resulted from the high temperature of the fertilizer in combination with easy ignitability of the duplex paper sack."[11] His memo was filed and ignored.

THE EXPLOSIONS AND FIRES

A month later, on the morning of April 16, 1947, the *Grandcamp*'s holds had been partially loaded with its cargo of ammonium nitrate, and eight stevedores descended into hold No. 4 as the ship's crane lowered in a load of bags.

Julio Luna, Jr., was the first to notice the odor of smoke. He called up to ask if anyone was burning paper on the deck before realizing the odor was coming from the cargo underneath his feet. The stevedores began to pull up the sacks—many of which broke in their hands and spilled their contents. After digging through four or five layers, they could see a small fire, about two layers farther down.[12]

The stevedores poured two one-gallon bottles of drinking water on the fire without result. They tried a couple of fire extinguishers, but the fire continued to spread. It did not seem to be an emergency. They believed they were standing atop inert fertilizer with the fire probably on wooden brackets under the bags. Soon the acrid smoke forced them out of the hold.

Sirens moaned, one on the dock and one in the distance, summoning Texas City's volunteer Fire Department. Twenty-seven of its twenty-eight members showed up to race their engines down to the dock. Not knowing he was dealing with an explosives fire, the *Grandcamp*'s chief officer resorted to a standard method of fire suppression. Ordering the hatches closed, he directed that hold No. 4 be flooded with steam from the ship's boilers. If the fire had indeed been burning wood frames below an inert cargo of fertilizer, this would have suffocated the blaze. But ammonium nitrate is a powerful oxidizer; it does not need air to burn. If anything, confinement and the increased pressure accelerated the fire. The first clue that the approach was not working came when the hatch cover blew off.[13]

Julio Luna and some other stevedores decided there would be no work on the *Grandcamp* that day. They loaded into Luna's car and slowly drove away from the docks. Alerted by the Fire Department sirens, crowds came down to see the bright flames and strange orange smoke.[14] Safety Engineer H. B. Williams left the dock area to get gas masks for the firefighters; for the first hundred yards of his drive he had to slowly edge his car through streets filled with incoming spectators.[15]

Inside hold No. 4, the lethal mix of ammonium nitrate and petroleum jelly was burning and melting. The molten mix ran down the cargo and pooled in the bottom of the hold while the Fire Department tried to smother the volcano erupting from the hatch.

A block away, Mrs. Dalehite was saying her novena. Captain Dalehite was approaching the Seatrain offices. Seven blocks away, Julio Luna was driving his friends to a game of pool.

Somewhere in the burning pool of molten ammonium nitrate and petroleum jelly a bubble expanded with sufficient velocity to start a detonation. In an instant, the *Grandcamp*'s cargo became an enormous ball of superheated gases expanding at more than fifteen thousand feet per second, forming a massive shock wave that tore the ship's steel apart and rushed on toward the crowd. The shock wave was heard 150 miles away: the ground tremor felt like an earthquake fourteen miles away in Galveston and broke windows forty miles north in Houston.[16]

The *Grandcamp* vanished into millions of pieces, a giant fragmentation bomb that mowed down the spectators with brutal effectiveness. A Coast Guard investigation later found the following:

> The explosion generated tremendous pressure but appears to have lacked the shattering destructive characteristics of an equivalent amount of a nitro-high explosive. The board's observations at the scene were that within a radius of one-half mile from Pier "0" the missile pattern was a missile to every 2 square feet. Missiles ranged in size from a rivet head to a portion of the ship's structure estimated to weigh 60 tons.[17]

The Texas City Fire Department was simply vaporized; body parts of four firemen would later be identified, the other twenty-three firemen would remain forever "missing." The crowds on the waterfront were annihilated in an instant, shredded by a storm of steel fragments hurled into them at five times the velocity of a rifle bullet. Buildings were blown flat, and fires erupted in shattered chemical plants and petroleum storage facilities, where twenty storage tanks were soon in flames.[18] Overhead, the blast blew the wings off two sightseeing aircraft, which crashed into the chaos below. The *Grandcamp*'s 3,200-pound anchor fell to earth more than a mile and a half inland, driven ten feet into the ground.

The destruction was not yet complete. The explosion had smashed another ship, the *High Flyer*, moored about six hundred feet away. Hatch covers were torn off and blazing debris descended from the air; its cargo of ammonium nitrate mix likewise caught fire. Sometime past one in the morning, 961 tons of treated ammonium nitrate detonated. Most of the city's population was dead or fleeing, so additional deaths were few—they included a Catholic priest who was giving last rites to the dying and a mortuary student who had volunteered to help embalm the dead. The explosion did destroy more of the city's houses.

The aftermath was staggering. A quarter of Texas City's population was killed or wounded.[19] The city had only one funeral home, and it could accommodate only a few of the dead. A high school gymnasium was commandeered to house the bodies and body parts for identification. McGar's Garage became the embalming station. Survivors walked through the gym, looking at bodies and body parts in efforts to identify family members, friends, and coworkers. Students from a mortuary school and some survivors of the blast handled the embalming in the garage, with the floor awash in blood and embalming fluid.

Fires were still burning a week later; body parts were still being identified a month later. About ten days after the blasts, a surveyor took two sons into the shambles. Decades later, one son, Robert Baer, recalled houses and fences blown to bits as the Baers resurveyed much of the town.

"The city stunk like hell," Baer remembered, "the smell of death and rotting flesh." Bluebottle flies were everywhere, attracted by the hideous smell, laying their eggs wherever rotting flesh could be found. Bob and his brother climbed atop a damaged chemical silo to eat lunch away from the stench . . . and were confronted by a burned and mummified corpse, its blackened arms reaching into the air.

"That wasn't the end of it," Bob added. "We found pieces of two corpses in the rubble. One was a man, one was a woman, as best we could judge." Smaller body parts, all that remained of spectators fragmented by the blast and shredded by flying steel, were scattered in every direction.[20]

The psychological sequelae remained after Texas City's physical hell ended. Posttraumatic stress disorder (PTSD) was not yet a diagnosis, but there can be little doubt that thousands suffered its most severe form. Family members found their loved ones, or parts of them, on the gymnasium floor.

The pipe fitter who volunteered to help with embalming was near breaking after days of standing in blood. A husband carried his wife to the doctor, explaining that he couldn't just lay her down because he was holding her guts in. He then watched her die.[21] A funeral home director later recalled a surge in "natural deaths" that went on for months. "People were dying because they had taken all they could stand. They burnt themselves out working in the disaster and they just died."[22]

The government carried on as if nothing had occurred. The ammonium nitrate that had not been loaded onto the *Grandcamp* and *High Flyer* was sent to another port and loaded onto the *Ocean Liberty*. After lowering anchor in Brest, France, the *Ocean Liberty* caught fire and exploded, killing approximately thirty and injuring more than one thousand French civilians and sailors.

TEXAS CITY RESIDENTS APPEAL TO THE COURTS

In the aftermath of the disaster, building inspectors throughout Texas volunteered to inspect surviving houses while volunteer construction workers repaired those fit for occupation. The Salvation Army and other organizations provided emergency relief. Airlines flew medical workers and others to Texas City at no charge.[23] The Monsanto Corporation, whose refinery had been destroyed by the blast, kept its employees on the payroll and sent money to the families of those who had died. Informed that the wealthy Busch family wanted to contribute, a local banker formed a relief fund that ultimately distributed more than a million dollars in contributions.[24]

The federal government, whose negligence had caused the destruction, was less charitable. The surviving 8,485 residents of Texas City had to sue the United States for loss of their loved ones, bodily injury, or destruction of their homes and property. One might have expected the government's attorneys to be willing to compensate them; after all, the attorneys worked for the United States Department of *Justice*.

Instead, the government attorneys fought as if they were under personal attack. An attorney for the victims described the Justice attorneys as "fiercely aggressive" and driven by an "extreme feeling that 'this must be fought out and this must be defeated on any ground we can achieve.'"[25] The government attorneys claimed the explosion was due to sabotage, or maybe due to longshoremen smoking in the hold (although the fire started deep in the cargo), that it was an unavoidable accident, and even that the government "had no title or control" over the explosive at the time it detonated; ownership had passed to the French government and its agents. That last claim failed when the government had to disclose the sales contract: under it, the United States owned the ammonium nitrate until it was delivered and paid for—but even so, the government attorneys pressed the argument at trial.[26]

Federal District Judge T. M. Kennerly, who presided over the trial, had practiced law for thirty-nine years before serving eleven years as a federal judge. He heard Mrs. Dalehite's suit as a test case, with its findings to govern the remaining cases.

The trial lasted three months and produced twenty thousand pages of transcripts. Judge Kennerly ruled in Mrs. Dalehite's favor; the beginning of his Findings of Fact summed up his reasoning:

> The 80 or more charges against Defendant [the government] of negligence contained in Plaintiff's pleadings are substantially all supported and sustained by the evidence. This record discloses blunders, mistakes, and acts of negligence, both of commission and of omission, on the part of Defendant, its agents, servants and employees, in deciding to begin the manufacture of this inherently dangerous fertilizer. And from the day of its beginning on down to after the day of the Texas City Disaster, it discloses such disregard of and lack of care for the safety of the public and of persons manufacturing, handling, transporting and using such fertilizer as to shock one.
>
> When all the facts in this record are considered, one is not surprised by the Texas City Disaster (i.e., that men and women, boys and girls, in and around Texas City going about their daily tasks in their homes, on the streets, in their places of employment, were suddenly and without warning killed, maimed, or wounded, and vast property damage done). The surprising thing is that there were not more of such disasters.[27]

The court found that the ammonium nitrate/petroleum jelly mix was "inherently dangerous" and that prior fires and explosions had put the government on notice of its dangerous qualities. He added that the government had improperly labeled it and failed to inform the shippers that it was explosive.

Judge Kennerly faced one last barrier. The government had argued sovereign immunity vociferously. While Congress had consented to be sued under the Federal Tort Claims Act, Congress had not consented to damage suits that challenged the government's "discretionary functions." Any case challenging those functions would be subject to speedy dismissal. But what was a "discretionary function"? The government claimed that the decision to risk blowing up an American city was within the discretion of the agencies and officials involved, and the people who as a result were maimed or lost loved ones were simply out of luck.

Judge Kennerly chose to differ. He took the view that "discretionary function" related to high-level policy decisions. The Cabinet-level decisions to produce fertilizer and to send it to France were thus protected against lawsuit. But those decisions had not made the Texas City disaster inevitable; with reasonable care, those policies could have been carried out safely. What caused the disaster was negligence at much lower levels of government, by individuals who chose to produce a dangerous mixture at too high a temperature, to disregard repeated proof and warnings of its risks, and to avoid warning anyone of the danger to life and limb, and Judge Kennerly found the government to be liable for those acts and omissions.

The prospect of the government being civilly liable for killing its citizens was too much for the Department of Justice. The federal government appealed the ruling to the Fifth Circuit Court of Appeals, and then to the Supreme Court. The core issue became whether Judge Kennerly was right in deciding that the discretionary function exception immunized only high-level policy choices, or whether it broadly protected governmental negligence at almost every level, down to the government employee who decided what label to put on a bag of "fertilizer."

The choice between the two approaches was likely affected by a human factor. Courts and judges tend to be very conservative, not in a political sense, but in the sense of regarding change with worry and suspicion. This feeling is particularly strong when Congress, rather than the courts, changes court-created legal doctrines. The courts had created and extended the defense of sovereign immunity. The Supreme Court had proclaimed that allowing suits against the government would shackle its operations and endanger the public good. Then Congress allowed such suits anyway! What could it have been thinking?

From this standpoint, it made sense to interpret the discretionary function exception broadly, to protect virtually any government decision, great or small, whether the decision came from a Senate-confirmed Cabinet officer or a midlevel worker in a field office. On the other hand, a government "by the people and for the people" is not supposed to maim and kill the people.

When *Dalehite v. United States*[28] reached the Supreme Court, the majority of Justices ruled against Mrs. Dalehite and scrapped her and the other survivors' lawsuits. To their mind, the discretionary function exception covered decisions made at every level of government. The decision to use bomb-grade ammonium nitrate mixed with wax and petroleum jelly was discretionary, since "the considerations that dictated the decisions were crucial ones, involving the feasibility of the program itself, balanced against present knowledge of the effect of such a coating and the general custom of similar private industries." The decision to bag at dangerously high temperatures was discretionary, since cooling the ammonium nitrate to a safe temperature would have increased production costs: "This kind of decision is not one which the courts, under the Act, are empowered to cite as 'negligence.'" Even the decision to label the bags as fertilizer was protected, since it violated no regulation and thus was left to government employees' discretion.

The *Dalehite v. United States* ruling remains law to this day. In the six decades since *Dalehite*, the Supreme Court handed down three major decisions interpreting that ruling. The judicial pendulum swung back and forth, but overall tended toward expanding the protection given to government officials. The first, a 1955 decision in *Indian Towing v. United States*,[29] allowed the Coast Guard to be sued over a lighthouse whose light malfunctioned. The Court distinguished between planning decisions, which were immune from suit, and operational ones, which were not. Creating the lighthouse was a planning decision, repairing its light was operational.

Then came *United States v. Varig Airlines*,[30] a 1984 decision that involved FAA inspectors who failed to give a passenger airplane a safety inspection. We might think that would be subject to suit as an "operational" decision, but the *Varig* Court ruled against liability. *Dalehite*, it held, immunized all decisions based on "social, economic, or political policy," no matter how low the decision maker's rank.

Four years later, *Berkovitz v. United States*[31] pushed the *Varig* legal immunity still farther. Now, the government decision did not have to actually be based on social, economic, or political policy to be protected. It was enough that the decision "was susceptible to" such policy considerations. If the decision merely *could have been* made in light of such policy, it was legally protected. So if a government land manager allowed public use of a dangerous road, his decision would be legally protected if government attorneys could, in retrospect, think up a policy reason (such as allocation of government funds, or difficulty of enforcement, or perhaps an official could have worried that putting up "keep out" signs would attract more attention and lead to more use) that could have justified leaving a dangerous road open. That the bureaucrat responsible hadn't worried about any of this would not matter.

By the end of the Supreme Court rulings, there were only two classes of government negligence where a lawsuit was allowed: (1) decisions for which no one could conjure up a possible policy reason (e.g., bad driving, medical malpractice, or occasionally failure to warn of dangers), or (2) situations where the government decision maker had no discretion to act: his or her choice violated law, regulation, or direct orders from their superiors. Only in rare cases could a person who had been injured, or who had lost a loved one to official negligence, win compensation.

A citizen can sue if a government employee is negligent *and* their negligence violates a superior's orders. But courts require the orders to be very specific. In 1997, the Sixth Circuit ruled that the Forest Service Manual's directives to inspect sites annually, to "give health and safety related items highest priority," and "to the extent practicable, eliminate safety hazards from recreation sites" were not specific enough to allow suit when those orders were violated and dangerous fire pits were allowed to exist even after accidents occurred. The Manual's commands "did not mandate that the Forest Service maintain its campsites and fire pits in any specific manner."[32]

The Court's reading of the Federal Tort Claims Act moreover created a perverse incentive. In private industry, the risk of liability gives reason to operate safely, to have safety policies, and to make sure that all employees avoid unreasonable risk to the public. In 2010, a British Petroleum (BP) oil rig explosion killed eleven workers and resulted in an enormous oil spill in the Gulf of Mexico. BP was convicted of eleven counts of manslaughter, and paid a $4.5 *billion* fine with billions more set aside to pay damages.[33] The rulings remain a powerful incentive for BP and other drillers to avoid cutting safety corners.

But in government, the best protection against being sued consists of having *no* safety policies and giving *no* orders on safety! If there are no agency orders, no agency employee can violate them, so whatever is done is within an employee's discretion. The United States can never be sued. The more incompetent or negligent the agency, the more likely it will be insulated against legal liability.

Under the 1946 Federal Tort Claims Act, a federal employee has a license to kill, unless a superior ordered him not to kill—and the superior has an incentive *not* to give such an order. "I was only following orders" is indeed an excuse. But if you are in the government, so is "nobody gave me orders, I did it on my own."

> The Postal Service has regulations stating that mailboxes "must" be located so that they do not block a driver's view when he or she enters an intersection. But when a driver was seriously injured because mailboxes blocked his view, the Eighth Circuit ruled that the regulations were (despite the word "must") "guidelines and not mandatory" and the lawsuit must be dismissed.[34]

Ultimately, the victims of the Texas City explosion received some compensation. Nine years after the disaster, and after extensive hearings, Congress passed a private bill appropriating $16.5 million for the victims. The average claim was $12,195, about $128,000 in modern terms—a tenth of what Congress would appropriate for the 9/11 victims.[35]

The private bill clearly rankled the Department of Justice; during hearings on the bill, Assistant Attorney General Warren Burger testified: "As a lawyer I have made up my mind that this is why they sued the United States, because it was the entity that could be sued for an amount running into millions of dollars."[36] It did not seem to occur to the future Chief Justice of the Supreme Court Burger that the victims may have sued the United States because it had, by gross negligence, blown up their homes and killed their loved ones. Another Justice official testified that his agency would not oppose the bill so long as the bill was viewed as "a bounty, an act of grace."[37] Government negligence, six hundred deaths, thousands homeless—and Justice officials wanted it understood that paying compensation is "a bounty, an act of grace"? Any corporate CEO who spoke with that casual arrogance would have been lynched before he got out of the Capitol.

But this is just one example; there are many others where the government would have been put out of business if it were a giant corporation. We'll examine a four-decade chain of preventable deaths in chapter 2.

CHAPTER 2

WESTERN UNITED STATES: ATOMIC TESTING POISONS THE LAND AND THE PEOPLE

———————

I feel that we were used more or less as guinea pigs. The forgotten guinea pigs, because with guinea pigs they will come to the cage and check, which they never have.

—Martha Laird, testimony before the
House Committee on Oversight, 1980[1]

Just what the hell do you think you're doing, saying the amount of radiation we're allowing is causing cancer? I've been assured by the Atomic Energy Commission people that a dose of a hundred times what they're allowing won't hurt anybody. Listen, there have been others who have tried to cross the AEC before you. We got them and we'll get you.

—Rep. Chester E. Holifield (D-CA), Chairman, Joint Committee on
Atomic Energy, to Dr. John Gofman, after his testimony
on the hazards of atomic test fallout, 1970[2]

University-employed scientists complain that industry hire scientists to refute their findings when the findings might adversely impact the industry. Let me assure you that when the Federal Government is the polluter, it follows exactly the same strategy as any company. But the Federal Government has far greater resources and power than are available to companies.

—Dr. Joseph Lyon, medical epidemiologist, testimony before
the Senate Appropriations Committee, 1998[3]

May 19, 1953: They Called It "Dirty Harry"

The electrical signal left the concrete bunker, ran through thousands of feet of wire, and up the three-hundred-foot steel scaffold that towered over the desert. The journey took about ten nanoseconds, and the reaction it would initiate took about the same amount of time.

The signal reached its destination, a control unit connected to ninety-two high explosive charges arranged in a five-foot-diameter ball. Each charge was designed to focus its explosive energy inward toward the small hollow sphere of plutonium at the center.

The control unit sent the firing signal, and the explosive charges detonated in unison. Their enormous force, thousands of tons per square inch, crushed the plutonium into a smaller solid ball and compressed the metal into its denser delta state. The plutonium went supercritical, and in an instant a part of its mass changed into pure energy. $E=MC^2$; in this case, the E translated to the energy of thirty-two thousand *tons* of TNT, released from a metal ball a few inches in diameter.

In the first millisecond, a blast of light and x-rays vaporized the steel tower, even before the shock wave of the explosion could crush it. A few milliseconds later, the fireball, now burning at twenty thousand degrees Fahrenheit, gouged the desert, sucking up its soil, pulling it into the churning nuclear maelstrom, converting it into dozens of radioactive elements and compounds that mixed with the unconsumed plutonium.

Test Shot Harry, the thirtieth such detonation at the Nevada Test Site, was a success. At thirty-two kilotons, Harry was the most powerful atomic bomb exploded to date. Its devastating power would be proven not in a war zone, but in the peaceful western states that grow our grain and raise our cattle.

The fireball rose and formed the now-familiar mushroom cloud, topping out at more than thirty-eight thousand feet. The ninety-mile-per-hour winds at that altitude pushed the cloud eastward, and as it cooled, its vapors condensed back into solids—radioactive cobalt, cesium, strontium, iron, iodine, plutonium, and many other substances. The radioactive material descended to the ground as the cloud swept over ranches, farms, and small towns. The places were inhabited by people who had come to call themselves the "downwinders."

On the Whipple Ranch, about ten miles from the blast, Keith Whipple noticed what seemed to be bug bites on his arms, small, painful welts. Then he realized they were being caused by the fallout that was descending on the ranch.[4] Atomic Energy Commission (AEC) representatives had told him if the fallout got too bad he should go to the nearby town of Alamo, where AEC buses would evacuate people. He set out for Alamo, only to find that the bus drivers had driven away as soon as they realized how much fallout was coming down.[5]

His mother was driving a few miles to the north with his younger brother Kent when she was detained by a deputy sheriff, who explained that he had received orders to stop vehicles coming up the highway. She noticed that the air smelled terrible, but had no way to know that they were inhaling the by-products of an atomic detonation. Two decades later, Kent Whipple, a nonsmoker, would die of lung cancer at the age of thirty-eight.[6]

The cloud swept on. In a few hours, it had covered 150 miles and was depositing its radioactive load on the small town of St. George, Utah. The residents noticed fine ash falling and a strange metallic taste in their mouths. Agatha Mannering was on her knees weeding her garden as the ashes fell. Her shirt had ridden up, and the ash settled on the skin of her back, leaving radiation burns where it had landed.[7] Elma Mackelprang was watering her sheep when the strange material descended. She became nauseous and her hair began to fall out.[8]

East of St. George, rancher Elmer Jackson was moving his cattle to a new watering area when the ash began to settle. He, too, developed deep radiation burns that took years to heal. He would die of thyroid cancer twenty years later.[9]

A hundred miles north of St. George, Oleta Nelson and her family watched the pinkish-tan cloud sweep over them. That night, all the exposed areas of her skin turned beet red and she began vomiting. When she washed her hair a few days later, her husband Isaac heard her scream. Her long hair had slipped off her head and was lying in the washbasin. "She was as bald as old Yul Brynner to halfway back," Isaac would later recall. She had been a vigorous woman of thirty-one, but now her health began to decline, and she died of brain cancer in 1965, aged forty-one.[10]

The Public Health Service had stationed Frank Butrico in St. George as a radiation monitor. He watched in shock as the needle rose on his radiation measuring device, stopping only when it hit the peg at the high end of the scale. He notified the test site, and then tried to sound a warning. By the time he found the telephone number for a radio station in a nearby town, and the station began broadcasting calls to stay indoors, most of the fallout had come down. Butrico went to his hotel room to shower off and discard the clothes he wore.[11]

A CHERNOBYL IN THE SOUTHWEST

Those on the receiving end of Harry's fallout, the "downwinders," nicknamed the shot "Dirty Harry." Harry was indeed the dirtiest of the hundred atomic warheads detonated aboveground at the Nevada Test Site. To gain an idea of the contamination that resulted, we can take one particularly nasty form of fallout, radioactive iodine, or I-131. The I-131 fallout that lands on pasture grass can be ingested by cattle, which excrete it in their milk and thus pass it on to humans, especially children. Once people drink the milk, their bodies will concentrate the I-131 in the thyroid gland. This fallout component, I-131, is thus particularly dangerous, especially when children are in the fallout zone.

The Three Mile Island reactor accident released a mere twenty curies of I-131 and resulted in widespread panic and a voluntary evacuation of more than a thousand square miles.[12]

The 2011 Fukushima reactor incident, when a Japanese reactor complex was damaged by an earthquake and tsunami, released more than five million curies of I-131; three hundred thousand people were evacuated.[13]

The all-time record for reactor disasters is Chernobyl, where a reactor core exploded, blew open the containment vessel, and burned in the open air. Nearly thirty years later, the thousand square miles surrounding the site remain designated as an "exclusion zone" where only temporary entry is permitted. Chernobyl released about forty million curies of I-131.

The nuclear tests in Nevada released more than *150 million curies* of I-131. Dirty Harry alone made up thirty million of that total, far exceeding the contamination created by Fukushima and approaching that of Chernobyl.[14] No one was informed or evacuated, and unwarned Americans continued to eat crops and meat produced within the contaminated area, and to give their children milk from cows that grazed on contaminated grass. No one knows how many more Americans were exposed to radiation as these animals were sold and slaughtered.

The effects of that contamination were staggering. A 1984 study published in the *Journal of the American Medical Association* compared the health histories of Mormons (who avoid drinking and smoking) living in the most heavily hit fallout areas with those of Mormons living elsewhere in Utah. The study found that those from the fallout areas were 60 percent more likely to develop cancer. For forms of cancer particularly linked to radiation, the situation was much worse:

- Leukemia was 500 percent more frequent;
- Thyroid cancer rates were elevated by more than 800 percent;
- Bone cancers increased by a factor of ten;
- Brain cancer and melanoma rates more than doubled.[15]

Not that the downwinders needed to wait for a study. Josephine Simkins lived in the small town of Enterprise, Utah, just over a hundred miles downwind from the atomic test shots. She lost her husband and two other family members to cancer. Interviewed in 1988, she recalled: "One little girl, born and raised here, is dying of brain cancer. One little girl had bone cancer in her teens. There [are] others that died of leukemia. . . . Then the other cancers started showing up. Lots of breast cancer. They've realized now that nearly everyone who died for years died of cancer. There are hardly any other deaths in town beside cancer."[16]

The Real Issue

Was the atomic testing necessary? Certainly. In mid-1949, under Joseph Stalin, a mass murderer on a par with Hitler, the Soviets had detonated their own atomic bomb and trained more than a hundred infantry and tank divisions for action in Europe. Civil wars between pro- and anticommunist forces were ongoing in China and in Greece. A Communist government had just seized control of Czechoslovakia, and pro-Soviet forces had tried to take over Yugoslavia. The Korean War began in 1950, and an initial American victory was met by a massive Red Chinese counterattack.

The development of atomic weapons was still in its infancy and many questions remained. Several of the Nevada bombs "fizzled" because of errors in design. What were the best materials and construction techniques for a bomb? Could it be made small enough to be carried by a battlefield rocket or fired by an artillery piece? Could a uranium bomb be used to initiate a hydrogen bomb, a thermonuclear bomb, which would have far greater power? Only testing could answer these questions.

That these tests were necessary in the abstract cannot, however, resolve the question of whether the tests were carried out responsibly, with efforts to minimize the danger to Americans in the vicinity.

Even in the 1950s, government officials knew that radioactive fallout was deadly. Studies of the Nagasaki and Hiroshima survivors had shown massive increases—400 to 500 percent—in leukemia.[17] Leukemia is a fast-onset cancer—its rise began quickly and peaked about six years after the bombs were dropped—so it stood to reason that other, more slowly developing, forms of cancer would follow.

The government was certainly in no position to argue that it was ignorant of the risks posed by radiation. The tests had been set in a remote desert area for just that reason and were postponed whenever winds might cause the fallout to fall on more populous or important places such as Las Vegas or California. One explosion was postponed eleven times due to "unfavorable winds which would distribute radioactive fallout onto populated areas."[18] Downwinders joked that, since they lived in an "uninhabited" area, they must be "uninhabitants."

Perhaps, when a nation confronts a serious danger, a small number of people must be put at risk for the safety of the greater number. But shouldn't those put at risk be honestly informed, put in a position to protect themselves as best they can, and perhaps even be compensated for what they must endure for the good of all? The risks of fallout could be minimized *if* people were made aware of them. Stay indoors while the nuclear ash is coming down; shower and launder clothes afterward; don't drink or give your kids locally produced milk for a time. Cattle that ingest I-131 from their feed will excrete it in their milk, but it has a half-life of only eight days.

All these were simple protective measures that the downwinders would likely have taken if they had been candidly informed of the need for them.

THE GOVERNMENT MISLEADS THE PUBLIC

In advance of the tests, the Atomic Energy Commission (AEC) distributed handbills describing what might be expected. The handbills assured the reader that "health and safety authorities have determined that no danger from or as a result of the AEC test activities may be expected outside the limits of the Las Vegas Bombing and Gunnery Range. All necessary precautions, including radiological surveys and patrolling the surrounding territory, will be taken to ensure that safety conditions are maintained."[19] The AEC sought to assure area residents that everything was safe, and the press blindly accepted the assurances. When the AEC chairman claimed that the fallout's radiation was less than that of a wristwatch's luminous dial, the *Ogden Standard-Examiner*, a Utah paper, ran it without question under the headline "Derides Fear of Radiation."[20]

The AEC's own staff was issued film badges to measure their radiation exposure, but the agency showed little concern for the impact of radiation on the public. In May 1952, the *Salt Lake Tribune* ran an editorial titled "We Don't Know Enough," stating that the radioactivity was worrisome despite scientists' reassurances. The editorial mildly concluded: "One nagging thought is that we (the scientists, really) don't know enough about radioactivity to be absolutely sure of its dangers."[21]

The AEC responded in characteristic harshness with a letter to the editor that ran below the title "Controls Make Atomic Tests Harmless." The letter assured readers that the AEC "can state categorically that at no time has radioactivity from AEC test operations been harmful to any human, animal, or crop."[22]

Then came Dirty Harry. Geiger counters maxed out, cars were stopped at roadblocks, a town was told to stay indoors, and radiation burns appeared on children, adults, and animals wherever the fallout hit skin. People reported widespread nausea, hair loss, and other symptoms of radiation poisoning. It was hard to explain these things away as harmless. But the AEC gave it its best shot. AEC press releases explained that Harry's fallout was "slightly more than usual."[23] This was a doubtful way to explain a radiation release that approached that of the later Chernobyl disaster, but the United Press dutifully reported:

> Residents near the Nevada-Utah border were reassured today that there was no harmful radioactivity in "fallout" that drifted over that area after an unusually powerful atomic blast.

A few hours after yesterday's dawn atomic blast on the southern Nevada desert, radioactivity was detected along border highways and forced residents of one Utah town to rush indoors. . . . However, the Atomic Safety Commission said its monitors did not register radioactivity in the border area strong enough to harm human beings.[24]

A few days later, an AEC official spoke to a meeting of scientists, assuring them that measurements of fallout in Salt Lake City and Idaho Falls were consistently within permissible levels. The *Provo Sunday Herald* ran a summary under the headline "Radiation in Atomic Tests Held Negligible."[25] No one seems to have noted that Harry's fallout had swept westward across southern Utah, and Salt Lake City (let alone Idaho Falls) was never in its path. A nice trick if one can get away with it.

An article headlined "No Danger in Nevada Nuclear Tests" reported an interview with a government scientific advisor who treated exposure to radiation as a minor annoyance. He admitted that the tests had "caused some inconveniences by forcing people in southwestern Utah to remain briefly indoors," but promised that "we are trying to minimize the inconveniences."[26]

THE COVER-UPS BEGIN

In the months after Dirty Harry, some 1,400 pregnant ewes and nearly 3,000 lambs who had been grazing downwind (or about 12 percent and 25 percent, respectively, of those affected) died after showing symptoms of radiation poisoning. The surviving ewes often delivered grotesquely deformed lambs.[27]

Ranchers who depended upon their sheep herds for economic survival saw the effects within weeks. Adult sheep were left with strange skin burns and wool that fell off at the slightest touch. One rancher rented a bulldozer to dig a mass grave for his flock.[28]

Eventually, word of the sheep losses reached AEC headquarters, and it ordered an investigation, which immediately turned up evidence that the sheep had consumed massive quantities of radioactive iodine, I-131. When an AEC veterinarian applied a Geiger counter to the sheep's thyroids, the needle pegged at its maximum. "This is hotter than a two-dollar pistol!" he exclaimed in shock.[29] His report to the atomic test site management attributed the sheep losses to fallout. The test site management in turn arranged for a panel of veterinarians to review the evidence; the panel's preliminary report, authored by Dr. Arthur Wolff of the Public Health Service, concluded that the sheep losses were due to fallout, citing the high radiation levels found in the animals' thyroids and skin burns that matched those found in radiation experiments.

To understand what happened next, you must understand bureaucracy. Theoretically, an agency is run by a director or a commission, but there is a much more powerful force in any large organization. An agency is run by its permanent staff, the "Omnipotent Peons," or OPs, as some jestingly identify themselves, and their single-minded mission is to protect the agency and to grow it. This is partially a matter of self-interest and partially a matter of emotional investment in the agency's functions. To take an example with which I have familiarity: Park Service tends to attract people who like parks, and they quickly come to take the view that if operating and expanding parks require treating some people unfairly, that unfairness is just the price of advancing the public good.

The top dogs nominally run the agency, but the few dozen top dogs know only the information that the thousands of OPs, staff and middle management, allow them to see. This isolation of leadership from information was particularly acute with the AEC, where the commissioners themselves were headquartered in Washington, D.C., and the testing was being done in Nevada and in the Marshall Islands.

Dr. Wolff's report tied fallout to the sheep losses; the AEC's Omnipotent Peons realized that this was an undesired answer. The AEC commissioners in Washington might reason that what killed sheep might endanger humans and either stop atomic testing or require the agency to inform the people at risk, which would generate an uproar that might have the same effect.

There was only one solution. OPs worked hard to ensure the commissioners received the "right" information, the information that would let the agency continue atomic testing. All copies of Dr. Wolff's preliminary report were seized. Another member of the panel, Dr. Richard Thompsett, a veterinarian under contract with AEC, was ordered to rewrite the report and to "eliminate any reference to speculation about radiation damage on animals."[30] He did so, and all copies of the original Wolff report, even the one held by Dr. Thompsett, were destroyed.

Other possible indications that Dirty Harry had been dangerous were also covered up. Frank Butrico, the Public Health Service monitor in St. George, had reported that his radiation sensor had pegged its needle, reporting radiation levels greater than it was designed to measure. He was ordered to rewrite his report to say that radiation levels were "a little bit above normal but not in the range of being harmful."[31] The atomic test site staff told him, "Let's try to get this thing quieted down a little bit because if we don't, then it's likely that there might be some suggestion made for curtailing the test program. And this, in the interest of our national defense, we cannot do."[32]

The test site personnel were not the only ones covering things up; some middle-level management at AEC's headquarters had a role to play, as well. When the panel of veterinarians was created, an AEC headquarters staffer named Dr. Gordon Dunning was made its secretary. A Congressional investigation years later documented Dunning's role in burying the evidence. The Congressional subcommittee found a long-suppressed memo reciting that Dunning "believed it was imperative that he prepare a statement for Commissioner Zuckert of the AEC pertaining to the Utah sheep situation. Dr. Dunning opined that the statement was necessary 'before Commissioner Zuckert [would] open the purse strings' for future continental weapons tests."[33]

But, as the Wolff preliminary report had shown, the panel was inclined toward finding that fallout had indeed killed the sheep. Dunning had quite a problem.

He solved it with a direct approach. At a meeting of the veterinarians' panel, he asked the members to sign a document as proof of their attendance. The document was actually a memo that Dunning had written, absolving the AEC of all blame for the sheep deaths and claiming that the skin lesions and deaths "cannot at this time be accounted for by radiation or attributed to the atomic tests conducted at the Nevada proving grounds."[34] A note Dunning gave AEC's head of public relations, Morse Salisbury, shows how far he was willing to go to keep the atomic tests going. Dunning wrote:

> after prolonged discussions I was able to get the group to agree to a series
> of statements which I thought you would be interested in seeing. The
> members of the committee signed the original. The statements were

finally agreed upon just prior to departure time so that they are not in the most elegant grammatical form but do represent the most tangible statements to date.[35]

COVERING UP RADIATION'S HUMAN IMPACTS

The sheep ranchers' situation was thus disposed of, at the cost of official honesty. But there was another problem out there, one that would not be so easily evaded. The harm to the sheep—acute radiation poisoning—had been immediate and obvious. The harm to humans—largely cancer—was delayed and subtle. The first public warning came with a test shot named Sedan in the summer of 1962. Sedan was intended to explore peaceful uses for nuclear warheads and demonstrated nicely that if anyone needed a large radioactive hole in the ground, a buried atomic bomb was just the ticket.

Sedan's fallout cloud drifted over a group of students on a field trip led by Professor Robert C. Pendleton, director of the University of Utah's Department of Radiological Health. The group was measuring background radiation, and the readings increased a hundredfold as the fallout cloud swept past.[36] Pendleton got his students to safety and then began blowing the whistle, pointing particularly to the hazards posed by I-131. Utah health officials responded by dumping thousands of gallons of milk. The Kennedy Administration reacted to the public uproar by insisting there was no cause for concern, then it forbade agencies to release any fallout data without White House approval.[37]

The term "Atomic Veterans" is used to describe servicemen exposed to radiation in the line of duty; a majority of the 250,000 Atomic Veterans were exposed at the Nevada testing grounds or the tests in the Pacific. In Nevada, infantry were placed as close as half a mile from the detonations and sometimes marched through ground zero shortly after the detonation; in the Pacific, ships were posted as near as three miles from the ground zero and often drenched in radioactive water from underwater blasts.[38] A medical study showed that a sample of 3,027 soldiers exposed in one of the Nevada tests had a 300 percent elevated risk for leukemia.[39]

Professor Pendleton did not know that a controversy regarding I-131 levels was already brewing inside the AEC. In the late 1950s, geneticist Edward B. Lewis raised the question of the dangers of fallout and testified before Congress's Joint Committee on Atomic Energy.[40] The Joint Committee asked the AEC to report on the subject. AEC assigned the report to Harold Knapp of its Fallout Studies Branch. Knapp's conclusion was that the thyroids of infants in southern Utah had been exposed to as much as four hundred radiation absorbed doses (rads) at a time when the maximum safe level for infants was considered half a rad per year. Nor was the risk limited to southern Utah. As far off as St. Louis, infants were irradiated at five times the supposedly safe level.[41]

The Knapp findings had the potential to be explosive. Gordon Dunning circulated the report with a memo attached that noted: "The Commission has been telling the world for years that it has been conducting its operations safely. . . . [W]hat reaction can we expect from the press and public?"

Knapp, with more candor than tact, replied, "I expect somebody might want to hang Gordon Dunning from a sour apple tree."[42] A team of AEC scientists was formed to meet with Knapp and convince him to withdraw his study; instead they supported him. In the end, the AEC agreed to publish his paper. But when Dr. Knapp saw the published version, he realized that it had been trimmed to remove all his I-131 findings.[43]

Then, in 1965, the U.S. Public Health Service commissioned a study of cancer in the downwind areas of Utah and Nevada, conducted by Dr. Edward Weiss. Weiss looked at leukemia, which can be caused by fallout's radioactive strontium. He found that in the two Utah counties most affected by fallout there had been twenty-eight cases of leukemia, when statistics would have predicted only nineteen.[44] The study immediately generated worries—and at very high levels. Shortly after receiving a draft, a White House science advisor asked the Public Health Service "what would be the federal government's liability" for any injury caused. A joint AEC-PHS-White House meeting was held the next day, with three lawyers in attendance.[45]

Shortly thereafter, Weiss's study was deep-sixed; officially, it remained unfinished and unpublished until 1979, when the *Washington Post* discovered and released its findings. Its January 8, 1979, story revealed:

Federal health officials had evidence as early as 1965 that excessive leukemia deaths were occurring among Utah residents exposed to radioactive fallout from U.S. atomic bomb tests, according to documents obtained by The Washington Post.

But the U.S. Public Health Service apparently ignored the findings of one of its own investigators and withheld his study, which cited the leukemia victims' "extended residence" in the fallout area.

The long-forgotten and unpublished study, dated Sept. 14, 1965, was requested and obtained under the Freedom of Information Act.

Officials of the Department of Health, Education and Welfare—now involved in a major controversy over whether A-bomb tests caused leukemia and cancer—were described as "horrified" to learn from the Post request that such an unpublished study existed.[46]

How the informational dam was broken is a tale in itself. Gordon Eliot White was the Washington, D.C., bureau chief for *Deseret News,* Salt Lake City's largest newspaper. During a slow news period in June 1977, word came of Sgt. Paul Cooper, an "Atomic Veteran" who was dying of leukemia and blamed his exposure to fallout at the Nevada Test Site.[47]

White acquired fallout-level charts and compared them to figures on leukemia deaths he obtained from the National Cancer Institute. He found leukemia rates were exceptionally high in the parts of Utah most affected by fallout; one hard-hit county had nearly twice the national rate.[48] He thought the matter was worth a story.

White's story came to the attention of Dr. Joseph L. Lyon, director of the Utah Cancer Registry. Dr. Lyon had thought the idea of a fallout-cancer connection was "nutty" and conducted his own research, expecting to refute the connection. Rather than comparing leukemia rates in counties with and without fallout, he would take counties affected by fallout and determine whether leukemia rates had increased during atomic testing and declined after it ended. Where White had compared leukemia rates in a geographical sense, Dr. Lyon would compare them over time.

To his surprise, Dr. Lyon found that the data confirmed the connection between atomic testing fallout and leukemia. Published in the prestigious *New England Journal of Medicine*, his results indicated that downwinder children born during the atomic tests had a 244 percent greater risk of dying from leukemia than children born before or after the tests.[49] Lyon had unknowingly replicated the results of the still-suppressed Weiss study.

The genie was out of the bottle. The downwinders had an explanation for the remarkable rates of cancer in their communities. They began to organize.

THE DOWNWINDERS TURN TO COURT

Before long, the downwinders had linked up with a legal team headed by the late Dale Haralson of Tucson, Arizona, an experienced personal injury trial attorney, and Stewart Udall, former Secretary of the Interior and lobbyist. Haralson had a personal stake in the matter: he would try the case while recovering from radiation treatment for throat cancer. Ultimately, 1,200 persons, injured downwinders or survivors of those who had died, joined in the case.

The suits focused not on the testing itself, but on the government's failure to warn. There was little sense in challenging the decision to test; if the discretionary function exception covered anything, it would certainly cover a presidential decision to initiate testing of weapons essential to the national defense. But failure to warn was a different sort of issue; it was hard to see what policy decisions were implicated in not warning people there was dangerous radiation headed their way. Indeed, the government had not only failed to warn, it had led the downwinders to believe that the fallout was harmless, promised that it *would* warn them if levels were likely to become dangerous, and actively suppressed any suggestion that the downwinders were in danger.

Lawsuits involving 1,200 plaintiffs were unmanageable, so it was decided that twenty-four plaintiffs would serve as a test or "bellwether" case to establish general legal doctrines. The lead plaintiff, Irene Allen, had twice been widowed by cancer. Other plaintiffs included the families of four children who had died from leukemia while in their early teens, and adult plaintiffs who had suffered from malignant melanoma or cancers of the colon, breast, bladder, kidneys, lung, and thyroid. The plaintiffs were almost all rural and Mormon, did not smoke or drink liquor, ate food fresh from their farms, fed their children milk from their own cows, and, in short, led lives that any health-food advocate would envy—except their food had been coated, and their children's milk laced, with radioactive fallout.

The initial hope was for a settlement. Stewart Udall had served in the Cabinets of Presidents John F. Kennedy and Lyndon Baines Johnson and retained powerful Democratic connections. The lawsuits were begun under the Jimmy Carter Administration, and Carter had been pressing for a comprehensive nuclear testing treaty. But the White House apparently did not want to get involved, so Udall dealt with the U.S. Department of Justice. USDOJ's OPs were attorneys rather than politicians, so they thought of settlement in terms of "what's the risk of our losing, and for how much?" Udall was a politician with a law degree, and approached matters as a lobbyist would, trying to use his connections and convince the government that settling was the fair and politically beneficial approach. As a result, the settlement negotiations quickly went nowhere. "He seemed to have the idea that if he knocked on the right door, had gone high enough, and had created enough adverse publicity, the legal and factual issues would just go away," the head of USDOJ's Torts Branch later recollected.[50]

The trial consumed thirteen weeks. The downwinders' case was strengthened by several remarkable discoveries. Some residents had been given "film badges" that measured the exposure of their wearer to radiation. The government had kept the measurements secret. When the government was forced to release the data, the reason for the secrecy became obvious. Plaintiff Willard Lewis Bowler was one of those issued a badge. He later died of metastatic melanoma, an especially deadly skin cancer. The government records showed his skin had been exposed to thirty-one thousand millirems of radioactivity, the equivalent of three to four thousand chest x-rays.[51]

Frank Butrico, the Public Health Service radiation monitor who had reported the fallout in St. George, Utah, testified that a government report he had supposedly authored was a forgery. The report, found in the AEC files, had him claiming that all children were indoors when the fallout cloud passed over, when actually he had reported school children playing outdoors.[52] The forged report added, in words Butrico testified he never would have used, that "the effectiveness of the safety program was amazing."[53] Butrico testified that he was shocked to see "that [his] name is over a report that contains statements unknown to [him]."[54] Almost any private attorney who discovered that his client had forged an exhibit would have, at the very least, moved to withdraw from the case, but the USDOJ lawyers were unfazed.

Judge Jenkins took seventeen months to rule, and then he released a thorough and lengthy decision. Federal trial court rulings typically run about ten pages printed in the *Federal Supplement*, but Judge Jenkins's ruling in *Allen v. United States*[55] ran a staggering 225 pages.

The critical question: Was the failure to warn absolutely protected by the Federal Tort Claims Act exception for "discretionary functions"? Judge Jenkins ruled that it was not. First, in his view the discretionary function exception covered policy decisions. The decision whether to test atomic bombs was protected, but the failure to warn people so they could take precautions was operational negligence, not policy making. "At no time has the defendant [the government] ever asserted that as a matter of conscious choice it deliberately adopted a policy of not warning, not measuring and not educating the populace at hazard," he ruled.[56] It was a refinement of the district court ruling in the Texas City case. There, the judge had argued that only high-level policy decision making was protected, and his decision had been overturned. Judge Jenkins's ruling was narrower. Policy making at any level would be protected; what was not protected was a *failure* to consider safety, to make safety policy. Judge Jenkins found in favor of ten plaintiffs; the others, he concluded, might have gotten cancer by sheer chance.

The government was not pleased; even ten winning plaintiffs were too many. It took an appeal to the Tenth Circuit, which reversed Judge Jenkins's ruling. The Circuit's ruling hinged on the recently decided *United States v. Varig Airlines*,[57] where the Federal Aviation Administration had negligently certified as safe a passenger plane that caught fire and crashed, killing 123 people. The Supreme Court had ruled that the discretionary function exception protected supervisors and inspectors who had decided to skip inspecting the airplane for fire hazards: "[I]t is the nature of the conduct, rather than the status of the actor, that governs whether the discretionary function exception applies in a given case."[58] As the Court saw it, the FAA OPs might have made "certain calculated risks, but those risks were accepted for the advancement of a governmental purpose."[59] The agency simply did not have enough resources to completely inspect every aircraft, and the low-level decisions to inspect one plane or another were protected as policy making.

In short, whether Americans died by the bad judgment of a Cabinet official or negligence of a "grunt" in the federal machine, the government was protected against lawsuits.

With the Supreme Court ruling in hand, the Tenth Circuit had no difficulty disposing of Judge Jenkins's ruling in favor of the ten downwinders.[60] Yes, government employees had known that the downwinders would be drenched in radioactive fallout. Yes, they had negligently failed to warn the downwinders of the danger; in fact, they led them to believe that fallout was nothing to be concerned about. Yes, people had died as a result. But no, the government was not liable for the result. Killing people and lying about it to the citizens and to the court was a "discretionary function" of federal employees.

Contrast the government response to its tests irradiating people *other than* American citizens. In addition to the Nevada Test Site, there was a test site in the Marshall Islands. In March 1954, a blast there proved much more powerful than expected, and a Japanese fishing vessel, the *Daigo Fukuryu Maru*, was covered in fallout. One of its crewmen died as an indirect result,[61] and a considerable amount of tuna was dumped due to fears of radiation. The United States agreed to pay $2 million ($18 million in 2017 dollars) as compensation.[62]

CHAPTER 3

TUSKEGEE, ALABAMA: DYING "FOR THE GLORY OF SCIENCE"

For the most part, doctors and civil servants simply did their job. Some merely followed orders, others worked for the glory of science.
　—Dr. John Heller, Director, Division of Venereal Disease, U.S. Public Health Services (USPHS), 1972[1]

[I]f the colored population becomes aware that accepting free hospital care means a post-mortem [an autopsy], every darkey will leave Macon county and it will hurt Dibble's hospital. This can be prevented, however, if the doctors of Macon County are brought into our confidence and requested to be very careful not to let the objective of our plan be known.
　—Dr. O. C. Wenger, U.S. Public Health Services, 1933[2]

SYPHILIS IS A STRANGE DISEASE. UNLIKE most diseases, its European outbreak can be fixed precisely in time—Naples, the winter of 1494–95. Scientists still debate whether it was brought back by Columbus's sailors, was a deadly mutation of an existing disease, or was brought by Columbus's crews *and then* mutated into a deadly disease.

Also unusual is that scientists can track the evolution of syphilis and show how it keyed upon "survival of the weakest." Syphilis arrived in a horrifying form—"its pustules often covered the body from the head to the knees, caused flesh to fall from people's faces, and led to death within a few months."[3] The face was often the first target, with the sufferer's nose and oral cavity caving in as the underlying tissues were destroyed.

Hideous disfigurement and swift death might do for some diseases, but they were a lousy business plan for a disease spread by sexual contact. The more aggressive strains of the germ died with their hosts; strains that killed slowly, or let their host survive until something else felled him, were the ones that continued to spread. In 1575, some eighty years after the disease's origin, the noted surgeon Ambroise Pare could write:

> Generally, the lues venerea [venereal plague] which now reigneth is far more mild and easy to be cured than that which was in former times, when it first began among us; besides, each day it seemeth to be milder than other. Astrologers think that the cause hereof to be this: for that the celestial influences that first brought in this disease, in success of time by the contrary revolutions of the stars, lose their power and become weak; so that it may seem somewhat likely that, that at length after some few years it may wholly cease.[4]

Pare is likely overstating matters: the disease was still fearsome enough that his patients were willing to undergo his cure, which involved cauterizing the sores with the equivalent of small branding irons (patients squeamish about having red-hot irons applied to their genitals were treated with acid or molten sulfur applied to the same body part).[5]

Fast forward three hundred years to the nineteenth century. By now the spirochete that causes the disease has reached an accommodation with its human host, a dance of death in three stages. In the primary stage, a small, usually painless, sore develops at the site of the infection. After it vanishes, a secondary stage begins, characterized by a rash and flu-like symptoms. The bacteria—a spirochete—is loose in the blood. Then those symptoms, too, go away.

The disease then seemingly becomes dormant. In most cases, the dormancy lasts for a lifetime, and the infected person may never realize that his body is harboring the spirochete and passing the disease on to other victims through sexual contact. Whatever damage the bacteria do is not enough to cause symptoms.

In the other cases, after ten or twenty years of supposed dormancy the disease's impact becomes apparent. About 10 percent of all syphilis cases are of the mildest form, where the victim develops sores and painful tumorlike pockets of inflammation that can affect skin, bones, and sometimes internal organs. They are often disfiguring but rarely life threatening.

Another 10 percent of all untreated infections progress to neurosyphilis, where the spirochete attacks the brain and nervous system. The process usually begins with problems with coordination and muscular weakness, and often headaches. Sometimes the optic centers and optic nerve are attacked, leading to blindness. From there the disease progresses to insanity, dementia, paralysis, and death. The process is not mercifully quick: nine years passed between gangster Al Capone becoming psychotic in prison and his 1947 death at home in Miami Beach.

Cardiovascular syphilis develops in another 14 percent of untreated syphilis cases. The bacteria attack the victims' circulatory system and erode the heart valves, causing congestive heart failure, and inflame and narrow the coronary arteries, which can cause a heart attack. Or they may attack the aorta, the body's main artery, weakening its walls and causing it to balloon out in failures known as aneurisms. If an aortic aneurism bursts, the victim bleeds out and dies in seconds.

Syphilis was once astonishingly widespread in America. One 1915 study concluded that about 5 to 10 percent of America's adult population was infected and that it caused 20 percent of the country's mental commitments.[6] During the World War II draft, 5 percent of draftees tested positive.[7] The spirochete was at least egalitarian, as the 2014 *Journal of Medicine and Life* explains:

> The writers were among the most affected category. . . . Alphonse Daudet, Thomas Chatterton, Keats, James Boswell, Baudelaire, Heinrich Heine, Dostoyevsky and Oscar Wild (sic) are only a few examples of writers suffering from syphilis. Romanian poet Mihai Eminescu was diagnosed with syphilis, too. He died in a mental institution at the age of 39 years. Even the philosophers, who were usually considered superior minds, and insensitive to women's charms, also have suffered for syphilis. The most famous of them were Friedrich Nietzsche (1844–1900) and Arthur Schopehnauer (1788–1860).[8]

As might be expected, there had long been attempts to find a cure. By the seventeenth century, it was known that syphilis seemed to be affected by high fevers and mercury poisoning ("A night with Venus, a lifetime with Mercury," went the saying), so sufferers were sometimes dosed with the chemical and heated in special ovens that left their head protruding. The approach had two drawbacks: it rarely killed the disease and often killed the patient. The mercury "therapy" lasted into the early twentieth century; at one point, it was estimated that in the United States mercury treatment killed thousands annually.[9]

Then, in the early 1900s, a German doctor named Paul Ehrlich became fascinated by the process of staining germs to identify them, a process that was being advanced by Germany's new and rising chemical industry. If there were chemicals that would *color* only one type of cell, he reasoned, there might be ones that would *kill* only one type of cell. What he wanted was a "magic bullet" of a chemical, one that was toxic to disease bacteria but not to normal cells. With that as his goal, he set to work with Teutonic thoroughness, testing one likely chemical after another to see if it would kill the syphilis spirochete. He invented a term for what he was seeking to create: "chemotherapy."

The search was exhaustive and, we may assume, exhausting. He set out to modify the toxic stain atoxyl, which was based on arsenic and known to affect bacteria similar to the syphilis spirochete. He and his assistant, Dr. Sahachiro Hata, tested 605 compounds without finding what they sought—but Number 606 hit the mark.

The 606 chemical was arsphenamine, soon given the trade name of Salvarsan, and its impact was enormous; a cure had been found to one of the major banes of humanity. In 1910, its first year of production, sixty-five thousand doses had been given to twenty thousand patients.[10] Two years later, Ehrlich brought out Neosalvarsan, an improved form of the medication.

Salvarsan was far from perfect. In the presence of oxygen, it decomposed into a very toxic compound, so it had to be packaged under carbon dioxide and quickly mixed and administered. The injections could be so painful that they required treatment with narcotics. It did have side effects (including liver damage—after all, it was based on arsenic), and it did not cure every case, but it did raise the chances of symptom-free survival to 85 percent.[11] In the 1920s, it was discovered that those odds could be raised by combining Salvarsan injections with those of bismuth, a heavy metal that is much less toxic than mercury.[12]

Salvarsan remained the standard treatment for syphilis for more than thirty years. In 1943, it was proven that the new drug penicillin would cure syphilis with only one injection if caught during the disease's primary stage and only a few injections if caught later. Penicillin was easily administered and, as long as the patient was not allergic, it did not cause side effects.

BEGINNINGS OF THE TUSKEGEE STUDY

The Tuskegee Syphilis Study began in 1932, a decade before penicillin. The initial study was hardly objectionable, but "mission creep" swiftly made it otherwise. A plan to cure untreated syphilitics while documenting what damage the disease *had already done* instead became a plan to leave the patients uninformed and untreated, and to document what damage the disease would do to them *in the future*. The new approach was not only horrifying, it also put the government doctors in violation of the ethical imperative "first do no harm." That almost forty years passed with no doctor "leaks" is a sad part of our history.

In 1929, the charitable Rosenwald Foundation provided a grant to the U.S. Public Health Service (USPHS) to study the seriousness of syphilis in the population of six rural counties, including Macon County, Alabama. The county's residents were impoverished black sharecroppers who could rarely afford medical care, so it was a safe wager that untreated syphilis would be a major problem. Macon County had a regional Veterans Administration hospital and was home to a teaching hospital at Tuskegee University, a historically black college, where blood samples could be analyzed.[13]

The initial study found that 25 percent of the adult test population had syphilis, and 90 percent of them had received no medical treatment for the disease.[14] The authors of the study began to write a plan to treat the ten thousand individuals who had tested positive—given the numbers, it was going to require a Herculean effort.[15]

On September 17, 1932, Eugene Dibble, the medical director of the Tuskegee Institute, wrote to another Tuskegee official about the survey:

> The experiment was very successful but was discontinued due to the lack of funds. The U.S. Public Health Service however, is very anxious to extend its research further into this problem, so they can find out just

what effect syphilis is having on people who have been untreated over a period of years. As you know, there are hundreds of people in this section who probably have certain forms of syphilis and have never had any treatment whatsoever. . . .

The cost of the treatment of this disease is very high, so that it would be of world-wide significance to have this study made.[16]

This approach still envisioned curing the patients after studying them; Dibble added that the USPHS "would furnish the necessary dressings, cotton, X-Ray films and the Neo-Salvarsan for any treatment given."[17]

High-level planning for the study was already in process. There were two major sponsors. One was Dr. Joseph Moore, of Johns Hopkins University, a leading student of venereal disease who was then writing his treatise *The Modern Treatment of Syphilis*. The other was Assistant Surgeon General Taliaferro Clark, who led the U.S. Public Health Service's Venereal Disease Division. On September 28, 1932, Dr. Moore sent Assistant Surgeon General Clark a comprehensive plan to combine research with cures. He suggested setting aside those patients who could give a definite date to the beginning of their infection. They would receive an extensive examination and workup to determine whether and how much their bodies had been damaged; then they would be given medication in hopes of curing the disease. The remainder, who could not date their infection, would skip the workup and proceed immediately to treatment.[18] Given the state of the art as it then existed, this would have been a humane approach. Patients would also have been given a number of incentives to participate. First, of course, would be treatment for their disease. Beyond that, there would be free medical care at a point in time when medical care was a luxury.[19] Participants also were given rides in automobiles, a rare luxury for black sharecroppers in the 1930s, hot meals at the hospital, and (later in the study) an allowance for burial expenses.[20] Yet even at this early stage, the study arrangements had an ominous undertone that suggested the study participants were being seen as experimental subjects rather than as human patients. The participants were never told that they had syphilis. At most, they were told they needed treatment for "bad blood" (a meaningless term from centuries ago, but which was still current in the rural south). They were given an iron tonic and sometimes pills that were actually aspirin.[21]

Dr. R. A. Vonderlehr of the USPHS was put in charge of the project. He wrote Dr. Clark, estimating that five hundred patients were already receiving treatment, and making plans to recruit new volunteers for the study as participants were cured: "The completion of the course of arsenic [Salvarsan] will automatically eliminate large numbers of patients each month, equalizing the new numbers acquired."[22]

The costs of this approach quickly became a problem. In January 1933, Assistant Surgeon General Clark wrote to Dr. Vonderlehr: "It never occurred to me that we would be called upon to treat a large part of the county as a return for the privilege of making this study." While treatment would continue (if only as the price of getting volunteers for the study), Clark called for limiting its cost "as greatly as can be done without prejudice to our study."[23] The patients came to be given eight doses of Salvarsan (instead of the standard twenty doses), plus "more or less of heavy metal" (bismuth or mercury).

The eight-dose plan was cheaper but almost useless in curing the patients. Diagnostic Wassermann tests given to "treated" patients revealed that 97 percent were still positive for syphilis.[24] This does not seem to have disturbed anyone: the object of the treatment had become to get people in so they could be studied, not to treat and actually cure them. The administrators of the study were, consciously or unconsciously, beginning to treat the volunteers not as patients but as experimental lab animals, as numbers to be manipulated for the good of science.

The purpose of the initial phase of the study was to establish a baseline for the persons being studied. One test procedure was deliberately delayed to the end of the initial phase: conducting spinal taps to determine if neurosyphilis was beginning to develop. This required insertion of a needle into the spinal canal to retrieve some cerebrospinal fluid. The tap itself is painful, and its aftermath is often worse: days or weeks of terrible headaches as the brain, deprived of some of the cushioning given by the cerebrospinal fluid, bumps the inside of the skull. The Tuskegee subjects were given one night in the hospital after the tap and then driven home down rutted dirt roads.

This procedure was saved for last, lest those experiencing it lose enthusiasm for the study, and deception was used to get the patients involved. Dr. Vonderlehr explained to Assistant Surgeon General Clark: "The idea of bringing them in large groups is to get the procedure completed in a given area before the negro population has been able to find out just what is going on. . . . [D]etails of the puncture procedure should also be kept from them as far as possible."[25]

Vonderlehr later admitted he planned to "rush through all the punctures as rapidly as hospitalization will permit because if sufficient time is permitted to elapse for news of reactions to spread before a neighborhood is completed the remaining patients will default."[26]

When the time came, letters were sent to each patient announcing they were being given their "last chance to get a second examination." The letter continued, "This examination is a special one and after it is finished you will be given a special treatment if it is believed you are in a condition to stand it." Some were told the spinal tap was actually an injection of medicine.[27] The rushed spinal taps were quite painful; some patients required two or three "sticks" to get the fluid, most experienced terrible headaches, and at least one had temporary paralysis.[28]

An uninfected 201 men chosen as controls, and 399 infected but untreated volunteers, had been examined, x-rayed, and if infected, had had their symptoms recorded and correlated to the duration of the infection. The USPHS had gotten the data it desired, although 97 percent of the infected patients were left with a potentially fatal and untreated disease.

THE STUDY'S NADIR: INADEQUATE TREATMENT BECOMES NO TREATMENT AT ALL

In April 1933, Dr. Vonderlehr wrote to Dr. Clark to outline a new idea: deliberately leave the patients with no further treatment at all, follow them over the years, and find out what the disease did to them in terms of death and destruction. Think of what science could gain!

> At the end of this project we shall have a considerable number of cases presenting various complications of syphilis [with patients] who have received only mercury and may still be considered as untreated in the modern sense of therapy. Should these cases be followed over a period of five to ten years many interesting facts could be learned regarding the course of complications [of] untreated syphilis. The longevity of these syphilitics could be ascertained, and if properly administered I believe

that many necropsies [autopsies] could be arranged. . . . [I]t seems a pity to me to lose such an unusual opportunity.[29]

Dr. Vonderlehr wrote this before penicillin became known as an easy cure for syphilis, but Salvarsan was available. Even in this period, to quote from an article in *The Medical Bulletin*, it was "no longer justifiable to withhold specific therapy from patients with cardiovascular syphilis, even when the situation seems hopeless; for treatment can be adjusted so as to do no harm to the patient and good results may be obtained."[30]

What would be done to the Tuskegee participants may be contrasted with what was done for Al Capone, America's most murderous gangster, while the Tuskegee study was under way. When Capone developed tertiary syphilis, the Alcatraz Bureau of Prisons doctors gave him forty doses of Neosalvarsan and forty-two doses of bismuth.[31] Sitting in Alcatraz, the infamous gangster was receiving the medical treatment that the USPHS was withholding from its Tuskegee patients!

In July, Dr. Vonderlehr wrote Dr. O. C. Wenger, who headed the USPHS office in Hot Springs, Arkansas, stating that he had presented his plan to the Surgeon General, and believed it would be approved. Wenger replied with suggestions to minimize costs: "As I see it, we have no further interest in these patients *until they die*." (Emphasis in the original.)

Wenger suggested they request any local doctors, from whom a subject of the study might request treatment, to refer the subject to Tuskegee, thus ensuring that a complete record of their medical condition would be in one place, and that after a patient died there would be "more time to persuade a family to have a postmortem performed." Yet Wenger added a *caveat*:

> There is one danger in the latter plan and that is that if the colored population becomes aware that accepting free hospital care means a post-mortem, every darkey will leave Macon county and it will hurt Dibble's hospital [Tuskegee]. This can be prevented, however, if the doctors of Macon County are brought into our confidence and requested to be very careful not to let the objective of our plan be known.[32]

There were only ten medical doctors in all of Macon County, making it easy to get such an agreement. Wenger took matters a step further. The sharecroppers trusted the federal government and respected its employ-ees, so Dr. Dibble, medical director of the Tuskegee Institute, received a nominal USPHS appointment. Dr. Wenger wrote: "One thing is certain. The only way we are going to get post-mortems is to have the demise take place in Dibble's hospital and when these colored folks are told that Doctor Dibble is now a Government doctor too they will have more confidence."[33]

One problem remained. The whole purpose of the study was to track the sickness and death inflicted by *untreated* syphilis. But the human beings who were its subjects were not always cooperative with this goal. As the years passed they got sicker, and some seemed to take a dim view of dying of dementia or from a burst aneurism. They tried to get real treatment for their ailments, sometimes from doctors who hadn't been tipped off to the study and were willing to give them real medication. The USPHS staff sought to block such interference. Dr. Reginald James, a USPHS doctor working in Macon County, later told the *New York Times* of his experiences:

> I was distraught and disturbed whenever a patient in the study group appeared. . . . I was advised the patient was not to be treated. Whenever I insisted on treating such a patient, he never showed up again. They were being advised that they shouldn't take treatments or they would be dropped from the study. At that time certain benefits were proffered the patients such as treatment for other ailments, payment of burial expenses, and a $50 cash benefit. To receive these benefits, the patient had to remain in the study.[34]

A bigger threat to the study loomed as World War II broke out, and the military got in the way. In 1942, Dr. Vonderlehr received a letter informing him that military draft boards were requiring that draftees take syphilis tests and, if infected, be given treatment. Vonderlehr responded:

> Some time ago Doctor Murray Smith wrote to me about this matter. I suggested to him that he confer with the chairman of the local Selective Service Board, Mr. J. F. Segrest, and explain to him that this study of untreated syphilis is of great importance from a scientific standpoint. It represents one of the last opportunities which the science of medicine will have to conduct an investigation of this kind.

Doctor Smith replied that he had furnished the local board a list containing 256 names of men under 45 years of age and asked that these men be excluded from the list of draftees needing treatment. During his conference with the board they agreed to this arrangement . . .[35]

By 1942, everyone who was found with syphilis was being treated, so the Tuskegee subjects (we can hardly call them patients at this stage) were dying and being ruined to obtain knowledge that was of no conceivable future value.

The now-worthless nature of the data being generated was underscored by the 1943 announcement that penicillin cured syphilis quickly and with no noteworthy side effects.[36] The dreaded disease was being cured with one or two inexpensive injections—unless the patient was a Tuskegee test subject. Some of the 399 received the treatment anyway, when they happened to consult doctors outside Macon County; and in 1952, Dr. Vonderlehr shared a worry with another doctor: "I hope that the availability of antibiotics has not interfered too much with this project."[37]

THE TUSKEGEE STUDY IN THE MEDICAL LITERATURE

In retrospect, it is strange to note that, while the nature of the study was a secret to its human subjects, there was no cover-up of the Tuskegee Syphilis Study in the medical world. The USPHS seemed inexplicably proud of its work, and the doctors conducting the study published numerous articles in medical journals that documented its results. The first article appeared in 1936, when the study was just beginning. Authored by Dr. Vonderlehr, Dr. Taliaferro Clark, and Dr. J. R. Heller, it described the study's background: "The administration of adequate treatment in early syphilis is recognized as the most important factor in the prevention both of communicable relapse and of the early complications so detrimental to the health of the individual patient."

That does seem logical. However, the doctors carefully worded the next section as if they are simply finding their study subjects, not creating them:

As a result of surveys a few years ago in southern rural areas it was learned that a considerable portion of the infected Negro population remained untreated during the entire course of syphilis. Such individuals seemed to offer an unusual opportunity to study the untreated syphilitic patients from the beginning of the disease to the death of the infected person.[38]

The article appeared in the *Journal of the American Medical Association* as "Untreated Syphilis in the Male Negro." As the years went on, more reports of the study documented the damage being done to its human subjects. A 1946 report found that 25 percent of the untreated syphilitics were already dead, versus 14 percent of noninfected persons chosen as controls. It estimated that the disease would reduce the life expectancy of the untreated syphilitic patients by 20 percent.[39] That 20 percent figure was cited by USPHS's Dr. O. C. Wenger addressing a seminar in 1950. He added the following:

> Remember these patients, wherever they are, received no treatment on our recommendation. We know now, where we could only surmise before, that we have contributed to their ailments and shortened their lives. I think the least we can say is that we have a high moral obligation to those that have died to make this the best study possible. This is the last chance in our country to make an investigation of this sort.[40]

Dr. Wenger's reference to "high moral obligation" is shocking. The obligation, as he sees it, is not to treat the patients, but to do the best possible job of studying them as they die.

A follow-up study in 1956 found that the syphilis damage was steadily expanding. Among the 159 surviving patients, ten were dying from neurosyphilis, six were going blind, six had aneurisms, four were dying from congestive heart failure, and twelve had syphilitic destruction of the skeletal system. Compared to the controls, the untreated syphilitics had more abnormal electrocardiograph readings (33 percent versus 20 percent) and were more likely to have enlarged hearts (64 percent versus 37 percent), high blood pressure (58 percent versus 33 percent), and hardening of the arteries (72 percent versus 50 percent). Twenty years of untreated syphilis were ruining the men's circulatory systems. The study concluded: "Review of those still living . . . reveals that an appreciable number have late complications of syphilis which probably will result, for some at least, in contributing materially to the ultimate cause of death."[41]

A 1964 article wrote of the thirty-year follow-up. Its summary began: "The syphilitic group continues to have higher mortality and morbidity than the uninfected controls, with the cardiovascular system most commonly affected. As of Dec. 1, 1963, approximately 59% of the syphilitic group and 45% of the control group were known to be dead . . ."[42]

The 1964 article had an unexpected result: someone actually objected to the morality of the study. A young Michigan cardiologist, Irwin Schatz, wrote to the primary author:

> I am utterly astounded by the fact that physicians allow patients with a potentially fatal disease to remain untreated when effective therapy is available. I assume you feel that the information which is extracted from the observations of the untreated group is worth their sacrifice. If this is the case, then I suggest that the United State Public Health Service and those physicians associated with it need to reevaluate their moral judgments in this regard.[43]

The letter got bucked down the chain of command to a coauthor, Dr. Anne Yobs, for her to answer. She noted on the routing slip, "This is the first letter of this type we have received. I do not plan to answer this letter."[44] The study had been ongoing for thirty years, had repeatedly been publicized in the medical literature, and only one person had objected—and that in a private letter.[45] But the study was about to find its whistleblower.

In 1966, Peter Buxtun was a new investigator for a USPHS venereal disease clinic in San Francisco. The military had trained him to be a combat medic, then a psychiatric social worker, so the USPHS had sounded like a good career move. While eating lunch in the facility's coffee room one day, he overheard a conversation between two nurses and a professional officer who worked for the Centers for Disease Control. Fifty years later, he still could remember distinctly what the officer told the nurses:

> He spoke of a patient who was elderly and insane, so his family, not knowing what else to do, took him to a doctor some distance away. The doctor didn't know of the Tuskegee study. He gave the patient a blood test, a VDRL test [for syphilis] and found he had a high titre, so he gave

him a big shot of penicillin. The next thing the doctor knew, the county medical society and the county board of health were jumping all over him, "look what you've done, you've ruined our study!"[46]

The nurses left and Buxtun spoke with the CDC staffer. It became apparent that the study involved using a group of ill-educated rural people as human guinea pigs.

Buxtun's job left him time for administrative details, in which he could request files from other offices. He called the CDC and asked for copies of the Tuskegee Study. The files arrived in a large manila envelope. While the study described its patients as "volunteers with social motives," reading the documentation made it quite clear that no one had volunteered in any real sense; they thought they had something called "bad blood" and were receiving treatment for it.

Buxtun told his immediate superior, Dr. John Harper, that he was going to send a letter to Dr. William Brown, head of the CDC's Division of Venereal Disease, suggesting that the study be brought to a halt and all the patients be given real treatment. Dr. Harper nervously replied that he had a family and needed to keep his job—"Don't mention my name when you get fired." Buxtun wrote the letter as a private citizen arguing that it was not appropriate for the Public Health Service to leave citizens ignorant of their condition and untreated.[47]

The CDC's first response came in about a month. A CDC headquarters staffer was coming to San Francisco for a Christmas visit with family, and Dr. Brown asked him to interview Buxtun. The staffer read questions off a clipboard, the first of which was "Why did you send that letter to Dr. Brown?"

Around a month after the interview, Buxtun received a letter directing him to fly to CDC headquarters in Atlanta. He knew that the Venereal Disease headquarters staff had meetings; presumably a decision was going to be made at one of those meetings. After arriving at headquarters, he was told he would not be taking part in any such meeting. He was ordered to sit in a chair in the corner, and at 5:00 p.m., five men came up and told him to come with them.

In the basement, Dr. John Cutler, who headed the Tuskegee Study, began giving Buxtun a tongue-lashing. The study was yielding important data, Cutler claimed, and everyone in it was a volunteer. Buxtun produced a document from the files, which stated that without "suasions" (the free medical care and other benefits promised to the subjects), it would be impossible to secure the cooperation of the subjects of the study.

Buxtun later said, "The look on their faces—it was as if you could see lightbulbs go on over their heads. They realized 'we have a problem here.'" The study scientists discussed what to do for about twenty minutes before they remembered that Buxtun was listening to everything and dismissed him. By then, Buxtun was tiring of the USPHS. Switching careers entirely, he won admission to Hastings Law School.

USPHS eventually appointed a "blue-ribbon panel" to look into the study. The handpicked panel wound up more concerned with improving the study's scientific quality than with its deep moral problems. As part of the improvements, USPHS delegates persuaded the Macon County doctors to reaffirm their decision to withhold antibiotics from any study subject that consulted them.[48]

In 1950, Edward Nevin died in a San Francisco hospital, after being infected with an obscure bacterium, *Serratia marcescens*. Decades later, his descendants discovered that the military had conducted experiments in biological warfare that included releasing an enormous fog of that bacterium over the city.[49] They sued the government, but the Ninth Circuit ruled that the government's choice to infect its own citizens was protected by the discretionary function exception.[50]

Buxtun waited for a year, then sent another letter to the chief of the Venereal Disease Branch. Trying hard to sway him, he pointed out that the study group is "100% negro," making it "political dynamite" for the agency. The subjects of the study were not willing volunteers; they had little medical knowledge and had been swindled into signing up. This was not a question of "informed consent": the subjects had not even been told they had syphilis, so they had given no consent at all. Buxtun argued that anyone today would regard it as "morally unethical" to do such a thing. He ended, "I earnestly hope that you will inform me that the study group has been, or soon will be, treated."[51]

He received no reply. Four years later, Buxtun mentioned the study to a friend who worked for the Associated Press. Then, suddenly, things got quite lively. On July 25, 1972, AP reporter Jean Heller's story broke across the country. The *Washington Star*, then D.C.'s afternoon paper, carried it on page one under the headline "Human Guinea Pigs / Syphilis Patients Died Untreated."[52] The next day the *New York Times* carried it, also on its front page, under "Syphilis Victims in U.S. Study Went Untreated for 40 Years."[53] The stories quoted the head of the CDC's Venereal Disease Branch, Dr. J. D. Millar, as saying that he had "serious doubts about the program." He added that the patients were not denied drugs, they just weren't being offered drugs—which was both irrelevant and untrue.

The Department of Health, Education, and Welfare convened a committee to investigate,[54] which found that the study was "ethically unjustified in 1932," and that the study subjects should have been treated with penicillin no later than 1953. Two doctors on the committee went on record to note that at least forty participants had had their life spans shortened by the failure to treat. They added that the patients in the study had been "exploited, manipulated, and deceived. They were treated not as human subjects but as objects of research."

No one was held accountable. The creators of the Tuskegee Syphilis Study were long retired, and likely deceased, by the time Peter Buxtun could get any attention. There is no indication that any of the persons who extended the study to its termination in 1972 were disciplined, let alone prosecuted.

After the story broke, a survivor named Charlie Pollard sought out civil rights attorney Fred D. Gray, who had years before represented Rosa Parks and who, as it turned out, had read the AP story.[55] Gray accepted the case and took an unusual approach.

The discretionary function exception would probably have voided any Federal Tort Claims Act (FTCA) suit. Did any law or regulation command USPHS staff to treat every case of syphilis they encountered? No. In withholding treatment, did the staff violate any binding orders? No, in fact, the study had been approved by the highest levels of USPHS leadership. Then Dr. Vonderlehr, Dr. Clark, and all the others who withheld treatment were exercising governmental discretion, and they and the USPHS were immune from lawsuit.

But, Gray realized, the USPHS seemed to have gone out of its way to recruit only black participants. Of the six hundred persons enrolled, not a single one was white. Notices seeking participants for the study were circulated only at black schools and churches (segregation was legal in the 1930s). The published articles detailing the results uniformly referred to effects of nontreatment "in the male negro." If the government physicians responsible for the study were not racists, they had done an uncommonly good job of acting like ones. So Gray brought the suit on a racial discrimination theory, rather than as an FTCA suit. This approach had an additional advantage: jury trials are allowed in civil rights actions, but not in FTCA suits. The government would have to explain its decision to treat four hundred black Alabamians as if they were human lab rats to a mixed-race Alabama jury.

The case ultimately settled for $10 million, but spread across all the victims, which meant surviving infected persons only received $37,500 and the heirs of deceased $15,000.[56] Still, it was $10 million more than the victims would have gotten under the FTCA and its discretionary function exception.

CHAPTER 4

RUBY RIDGE, IDAHO: FBI OBEYS "SHOOT ON SIGHT" ORDERS

What the plan boiled down to was this: we'd gas the place and rip it up until everybody inside was too hysterical to think straight, and then HRT [FBI Hostage Rescue Team] operators would go into close-quarters battle with women and children.
> —Danny Coulson, Deputy Assistant Director,
> Federal Bureau of Investigation[1]

You killed my wife! Vicki's dead! You murdered my boy Sam and wounded my other son Kevin! He may die tonight! Aren't you a brave bunch of bastards?
> —Randy Weaver, shouting to FBI Hostage Rescue Team[2]

SOME PEOPLE MARCH TO THE BEAT of a different drummer. Randy and Vicki Weaver, the unfortunate victims of Ruby Ridge, had their own marching band. Not that it started out that way—quite the contrary.

Randy Weaver grew up in small-town Iowa, where he attended community college. At age twenty, he volunteered for a three-year hitch in the Army and qualified for the Special Forces, the "Green Berets." His technical engineering assignments kept him stateside through the height of the Vietnam War.

At the community college, he'd developed an interest in Vicki Jordison, a similar small-town student who was beautiful, intelligent, and strong willed. They married a month after his discharge, and over the next ten years she bore three children—two daughters, Sara and Rachel, and a son, Sammy.

In 1983, the Weavers announced to friends that a drastic change would soon occur in their lives. They sold their Iowa homestead, relocating to northern Idaho to live a life apart, raising their family without the corruptions of ordinary society. Randy would later write:

> Quitting your job, leaving family and friends, selling most of what you own to move to a place you have never been, is more risk than most people are willing to take.

> Vicki and I had come to the conclusion that we wanted to raise our children away from the rat race and the ever-increasing intrusions of government. I could no longer envision spending the rest of my life working in a factory for forty or fifty hours a week and waiting all year for my three-week vacation.[3]

The Weavers had another motivation: they were convinced that the end of the world was approaching, the "Days of Tribulation," when the faithful would be persecuted by the forces of evil. Vicki believed the persecution would begin with a multinational attack arriving through Canada and thought that a self-sufficient family located away from population centers and other potential targets would have the best chance of survival.

That summer, the Weavers lived in a rented trailer while building their cabin on twenty acres they had purchased at a location known as Caribou Ridge or Ruby Ridge. The construction took months. Kevin Harris, a teenager separated from his parents, usually stayed with the Weavers and helped with the construction. The children acquired a new sibling when Elisheba was born in late 1991.

The cabin grew into a comfortable two-story affair, situated on a knoll with excellent views. The location was isolated but not too remote. A general store with a post office stood about a mile distant, and Bonner's Ferry (population 2,500) was eight or nine miles away.

The locals tolerated eccentric beliefs; after all, Bonner's Ferry is home of the 1974 Kootenai Indian War, when the tribe's sixty-five members declared war on the United States. (The war consisted of charging ten-cent tolls for use of a nearby highway.) The tribe ultimately settled for a six-square-mile reservation on which they built a prosperous casino, a very favorable outcome for people who had declared war on a superpower.

The Weavers remained self-sufficient for eight years, growing crops, raising chickens, and homeschooling the children. Apart from Randy's unsuccessful campaign for sheriff, their only contact with government came when they paid their taxes. They were, in short, a decidedly eccentric but harmless family . . . that would shortly become the target of three federal law enforcement agencies.

Randy Weaver was a racial separatist but insisted he was not a racist, saying that "to hate someone just because they're of another race is sheer ignorance."[4] He would sometimes attend the Aryan Nations' annual meetings, staying outside to talk.[5]

It was a safe bet that some, maybe most, of the Aryan Nations' leadership were violating federal gun laws, which are enforced by the Bureau of Alcohol, Tobacco and Firearms, or BATF, an agency then in the Department of the Treasury. (The agency is today known as the Bureau of Alcohol, Tobacco, Firearms and Explosives, and its law enforcement operations are part of the U.S. Department of Justice.) BATF had one low-level informant inside the Aryan Nations and wanted more access for him, as well as additional informants. Weaver seemed like a person who could be useful for both objectives, but he turned down the offer. Federal agencies know how to deal with stubbornness: set the person up as a lawbreaker then make them an offer they can't refuse.

ENTRAPMENT AND A REJECTED OFFER

BATF soon found its opening. The Weavers were exceptionally short of money when Randy Weaver offered to sell two shotguns to a friend. The friend happened to be a BATF informant. The informant offered Weaver a considerable sum, $700, two or three times what the guns were worth, if Weaver shortened the barrels to a point the informant indicated. The National Firearms Act of 1934 requires a permit and payment of a $200 tax before making or transferring a shotgun with a barrel of less than eighteen inches, and the informant indicated a length well below that measurement. When Weaver modified the shotguns to the informant's specification, he committed a federal felony that carried penalties of up to ten years' imprisonment.

BATF now had Weaver on a leash, but months passed before it pulled the leash tight. The case was probably not a high priority, and Weaver would have had a solid entrapment defense—he had proposed a legal transaction, the BATF informant had proposed making it an illegal one, offering an inflated price to a man desperate for money. Better to work more solid cases.

Things changed when BATF's existing Aryan Nations informant had his cover blown, and the agency needed a quick replacement. A BATF supervisor tracked Randy and Vicki down at a friend's house and demanded that he become an informant or be charged with multiple federal felonies. Weaver refused.

Again, months passed. Driving down an isolated road, the Weavers encountered a couple with a seemingly disabled truck. When they stopped to render aid, they found themselves staring down the couple's pistol barrels while more BATF agents climbed out of the camper shell. The agents departed with a handcuffed Randy Weaver.

The following morning, Weaver appeared before a federal magistrate. The court quickly made two serious errors. First, the magistrate suggested that if he were convicted, Weaver's land and house would be forfeited. This was not the law, but Weaver thought, "I'd be sitting in prison and Vicki and the kids would be homeless."[6]

The court's second error had even more impact. During the hearing, the magistrate fixed Weaver's trial date for February 19. After Weaver left, the judge realized that February 19 was a federal holiday, President's Day, so he changed the trial date to February 20. But the court's Pretrial Services Division sent Weaver a notice that the trial date was changed to *March* 20, a month after the real date.[7]

When Weaver did not show up on February 20, the federal court issued a bench warrant, ordering his arrest. A few days later a newspaper reporter—possibly alerted by Weaver himself[8]—called Pretrial Services and pointed out that it had given Weaver a notice with the wrong date. Pretrial Services notified the court and the U.S. Attorney's Office, but remarkably, the court refused to withdraw the arrest warrant. The U.S. Attorney's response was even more high-handed. On March 14—that is, six days *before* the day when Weaver had been told to appear—it indicted Weaver on felony "failure to appear" charges. When U.S. Department of Justice (USDOJ) investigators later asked the U.S. Attorney why he did not wait to see if Weaver showed up when he had been told to, he responded cavalierly that if Weaver showed up, they could just dismiss the failure to appear charge.[9]

Believing he had to appear on March 20, Randy Weaver was startled to hear on the radio that a warrant had been issued for his arrest and the Marshals Service was announcing that it would bring him in. He decided to stay where he was and not come to court on March 20.[10]

To sum up the situation: an arrest warrant had been issued against a man who seemed to be holed up in a remote cabin with his family and a friend. He had harmed no one and seemed to be a danger to no one. After all, BATF would have been willing to forget about the charges they had filed if Weaver had agreed to become an informant.

What priority do you give such a case? Close to zero. If the defendant spends the rest of his life in his cabin, no one will be harmed except himself.

THE PURSUIT OF RANDY WEAVER

What the government actually did was the exact opposite. Now that Weaver had (seemingly) failed to show up for trial, the job of bringing him in passed to the U.S. Marshals Service, which is responsible for apprehending fugitives from justice. Idaho's Chief Marshal Ronald Evans did not wait to see if Weaver would show up on March 20 before he contacted the Marshals' Special Operations Group, or SOG, the agency's SWAT team that makes dangerous arrests.[11] Evans told the SOG leader that "'a very senior judge' was not going to tolerate delay in capturing Weaver."[12] (After the fact, Judge Ryan told USDOJ investigators that he saw Weaver's case as "just another case" and "thought scarce judicial resources were being wasted on the large number of gun cases brought in federal court."[13])

Judicial resources were not the only ones being wasted. The Marshals managed to wrangle a National Guard reconnaissance aircraft to snap photos of the Weaver cabin, which were analyzed by the Defense Mapping Agency. They installed $130,000 worth of solar-powered spy cameras to monitor the Weavers' life from a distance.[14] They hired a psychologist to give them a profile of Weaver (we may hope he was not overpaid—his report was filled with typographical errors and called Weaver "Mr. Randall").[15] In the end, SOG concluded that the plywood cabin could not safely be taken by assault, and there the matter rested.

A year after the bench warrant was issued, newspaper articles appeared in the Spokane *Spokesman Review* and the *Chicago Tribune* suggesting that Weaver was defying the government and becoming a folk hero.[16] The Chief Deputy Marshal for Idaho later told USDOJ investigators that "pressure from USMS headquarters to effect the arrest of Weaver increased substantially after these two articles."[17]

In 1996, FBI expert Frederic Whitehurst blew the whistle on the FBI crime lab's hair analysis section, which he alleged was routinely and falsely claiming that defendants' hair samples matched hair found at crime scenes. In 1997, DOJ's Office of Inspector General confirmed his assertions, finding that as much as 90 percent of the lab's hair analyses were flawed. But the FBI took years to notify those who had been convicted based on the analyses, and three were executed; three more served over twenty years each before DNA testing exonerated them.[18]

Planning began for an undercover operation to grab Weaver after luring him outside his cabin. The agency wanted more information so a team of six Marshals, headed by SOG member William Degan, flew in to scout the area. They made their approach shortly before dawn on August 21, 1992, dressed in camouflage and with faces hidden by ski masks. Most were carrying M16s, the standard military assault rifle; Deputy Marshal Larry Cooper carried a silenced 9 mm submachine gun.

Three Marshals took up observation posts, while the other three began throwing rocks up toward the cabin, hoping to attract the attention of the Weavers' dogs. The combination of a silenced gun and an attempt to attract the dogs' attention suggests that the plan was to lure the dogs away, then kill them silently, depriving the Weavers of their canine alert system. Camera surveillance of the Weavers had demonstrated that when visitors approached, the dogs heard them and barked, whereupon one or two of the young Weavers would climb the rock outcropping to see who had arrived. Eliminating the dogs would make a close approach possible.

The dogs did not alert to the rocks, and the Marshals moved in closer. How close the Marshals got to the cabin is unknown. The Marshals claimed that they stayed 100–150 yards away, but this seems questionable. It is hard to see how a four-feet-eleven fourteen-year-old Sammy could have chased down professional law enforcement if they had a hundred yards' head start.

The plan succeeded up to a point. Striker, the Weavers' yellow lab, detected the Marshals and ran downhill toward them. They retreated, drawing Striker further into the forest. What the Marshals hadn't counted on was that the Weavers were short of meat and thought Striker might have detected game. With winter approaching, a deer or, better yet, a bear would improve their diet. Sammy Weaver and Kevin Harris followed the dog while Randy Weaver went down a different trail, in hope of catching the game between them.

THE MARSHALS AND THE WEAVERS COLLIDE: TWO DIE

What happened next was vigorously disputed at the criminal trial that followed the confrontation, but the most reasonable reconstruction is as follows.

The Marshals fled for a time and then took up defensive positions. The dog Striker caught up, circled Marshal Cooper, then left him to find Marshal Arthur Roderick, who was farther away. (That the dog circled Cooper and left him suggests its motivation was friendly curiosity rather than aggression.) Before reaching Roderick, the dog turned away, possibly in response to a human call, and Roderick shot Striker dead. Roderick's bullet struck the dog from its rear. Striker let out one yelp, may have been shot again, and died.

The Marshals contended that Roderick's shot came *after* Kevin Harris fired the first shot. As will be noted below, this sequence is impossible to believe. It requires us to believe that, after a firefight has begun at close range, Roderick stopped to shoot a dog that posed no threat to anyone.

Sammy Weaver shouted, "You shot my dog, you son of a bitch!" He fired at the Marshals and Marshals Cooper and Degan fired back. One of their bullets damaged Sammy's rifle and mangled his arm, and he broke off the fight. Randy Weaver testified that he had called for Sammy and Harris to retreat to the cabin, and he heard Sammy call that he was coming back.

At that point, Marshal Cooper shot and killed the fleeing Sammy: the fatal bullet entered Sammy's back and was ballistically linked to Cooper's silenced submachine gun. When found, the bullet had traces of Sammy's shirt in its hollow point.[19] That Cooper thought he shot Harris, who fell "like a sack of potatoes,"[20] is indicative of how stress distorts the memory. Harris was not wounded during the fight; the teen Sammy Weaver, shot through the heart, likely fell as Cooper described.

Seeing the camouflaged men firing on his friend Sammy, Kevin Harris shot Degan, using his .30-06, a powerful deer rifle that punched a two-inch hole through Degan's chest. The government contended that Harris's shot had started the battle rather than ended it—but Degan's gun had fired seven shots, whose fired casings were found spread for twenty-one feet moving in Sammy's direction. It is hard to believe that a man with a two-inch hole in his chest and a deflated lung would have been running forward and continuing a gun battle.

All of the above happened in perhaps two seconds, so rapidly that Kevin Harris shot from the hip without shouldering his rifle.

Everyone involved then retreated. The Marshals recovered Degan's body, and the Weavers recovered Sammy's, which they put in a shed. Then the Weavers retired to the cabin to mourn the loss of their only son, a small boy whose voice had not yet changed.

Elsewhere, the groundwork for further tragedy was being laid. Hungry for news, the media reported what information the government provided, and did not trek through the woods to get the other side of the story. In the government's releases, the Weavers' plywood and two-by-four cabin became a fortress, and Weaver himself a homicidal fanatic whose gunfire had kept Marshals pinned down for hours. "He has vowed to die, and to take his three daughters and his wife, Vicki, with him if necessary," went one story.[21] "Court documents said Harris, Randy Weaver, and Samuel Weaver chased and shot at six marshals who surprised them," went one Associated Press release.[22] "Six marshals were fired on Friday at the fortress-like cabin of Randy Weaver," went another.[23]

Things were also happening in Washington where the Deputy Director of the Marshals Service had alerted the FBI leadership to the case; the FBI was recognized as having lead responsibility in cases where federal officers have been assaulted. FBI headquarters initially ordered an FBI SWAT team call-up in its Salt Lake City, Portland, and Seattle Divisions.[24] The FBI also put its Hostage Rescue Team on alert. Shortly thereafter, FBI Assistant Director Larry Potts ordered the Team to deploy to Ruby Ridge.

The Hostage Rescue Team was not just a SWAT team (the FBI already had fifty-six of those). It was created as an elite force to give the FBI capabilities rivaling those of the Army's Delta Force or the Navy SEALs. Its members trained daily, six days a week, on dynamic entry—kick in or blast through the doors, "break and rake" the windows, and then charge in for an incredibly intense battle whose duration would be measured in seconds rather than days. Hopefully, at the end of seven or ten or twenty seconds, the terrorists or other targets would be dead, the HRT members alive, and hostages (if any) rescued. Needless to say, it was a job that beckoned to adrenalin junkies.

The HRT was founded by Danny Coulson, who became its first commander.[25] Coulson had the brains and judgment to control any adrenalin oversupply; he came from an FBI SWAT sniping team. Sniping requires not only marksmanship, but near-superhuman patience and self-control. By 1992, however, Coulson had been promoted to Deputy Director of the FBI, where he would oversee the new HRT commander, Dick Rogers, but he would not directly command or deploy with the team. Unfortunately, Coulson's wisdom and restraint were not present in his replacement. Rogers had been a noncom in Vietnam, and FBI Agent Gary Noesner notes that his FBI nickname was "Sergeant Severe": "[H]e epitomized the tough-guy school of law enforcement."[26]

The attitude at FBI headquarters at the time was one of near panic, or what could be called "institutional paranoia." The menace posed by Randy Weaver and Kevin Harris—supported by Mrs. Weaver, two teenage girls, and an infant—was inflated to incredible levels. The Justice Department investigation later summarized the headquarters' understanding of the situation as follows:

> It was their understanding that one law enforcement officer had been killed and others remained "pinned down," unable to be extricated. The attack on the retreating DUSMs [Deputy U.S. Marshals] had been extremely aggressive in nature, with a "barrage of gunfire" having been directed at them. The situation was so severe that these USMs, who were specially trained, were afraid to move. They were located in a remote area of rugged terrain, which was well known to the subjects. The family

of Randy Weaver was armed, including his children. It was unknown whether the surviving DUSM's were still receiving fire and it was not known whether the subjects had reinforcements, were in the Weaver cabin, in the woods near the cabin, or whether they had escaped. Because of Randy Weaver's military background, it was believed that the subjects may have built tunnels and bunkers, making any approach to the area exceedingly dangerous.[27]

One of the HRT snipers would testify that their briefings depicted Randy Weaver "as a Rambo-like figure, commanding an unknown number of heavily armed white separatists who had fired indiscriminately at the Deputy Marshals the previous day, killing Deputy Marshal Degan."[28] Like a good legend, the danger of the two men with deer rifles, holed up in a plywood cabin, seemed to grow with each telling.

HRT hitched a ride to Spokane in two Air Force C-141 "Starlifters" and drove to Ruby Ridge from there.[29] On the flight, HRT commander Dick Rogers worked out with FBI Assistant Director Larry Potts (who remained at headquarters) the rules of engagement; Rogers then met with the on-scene commander, Agent Gene Glenn, to draft an operations plan. Both the rules and the plan favored a quick and violent end.

The rules of engagement—a term, significantly, borrowed from the military—defined how and when lethal force could be employed. The FBI's normal rules of engagement track what the Supreme Court had ruled was permissible. Law enforcement cannot kill an offender just to stop his escape. Lethal force may only be used if an offender "poses a significant threat of death or serious physical injury to the officer or others."[30] The Court outlined two circumstances that met this test: where the suspect threatened the officer with a gun and where the use of lethal force was necessary to prevent escape of a violent offender, with warning ("halt or I'll fire!") having been given, if feasible.

The rules of engagement for the Weaver household were at odds with Supreme Court guidance. The early drafts instructed HRT agents that any adult males seen with arms "could" be shot on sight, even before the HRT announced its presence and demanded surrender. This permitted the illegal killing by ambush—a polite term for murder—of Randy Weaver or Kevin

Harris. HRT commander Dick Rogers thought "could" was too mild and changed the wording to "could, and should," converting the authorization to murder into an order.[31] As finally given to the HRT, the rules of engagement contained a slight variation on this:

1. If any adult male is observed with a weapon prior to the announcement, deadly force can and should be employed, if the shot can be taken without endangering any children.
2. If any adult in the compound is observed with a weapon after the surrender announcement is made, and is not attempting to surrender, deadly force can and should be employed to neutralize the individual.
3. If compromised by any animal, particularly the dogs, that animal should be eliminated.
4. Any subjects other than Randall Weaver, Vicki Weaver, Kevin Harris presenting threats of death or grievous bodily harm, the FBI rules of deadly force are in effect. Deadly force can be utilized to prevent the death or grievous bodily injury to oneself or that of [sic] another.[32]

According to the USDOJ report, the FBI's negotiator told Justice investigators that he was "surprised and shocked by the rules of engagement. The Rules were the most severe he had ever seen in the approximately 300 hostage situations in which he had been involved."[33] The USDOJ review would later note the following:

> Denver SWAT team leader Gregory Sexton recalled the Rules as "if you see Weaver or Harris outside with the weapon, you've got the green light." He had never seen such severe Rules of Engagement . . . Another member of the Denver SWAT team characterized the Rules as "strong" and as a departure from the FBI's standard deadly force policy. A third member of Denver SWAT . . . remembered the Rules of Engagement as "if you see 'em, shoot 'em."[34]

So far as the Weavers knew, they were alone on the ridge; after the firefight, the Marshals had vanished. The HRT plan was for the snipers to get into position before the HRT announced its presence; only at the announcement would the Weaver household even know that the FBI was there. The FBI knew, from the surveillance videos and photos taken by the Marshals, that no one in the Weaver cabin ventured outdoors without at least a handgun—a reasonable approach for anyone living in bear country. The rules of engagement assured that Randy Weaver and Kevin Harris were to be killed out of hand if they were outside, before they knew that federal threats existed and before anyone had asked them to surrender.

One of the FBI snipers later told USDOJ investigators:

> Q: Were you advised that the folks there had a habit of coming out of the
>   house with the weapons?
> A: Yes, sir, I believe that was [in] one of the briefings.
> Q: So you knew that sometimes they came out, the dogs barked, they
>   came out with their weapons, you knew that, didn't you?
> A: Yes, sir.
> Q: Under your rules of engagement, you could then and should, if they
>   came out of the house, you could and should use deadly force?
> A: Yes, sir, it is true.[35]

The operations plan laid out the intended, and violent, confrontation. Essentially, the HRT snipers would take position. Two armored personnel carriers would approach the Weaver cabin and demand surrender. If Weaver or Harris (misidentified as Weaver's older son) exited the cabin while armed, the snipers would kill them. If there was no response to the demand to surrender, the armored personnel carriers would return the next day with the same demand. If it was not heeded, they would demolish the outbuildings by ramming and crushing them. If that did not work, they would gas the cabin with tear gas.[36]

Negotiations? We don' need no stinkin' negotiations! USDOJ's own report described the FBI negotiator's observations:

> He had attended Rogers' 9:00 a.m. briefing of the sniper/observers and
> heard Rogers tell the group that there would be "no long siege" and that
> the "Rules of Engagement" were to shoot armed adult males, if there
> was a clear shot. After attending this briefing, Lanceley [the negotiator]
> concluded that a tactical solution would be sought without negotiations.

While in [sic] route to the crisis site, Lanceley told Rogers that he would work with HRT Intelligence because there was not going to be a negotiation effort. When Rogers said, "Good," Lanceley felt that his impression had been confirmed.[37]

The plan was faxed to FBI headquarters where, by good luck, Deputy Assistant Director Danny Coulson was on duty and demonstrated wisdom to temper his offensive drive. The USDOJ investigation stated that Coulson rejected the plan because it had no provision regarding negotiations. In his memoirs, Coulson is rather blunt:

> As I read the fax, my jaw locked. My God, we've got a problem, I said to myself. Well, this is just not going to happen. I thought thoughts that would've earned me about a hundred letters of censure, the cleanest of which was, Those dumb shits. Have they got their heads up their ass or what?

> What I had in my hand didn't resemble anything the HRT or any law enforcement agency should do. It was a military assault plan. . . . What really fried me was that somebody in the HRT had put this op on paper in the first place. They know better. Had everything I'd said and done and stood for been lost on these guys? How many times had I said that a tactical assault is always the last, worst, option, that every nonviolent, nonconfrontational option has to be thoroughly explored, no matter how long it takes? . . . What the plan boiled down to was this: we'd gas the place and rip it up until everybody inside was too hysterical to think straight, and then HRT operators would go into close-quarters battle with women and children.[38]

Those on the scene responded to Coulson's rejection with a negotiation plan, which Coulson quickly approved. Matters would open with a negotiator going up to the cabin in an armored personnel carrier and informing the occupants that the FBI had arrest warrants for Randy Weaver and for Kevin Harris, while dropping off a portable phone so negotiations could begin.

But the special rules of engagement remained in effect while the negotiation plan was being drafted. Because of this, events were about to occur that would make any negotiation plan useless.

The HRT snipers were soon in position. Each had a four-thousand-dollar custom rifle topped by a three-thousand-dollar telescope sight. The range to the cabin was less than two hundred yards, at which distance the snipers were trained to hit a mark the size of a dime.

The family in the cabin had no idea law enforcement had returned. The battle with the Marshals had occurred the day before, and since then they had been left alone in stunned disbelief and grief. Late that afternoon, the two surviving dogs began to bark. Randy Weaver, Kevin Harris, and sixteen-year-old Sara Weaver climbed the rock outcropping for a better view, but saw nothing unusual. The HRT snipers were well concealed.

One of the snipers, Lon Horiuchi, was watching through his scope sight. The day was foggy, but he could make out two males carrying rifles, who had to be Weaver and Harris. He picked one male and rested the crosshairs of his Schmidt & Bender scope sight on him.[39] They were adults and armed, fair game under the rules of engagement. Indeed, under the "could and should" standard of those rules, the snipers were not merely authorized to shoot, they were under orders to kill them.

Randy Weaver walked over to the shed that held Sammy's body; he wanted another look at the face of his only son. He reached up to unlatch the door. Then it happened. "A bloody mist smelling like fresh hamburger crossed my face," Randy Weaver would later write, "accompanied by a loud bang and a very sharp pain. It felt like I had been kicked in the shoulder by a mule."[40] Weaver realized he had just been shot. Sara shoved him toward the cabin, staying close to her father, thinking, "If you want to murder my dad, you're going to have to shoot another kid in the back first!"[41] Kevin Harris followed them as they sprinted toward the cabin.

Ahead of them, Vicki Weaver clutched the infant Elisheba to her breast with one hand and held the cabin door open with the other, calling out. The cabin door had a row of windows at its top.

Horiuchi was off to the side of the cabin, at a fairly steep angle. The open cabin door blocked part of his view as he prepared to take a second shot. What he saw in that instant will never be known, though we do have a sketch that he made. In the sketch, a stick figure (presumably Kevin Harris) stands in front of the open door, running toward it. The crosshairs of Horiuchi's scope are shown, together with the "mil-dots" on it, which suggest that he was leading (shooting ahead of) the moving Harris by about fourteen inches.[42] The crosshairs, and thus the point of the bullet's arrival, would be through the window of the opened door, which extended at right angles across the sniper's view.

That sounds quite sterile. What is not sterile is that in the window of the door the sniper drew his scope sight's crosshairs, and also two semicircles. Heads sticking up: Vicki and someone else, either baby Elisheba in her arms or Randy passing her as Vicki bent outward and held the door open. The sniper could see that there were one or two other people in his line of fire as he squeezed the trigger. One of the first safety rules any hunter or shooter learns is to be sure of your target—and of what's in front of and behind it. The sniper was about to violate that rule.

The bullet left the muzzle at over 2,600 feet per second, carrying over 2,400 foot-pounds of energy. It arrived on target about a quarter second later and did horrifying damage. Randy and Sara Weaver had already plunged past the danger zone; Kevin Harris was just entering it. The powerful bullet penetrated the door, caught Vicki Weaver in the jaw and neck, and blew apart her carotid artery and jugular vein. She slumped to the floor still holding Elisheba, blood spurting from Vicki's head. The bullet continued onward, expanding, slamming into Kevin Harris's arm, penetrating it, continuing into his chest, and driving into his lung.

The HRT snipers heard a terrible female scream, lasting about thirty seconds, and then silence. One later wrote, "No words can describe the frantic abandon or immense horror of that scream. It was a banshee wail filled with death and rage and anguish."[43] It was Rachel Weaver, screaming in horror as her mother's blood poured across the floor.[44]

Sara Weaver later described the chaos of those seconds:

That's when I heard, or rather felt, the second shot. It sounded as if someone had fired a gun right by my ear. I thought I had been hit as fragments of something hit my cheek. My left ear was ringing.

The sniper's bullet had passed through the glass in the door and hit my Mom in the head destroying half of her face. The bullet then hit Kevin in the left arm and lodged in his chest. Mom dropped to the floor beside me still cradling Elisheba in her arms. Kevin fell to the floor in front of me. Mom's still body was holding the door wide open. She had died trying to save her family. . . . There was blood everywhere. Thick pools spreading across the kitchen floor and into the pantry. . . . Elisheba's face and hair were covered with her mother's blood and bone fragments.[45]

A few minutes later, the negotiator came up in the armored personnel carrier, announced his willingness to negotiate surrender, and dropped off a telephone. All the occupants of the cabin had to do was walk out in the open, into the sniper's line of fire, and pick up the phone. Can anyone wonder why they didn't?

Unannounced ambush is not generally the first step in a successful negotiation. Over the next few days, the FBI negotiator Fred Lanceley used a bullhorn to try to persuade the Weavers to step outside and pick up the telephone. From their standpoint that would mean volunteering for certain death. Trust was nonexistent.

The HRT is an action-directed organization, chosen and trained to break in and win a hyper-violent ten-second battle. Now they were being employed in a boring and sedentary siege, listening to a negotiator trying to work things out, day after day. They did not take it well, and began taking actions that made a well-negotiated end less likely. HRT leader Dick Rogers persuaded his superiors to let his armored personnel carriers demolish the outbuildings near the cabin.[46] The family could hear military vehicles smashing a bicycle and a generator within twenty yards of the cabin.[47] Then the HRT turned floodlights on the cabin, driven by noisy generators, to deprive the Weavers of sleep.[48] Someone (not the designated negotiator, so probably an HRT member) used a bullhorn to taunt them: "How did you sleep last night, Randall? How are Mrs. Weaver and the children? We are having pancakes for breakfast, I think."[49]

The FBI claimed that it did not at this point know that Vicki Weaver had been killed. But it had planted listening devices on the cabin and was quoted in the *Orlando Sentinel* and other media claiming that the sounds picked up showed that everyone inside was alive: "Electronic listening devices indicate Weaver, his wife, Vicki, Harris and Weaver's three other children are alive and in the cabin."[50]

Conditions inside the cabin were hellish. The air was dank with the odor of blood. Vicki Weaver lay where she fell, covered in a blanket. Baby Elisheba cried, "Mama, Mama!" whenever she awakened. Kevin Harris was in agony from his wounds and begged Randy Weaver to kill him and end the pain; Weaver refused. To get food without exposing herself to the snipers' gunfire, Sara crawled back and forth to the kitchen through the pools of blood.

Botched negotiation attempts, or perhaps intentionally sabotaged ones, continued. A tracked, remote-controlled bomb deactivation robot carrying a telephone climbed onto the porch and waited in front of the door. Negotiators used bullhorns to ask Randy Weaver to take the telephone from the robot.

The robot had a remote-controlled shotgun, used to disrupt bombs, and no one had removed it.[51] Did the HRT overlook the shotgun (hard to accept), or did it leave it on the robot to sabotage negotiations? Or was it really a booby trap—would Weaver have received a load of buckshot if he opened the door? Whichever scenario was planned, Weaver noticed the shotgun, which did little to inspire trust in the negotiators.

Seven days into the siege there was a breakthrough—*and it was Randy Weaver who made it.* He listened to the news with his battery-powered radio and had heard that there were crowds of protestors along the road outside the FBI lines. The program mentioned that James "Bo" Gritz was among them. Gritz was a Colonel of the Green Berets who had served in Vietnam and spent the postwar period searching for POWs. Weaver began crying out that he would talk to Gritz.[52] FBI's on-scene commander telephoned Deputy Assistant Director Danny Coulson, and Coulson approved the idea "in a heartbeat."[53]

Weaver and Gritz trusted each other and matters moved rapidly. Gritz's party expanded to include Weaver's friend Jackie Brown and militia leader Jack McLamb. Two days of talks persuaded Kevin Harris to come out and surrender, although Weaver still feared that he and his daughters would be shot down if they left the cabin. But the end seemed to be in sight.

At that point, Danny Coulson walked into FBI Assistant Director Potts's office just in time to hear the FBI's on-scene commander asking, over the telephone, for permission to gas the cabin because "negotiations were at a standstill" and things needed to end. Coulson later described the encounter:

> I lunged for Larry's speakerphone so fast I almost got whiplash. "This doesn't make any sense," I snapped. "Why do you want to do this if you have a possibility of getting them out? Besides, they have gas masks."

"Gritz didn't see any," was the reply.

"I don't care if he saw them or not," I said. "Every survivalist has a gas mask. . . . They are going to have gas masks. The only one we'd gas would be the baby. You've got the man he admires most in the world [Gritz] in there. You throw tear gas in there, and it'll be a disaster. They're gonna come out shooting, and we're going to shoot a man with three little girls. Well, we're not going to do this."[54]

Negotiations took just one more meeting. Gritz's party returned with two promises. Randy Weaver would be allowed to explain his side to a grand jury, and Gerry Spence, a flamboyant, theatrical, and very successful defense attorney, would represent him. By the end of the day, what was left of the Weaver family came out of what was left of their compound.

Showdown in the Courtroom

The battle in Federal District Court would pit a team of USDOJ attorneys, led by local Assistant U.S. Attorney Ron Howen, against two rather more colorful defense teams. Kevin Harris's defense went to David Nevin, a first-rate defense attorney and a relatively young man on the rise. Randy Weaver's team was headed by Gerry Spence, backed by Gary Gilman, Ellie Matthews, Chuck Peterson, and Kent Spence.

At the outset, the government followed its standard course: overcharge the hell out of the defendants, tacking on as many counts as possible to the indictment. The hope is that the defense will have to spread out its efforts, overwhelming the attorneys. Even with a weak case something might "stick to the wall." Government attorneys tend to disregard the risk that the jury may see this as an abuse of power, perhaps because with anything but a solid defense attorney they get away with this course of action. In no small measure, defendants lose because they run out of resources to fight unlimited government budgets.

For Randy Weaver, USDOJ started with the obvious: the sawed-off shotgun and failure to appear charges. Going further than that presented the obvious little problem that Weaver had shot at no one. He'd been shot, his wife and son had been killed, but he had done nothing beyond refusing to surrender for a time. That he'd done nothing was no barrier to an enterprising prosecutor—as prosecutors occasionally jest, "*anyone* can convict the guilty!" Weaver was charged with conspiracy to commit murder: since his 1983 move to Idaho, he, Vicki, and Kevin Harris had supposedly plotted to murder federal agents; even the move and the building of their cabin was part of this sinister plot. The government also accused Weaver of assaulting federal agents, obstructing justice, and murder for aiding and abetting Harris's killing of Marshal Degan. Under federal law, a person who aids and abets a crime—aids, counsels, or advises someone to commit it—is as guilty as the one who carries it out. Harris stood charged with murdering Degan and with conspiracy.

The combined conspiracy claims accused Weaver and Harris of masterminding a white racist terrorist network directed at luring federal agents to their deaths. With the conspiracy count, evidence of the Weavers' rather strange political beliefs became relevant. Weaver and Harris would, as coconspirators, be liable for each other's actions—thus Weaver could be blamed for Degan's death, even though he was not there and had no idea that Degan had been shot.

FBI Deputy Assistant Director Danny Coulson later wrote that he'd opposed the overcharging; so had Henry Hudson, chief of the Marshals Service and a former prosecutor. So, for that matter, did everyone of consequence in FBI headquarters. Even during the siege, Coulson had advised USDOJ officials that Weaver had a "pretty strong legal position":

1. Charge against Weaver is Bull S . . .
2. No one saw Weaver do any shooting.
3. Vicki has no charges against her.
4. Weaver's defense. He ran down the hill to see what the dog was barking at.[55]

But within USDOJ, the local U.S. Attorney has almost complete autonomy in filing criminal charges, and Washington's Main Justice refused to overrule the U.S. Attorney's Office.

Then the U.S. Attorney's Office announced that it wanted to seek the death penalty! Coulson and Potts opposed the idea. "But Potts and I didn't slug it out at the department. Once the conspiracy count was in the case, we figured Weaver's chances of acquittal were about 99 percent."[56]

Coulson's prediction came to pass. The prosecution put on fifty-six witnesses over a period of three months—another attempt to simply overwhelm the defense—but the defense counterattacks did the real damage. Marshal Cooper testified about the beginning of the firefight, and wept as he described the death of his friend Bill Degan, gunned down by Harris in what supposedly was the first shot of the fight. But Cooper had no explanation why, if Degan had died with the first shot of the firefight, Degan's gun was found to have fired seven shots. Nor was there a good answer to Spence's question: "Does it make sense to you that Officer Roderick would be shooting the dog *after* Mr. Degan is dead, *after* Mr. Degan is shot?"

HRT sniper Lon Horiuchi was another key witness; he testified that he had had no intent to kill Vicki Weaver and denied knowledge that anyone was standing behind the door. The view through the window on the door had been blocked by a curtain, he said.

The prosecutor Howen returned to his office that night to find a package awaiting him. It was from FBI headquarters in Washington, containing documents he'd requested long ago. In it was the sketch Horiuchi had made depicting what he had seen at the moment of firing with the stick figure representing Kevin Harris and with two semicircles in the window. *Horiuchi had seen two heads through the window, despite the window's curtain.*[57] This was the first Howen had heard of Horiuchi's sketch.

FBI headquarters had mailed the documents to Howen *by fourth class mail.* The documents had taken two and a half weeks to make it to Howen; obviously, the FBI had hoped to delay this damaging disclosure just long enough to convict Weaver.

In 2008, the Department of Justice indicted Senator Ted Stevens on charges he had failed to list a gift on a Senate-required form. He was convicted, but during and after the trial it was discovered that the Justice Department was hiding *a lot* of evidence. The judge appointed a special counsel to investigate; the counsel filed a 525-page report, showing the government had hidden dozens of pieces of evidence testimony that showed Stevens was innocent.[58] Stevens's conviction was set aside, the judge ruling that the Justice prosecutors had "abandoned all decency to win a conviction."[59] By then, however, Stevens had lost his bid for reelection. The two lead prosecutors went on to take lucrative jobs with major national law firms. Sidney Powell, one of Stevens's defense attorneys, wrote a book, *Licensed to Lie: Exposing Corruption in the Department of Justice*, about her experiences.

Howen disclosed the sketch to the defense, and they recalled Horiuchi to the stand. The judge was outraged at the FBI's conduct and imposed money sanctions on the government, finding that it had shown "a callous disregard for the rights of the defendants and the interests of justice."

A federal jury verdict must be unanimous—even an eleven-to-one for acquittal results in retrying the case. The jury deliberated for an incredible twenty-three days before returning its verdict. Kevin Harris was innocent of everything. Randy Weaver was guilty only of failure to appear on the shotgun charge. After giving credit for time served, the judge sentenced him to serve four more months.

FBI official Danny Coulson has the last word:

> [W]hat had started this crazy business? A lousy ATF case involving two guns that had nothing to do with crime in the United States. A bench warrant for nonappearance. What was the point? At the same time that we were trying to find more FBI agents to send into high-crime areas to reclaim our streets, we had a federal agency chasing after a mountain man who had produced a couple of sawed-off shotguns.[60]

WHO BORE THE CONSEQUENCES?

USDOJ commissioned an extensive report on the events at Ruby Ridge, which came to 542 pages and concluded that the prosecution was somewhat overzealous, the rules of engagement were illegal, and Horiuchi should not have fired his second shot. There the matter rested for three years until Congress began pressing the FBI for action. Then the FBI gave a ten-day suspension to HRT head Rick Rogers, who had issued the illegal rules of engagement and ordered his agents to commit murder. FBI negotiator Gary Noesner would later write:

> The disaster that followed from his [Rogers's] preemptive actions at Ruby Ridge had done nothing to tarnish that image within the FBI, at least

not yet. If anything, critical accounts of what had happened there created something of a bunker mentality among certain elements at FBI headquarters. For my own part, I was surprised that Rogers still had his job in spite of having overseen the debacle at Ruby Ridge. Then again, meting out punishment to the HRT commander would have been an admission of the gross errors of judgment that had taken place in Idaho.[61]

FBI Assistant Director Larry Potts was given a letter of censure for failure to monitor Rogers. It didn't hurt his career; he was soon promoted to Deputy Director, the second-in-command of the agency.[62] His deputy, Danny Coulson, who had done more than anyone to restrain the HRT and seek a bloodless resolution, was likewise censured for not doing enough. A few other officials received brief suspensions, letters of censure, or verbal reprimands.[63]

> Compare what happens to private attorneys who conceal evidence. In 2016, a federal judge imposed a $2.7 *million* penalty against a law firm representing Goodyear Tire & Rubber in a civil suit for hiding a study of tire failures.[64]

The surviving members of the Weaver family filed a civil action; the government settled for $3.1 million, while Kevin Harris received $380,000. The settlements were not paid by the FBI, however, but by the "Judgment Fund," a general appropriation shared by all agencies and ultimately financed by the taxpayer.

> All judgments or settlements against federal agencies that exceed $2,500 are paid from the Judgment Fund, not from the agencies' own budgets, and thus do not cost the agency anything. The $2,500 limit has not been adjusted since it was set in 1959, at a time when a new car cost about $2,000 and the median price for a new house was $12,000.

For once, there seemed to be a chance of some criminal consequences. Five years after the events of 1992, the Boundary County prosecutor filed involuntary manslaughter (homicide by extreme negligence) charges against sniper Lon Horiuchi for killing Vicki Weaver. The prosecutor had to "pass the hat" to find funds to hire a special prosecutor; there were only four attorneys in the entire county, and the county budget totaled $8.6 million.[65] Private donations enabled her to hire outside attorneys as special prosecutors.

USDOJ undertook Horiuchi's defense and moved to dismiss charges on Supremacy Clause grounds. The Supremacy Clause of the United States Constitution reads: "This Constitution, and the Laws of the United States which shall be made in Pursuance thereof . . . shall be the supreme Law of the Land; and the Judges in every State shall be bound thereby, any Thing in the Constitution or Laws of any State to the Contrary notwithstanding."[66] The effect of the Supremacy Clause is straightforward: a federal law, if constitutional, can override any state law and even a state constitution. So long as Congress stays within its constitutional limits, regulates interstate commerce, imposes taxes, etc., its enactments take precedence over those of the states.

The major Supreme Court ruling applying this clause of the Constitution to state prosecutions came in the 1890 ruling of *In re Neagle*,[67] discussed in the introduction. Neagle was a deputized U.S. Marshal who killed a violent but unarmed man who attacked U.S. Supreme Court Justice Stephen J. Field. Neagle was charged by California authorities with murder, but the U.S. Supreme Court ordered Neagle's release, because Field was carrying out his duties when he was attacked, and Neagle was within the scope of his federal duties when he shot. The Court ruled as follows:

> [I]f the prisoner is held in the state court to answer for an act which he was authorized to do by the law of the United States, which it was his duty to do as marshal of the United States, and if, in doing that act, he did no more than what was necessary and proper for him to do, he cannot be guilty of a crime under the law of the state of California.[68]

Essentially, the Supremacy Clause of the U.S. Constitution makes the Constitution, and laws made pursuant to it, the "supreme law of the land," overriding conflicting state laws. *Neagle* extended this, so that federal *law enforcement* functions would override conflicting state *law enforcement* functions. This 1890 ruling established, the government argued, that the FBI agents' actions were not subject to Idaho state law. Under this approach, even if Lon Horiuchi had *intentionally* aimed at Vicki Weaver, and then proceeded to whack her baby as well, he would have committed no crime punishable by Idaho law—or, for that matter, any law at all. While it is illegal for a private person to kill a federal agent, no federal law forbids federal agents to kill private citizens . . . or noncitizens.

The District Court dismissed the charges against Horiuchi. Boundary County appealed to the Ninth Circuit Court of Appeals, which upheld the dismissal two to one. The County took it one step further, and appealed to a special, larger, panel of the Circuit Court.[69] The panel divided narrowly six votes to five and allowed the prosecution to proceed.[70]

The Ninth Circuit ruled that in order to be protected by the Supremacy Clause, a federal agent must have reasonably believed that his conduct was necessary to the performance of his lawful and constitutional duties. Since the Supreme Court had ruled that deadly force could only be used to arrest a suspect under certain narrow conditions (largely self-defense), and there were legitimate questions about whether those conditions were met here, the District Court should hold a hearing and determine that issue. The opinion closed:

> Nor do we believe that allowing this case to proceed will open the floodgates to numerous state criminal prosecutions of federal agents, hampering federal law enforcement efforts. Assuming the facts alleged by the state, this is not a case where a law enforcement agent fired his weapon under a mistaken belief that his fellow agents or members of the public were in immediate danger. Rather, a group of FBI agents formulated rules of engagement that permitted their colleagues to hide in the bushes and gun down men who posed no immediate threat.
>
> Such wartime rules are patently unconstitutional for a police action. As soon as the incident was over, the FBI disowned the rules and disciplined the officers who approved them. The incident led to a lengthy investigation by the DOJ Office of Professional Responsibility; Congress itself conducted extensive hearings and published a bipartisan report that was highly critical of the FBI in general and Horiuchi in particular. There is nothing run of the mill about this case, and we cannot conceive that it will provide a precedent for state prosecutions in more ordinary circumstances.[71]

Yet, the inherent expense of fighting the federal government remains an overwhelming obstacle to justice; the Boundary County prosecutor lost her next election when voters decided that the county spending its time prosecuting an FBI sniper was too controversial and expensive. The new county attorney announced he was dropping the case to bring "closure."[72]

Gerry Spence's summation is apt: "No one was ever convicted for the murders at Ruby Ridge. That massacre proved that the Constitution can be set aside by Power at its whim, that the FBI could, and did change the law as if it, not the people, create the laws of the land."[73]

But worse was about to come. Much worse.

CHAPTER 5

WACO, TEXAS: "IT'S SHOWTIME!"

——————

The federal government was absolutely out of control there. We spoke in the jury room about the fact that the wrong people were on trial, that it should have been the ones that planned the raid and orchestrated it and insisted on carrying out this plan who should have been on trial.
—Sarah Bain, foreman of the jury, Waco criminal trial[1]

I really liked that guy [undercover agent Robert Rodriguez], too. I've always loved law enforcement, because y'all guys risk your lives every day, you know.
—David Koresh, wounded, speaking over the telephone to
BATF supervisor Jim Cavanaugh, February 28, 1993[2]

APRIL 19, 2016. THE BRANCH DAVIDIANS, an offshoot of the Seventh-day Adventist Church, are holding a memorial service at their religious center. Although the Mount Carmel center is not far outside of Waco, Texas, navigating there is no simple task: Route 340 to Elk Road, turn onto EE Ranch Road, then north until a few buildings are visible on a gently curving road, actually a driveway, to the right.

The setting is extraordinarily peaceful. Green farmland extends to the horizon on every side; the only other building visible is the "undercover house," on the other side of the road. Chirping birds remain the only sound. Your first indication of a special history is the monument to the eighty Davidians who died here—twenty-four men and fifty-six women and children. Then you encounter the Davidians' memorial for the four Bureau of Alcohol, Tobacco and Firearms (BATF) agents who died in the raid on their church. Yes, the Davidians are a forgiving lot.

Inside the church, the main speaker Clive Doyle explains that David Koresh taught them to regard the FBI agents who were besieging the place not as enemies, but as souls to be saved. Doyle was seriously burned and lost his eighteen-year-old daughter Sherri in the fire that ended the siege, but there is no rancor in his voice.

The Davidians believe we are in the "end times," but that those times will span years, centuries, even millennia, and that a person on the wrong side can, at any point, wise up and join the good guys. The persecutor of today might pray with them tomorrow. The Davidians' view of the end times is, in short, remarkably humane. As Doyle writes in his book *A Journey to Waco*:

> David [Koresh] stressed over and over that you don't want to be trying to put God in a box or limit his performance. If you say God will save only Branch Davidians or God will save only Seventh-day Adventists—which most Christians think—David said: you're limiting God, you're putting God in the losing position. Let's say, according to the mindset of most Christians, God gets every one of those Christians and the devil gets all the rest, that means the devil has the majority. David asked: You mean the devil wins? . . . He said, God's got a few tricks up his sleeve. God's in the saving business, He wants to save all who will be saved. . . . We believe God raised up Muhammad, he raised up Buddha, he raised up major teachers of thought. . . . God wants to save everybody.[3]

After the memorial service, the Davidians depart to eat a buffet lunch as the fields around their church return to their natural quiet. In 1993, those quiet fields saw gunplay, a tank attack, fire, and a fifty-one-day FBI siege that darkened the history of law enforcement in America.

FEBRUARY 25, 1993

It was nearly 9:00 p.m. when U.S. Magistrate Judge Dennis Greene signed the search warrant and handed it back to BATF Agent Davy Aguilera. The warrant authorized federal agents to search Mount Carmel for firearms, machine guns, bombs, and other weaponry.

Attached to the warrant was a lengthy affidavit from Aguilera, giving the reasons why he felt that evidence of a crime would be found. It discussed how the agency had been contacted by the sheriff's office, passing on a report from a local UPS delivery office that a package intended for Mount Carmel contained army surplus grenade casings and black powder. Both of these were legal, but BATF had thought the case merited investigation. Further probing had found that the Davidians had purchased large numbers of new semiautomatic rifles from a licensed firearms dealer in the area and bought gun parts from a number of suppliers.

But the core of the warrant was that the Davidians had bought dozens of AR-15 rifles, which could—with extra parts and work in a machine shop—be made to function as machine guns. The grenade hulls and black powder they had purchased could be combined to make improvised, low-power grenades.[4]

In short, the Davidians had rifles that *could* be turned into machine guns and components that *could* be turned into grenades; either action would be a serious federal crime.[5] Or the items could be left as they were, the rifles kept for investment, and the grenade shells sold at gun shows (which the Davidians would later claim was the case, and which was quite legal). Which was it?

That was where Aguilera's affidavit skated on thin ice. It cited a neighbor's statement that he had heard machine-gun fire from the area of Mount Carmel a year before. Aguilera added that a former Davidian had told him that she had seen David Koresh shoot a machine gun, some four years ago. The problem with these statements was that it is legal to own a machine gun, provided that it was made before 1986 and the owner registers it with the federal government. The owner can then let others fire it, so long as he is present. Aguilera's affidavit stated that he had checked the government registry of machine guns and found that Koresh had no machine guns registered to him. But the affidavit failed to deal with the possibility that the owner of a registered machine gun might have visited Mount Carmel a couple of times and let Koresh shoot his gun.

The Aguilera affidavit also alleged, at some length, that David Koresh had been having sex with underage girls. This seemed out of place: BATF's jurisdiction extends to gun crimes, not to sexual ones. On the other hand, nothing draws media coverage like sex and (incipient) violence.[6]

Early the next morning, a Friday, BATF Public Information Officer Sharon Wheeler began calling reporters to tip them off that a big operation would soon be going down, and making sure they knew how to reach her over the weekend. A few hours later, Christopher Cuyler, BATF's liaison to the Treasury Department, alerted Treasury headquarters to the operation, adding, "It is felt this operation will generate considerable media attention, both locally (Texas) and nationally."[7]

That would prove to be an understatement.

FEBRUARY 28, 1993

BATF Special Agent Robert Rodriguez had lived an undercover role for weeks, gathering information on the Davidians. He was one of several agents installed in the house across the street from the Davidian residence, pretending to be students at a local college (their cover did not last: the Davidians quickly deduced that the middle-aged men driving large cars were not there to attend the junior college). Rodriguez had regularly walked over to Mount Carmel and discussed religion, guns, and gun rights with David Koresh. Now he had a more difficult role. Several miles away, BATF was mustering a giant raid team of agents plus support personnel, a fleet of vehicles, and three borrowed military helicopters. The agents would climb into long horse trailers, drive up to Mount Carmel, emerge, and execute the search warrant. Just before the trailers pulled up, three military helicopters carrying BATF agents would make a loud, low-altitude run at the back of Mount Carmel as a distraction. Taken by surprise and distracted, the Davidians would submit rather than resist.

On that day, Rodriguez would visit Mount Carmel and see if its residents had a clue what was coming. He had a pleasant chat with David Koresh, who left the room to take a phone call . . . and returned in a state of shock, telling Rodriguez that a federal raid was incoming. In that instant, Rodriguez realized that Koresh knew he was undercover. But instead of snatching him as a hostage, Koresh shook his hand and wished him good luck.

Rodriguez returned hastily to the undercover house and called raid leadership to let them know the Davidians knew they were coming. Surprise had been key to the plan, he thought, and surely the raid would be canceled.

Except that it wasn't. An hour or so later, two trucks towing horse trailers loaded with seventy-six heavily armed BATF agents turned onto the dirt driveway. Moving slowly, they turned in front of Mount Carmel, halted, and agents charged out, guns in hand, while the three helicopters made a belated run at the back of the building.

Koresh ran out of the front door of Mount Carmel, calling for restraint. A few shots rang out, triggering a fusillade from both sides that lasted for hours. By the time a cease-fire was worked out and the agents trudged back up the driveway, four agents and six Davidians were dead and Koresh was seriously wounded.

The FBI's elite Hostage Rescue Team arrived to take over, backed by numerous FBI Special Weapons and Tactics (SWAT) teams. Soon Mount Carmel was ringed with barbed wire, sandbagged positions, and a collection of armored military vehicles headed by a state-of-the-art M1 tank.

APRIL 19, 1993

Fifty-one days later, armored vehicles came down the driveway with a purpose: injecting Mount Carmel with massive loads of "tear gas," technically described as liquid CS. CS causes much more than tears—the burning sensations sear the eyes and throat; an overwhelming feeling of suffocation, and violent retching, crying, coughing, sneezing, and temporary blindness ensue, among a host of other physical reactions.

Combat engineering vehicles, tanks designed to build or destroy things, tore holes in Mount Carmel with their elevated booms, then shot in liquid CS—CS dissolved in the toxic industrial solvent methylene chloride. Agents in Bradley fighting vehicles used 40 mm grenade launchers to fire hundreds of plastic projectiles filled with the same liquid. When that did not force the Davidians out, the combat engineering vehicles began to demolish the building, driving into it, tearing large holes and collapsing parts of it.

Six hours into the gassing, winds quickly whipped up a fire the length of Mount Carmel. Half an hour later when the Waco Fire Department was allowed to pass down the driveway, firefighters found the church building reduced to glowing ashes, with the seared bodies of seventy-four Davidians—men, women, and children—dead in the ruins.

All in all, a lot of history for a country driveway a couple of hundred yards long.

THE DEMONIZING OF THE DAVIDIANS

During the siege, twenty-four years ago, these quiet and tolerant people became the most hated group in America. As the review of a made-for-TV movie rushed out while the siege was under way summarized, "Religious fanatics are barricaded in a building, and surrounded by police. But they're not going to surrender, they prefer to die."[8] *Time* magazine issued a special report with the cover showing an artist's impression of a maniacally laughing David Koresh superimposed on the burning Mount Carmel. In the FBI archives is a foot-thick stack of letters from the public volunteering suggestions for dealing with the Davidians; most of the suggestions can be summarized as *crush them by whatever means are necessary.*

Department of Defense files list a staggering variety of military equipment loaned or given to the FBI to use against members of this church, a list capped by M1 tanks, with special Chobham armor, just in case the Davidians had somehow gotten TOW (tube-launched, optically tracked, wire-guided) antitank missiles.[9] All this to deal with a group that numbered barely eighty people, two-thirds of them women and children, and none with any military training.

How things came to that pass is simple. Reviewing the press coverage today would be comical, if it were not so tragic. During the siege, the FBI kept the media several miles away from Mount Carmel; reporters could only see the scene through telescopes raised on construction scaffolding, and could only relay the contents of daily government briefings, their sole source of information. From those briefings, the media learned and duly reported the following:

- The Davidians were a cult, blindly following the orders of self-styled apocalyptic prophet, David Koresh. Koresh was described as charismatic and cunning, a madman with a hatred for law enforcement and an insatiable lust for women and violence.
- BATF had tried to arrest Koresh peacefully, but Koresh was a reclusive paranoid who never left the "cult compound" at Mount Carmel. When BATF raided the compound, the agents were caught in a hail of bullets, as multiple Davidian machine guns raked them in a murderous crossfire.
- FBI negotiators attempted to reach a peaceful outcome, but for 51 days the Davidians resisted every effort. With negotiations thwarted, the FBI decided that a tear gas assault was the only hope for ending

the siege. The CS tear gas would be dispensed using fireproof injection systems that posed no danger to the children inside.

- Things did not go as planned. For six hours, the Davidians responded to the negotiators' pleas with a hail of gunfire. Then the maniacal Koresh ordered his followers to put the compound to the torch, and twenty-four children and more than fifty adult Davidians perished in the flames.

We could be sure of these events because they were confirmed in 1993 by official investigations launched by the Justice and Treasury Departments (BATF then being a Treasury agency); in 1994 by sworn testimony during a seven-week criminal trial that convicted most of the surviving Davidians; and in 1995 by three different Congressional investigations, one of which culminated in a seven-hundred-page report.

More than two decades later, we know there is one small problem with this history.

Scarcely a word of it is true.

The remarkable thing is how far the FBI and BATF were willing to go to try to prevent us from figuring that out.

THE INCREDIBLE VANISHING EVIDENCE

The February 28 raid had been the biggest law enforcement operation in the history of BATF; the following fifty-day siege was the largest such operation in the history of the FBI. The April 19 assault involved weeks of planning and coordination and was carried out in front of a ring of government closed-circuit television cameras, with aircraft circling overhead videotaping and taking photographs. After the fire, the scene was studied with techniques borrowed from archeology, such as using ribbons to divide the area into small boxes that could be searched individually. But the fire had hardly died down before the evidence began vanishing with a speed that would have amazed a professional magician. A few examples:

- On the first day's gunfight, BATF conceded to Congressional investigators that it had several video cameras recording the scene as the agents rushed Mount Carmel, cameras that would have recorded who fired the first shot. But BATF claimed that every camera had malfunctioned and no data could be salvaged.[10]

- BATF also claimed that it had no record of its radio traffic during the raid and gun battle.
- BATF Public Relations Officer Sharon Wheeler reported that she had taken some photographs—but her camera had been stolen off a table—*a table in BATF raid headquarters*, where everyone present was a sworn law enforcement officer.
- Although the FBI had ringed Mount Carmel with closed-circuit TV cameras, it insisted it had not a single video record for the day of the fire.[11]
- The FBI was known to have had an aircraft circling Mount Carmel on the day of the fire equipped with an infrared camera that recorded to videotape. The gassing began predawn, but according to the FBI no one thought to turn on the video recorder until nearly 11:00 a.m., leaving no tapes for the first five hours.
- The bodies of the deceased Davidians were autopsied by the Medical Examiner and then placed in a refrigerated trailer. Somehow the trailer warmed up, and the bodies decomposed.[12]
- One of the largest pieces of evidence to disappear was a *twenty-square-foot metal door*. The main entry into Mount Carmel was through a steel double door. The Davidians insisted that the battle began as BATF fired a blind fusillade *into* the right-hand door, and BATF insisted with equal fervor that the battle began when the Davidians fired a volley *outward* through the same door.[13] During the siege, the Davidians had (all too naively) told FBI negotiators that the right door's metal surface clearly showed that the bullet holes all came from the BATF agents outside.

After the fire, the right metal door vanished. Its twin left door survived and showed marks of having been run over by a tracked vehicle, but no fire damage.[14] A critical piece of evidence escaped from a tightly controlled crime scene, where searching authorities were said to have made a "fingertip to fingertip" search.[15] Years later, a Texas Department of Public Safety officer would reveal that while ashes were still smoldering and before any search could be made, FBI agents brought in a van and loaded it with material from the site. One of the items removed was an object the size and shape of the vanishing door.[16]

With virtually all the hard evidence (supposedly) nonexistent, the agencies were free to invent anything they wanted to fill the gaps. When the Secretary of the Treasury and the Deputy Attorney General commissioned blue-ribbon panels to investigate the events, the reports reflected the agencies' official stories.[17] Koresh could not be arrested peacefully, the Davidians had deluged the BATF agents with machine-gun fire, and the FBI had been helpless to stop the Davidians' mass suicide. The official reports are filled with errors and inventions; how we came to know that is a story in itself.

MIKE MCNULTY AND THE VIRTUES OF PERSISTENCE

The Waco debacle aroused the interest of the late Mike McNulty,[18] an insurance broker turned documentary film producer. Soon a team had formed—McNulty as producer, Dan Gifford as executive producer, and Bill Gazecki as director—a team that would create the Oscar-nominated documentary *Waco: The Rules of Engagement*. Mike's investigation spanned several years, and coordinated with the three years of Freedom of Information Act (FOIA) lawsuits conducted by this author. Archives of information that the official Treasury and USDOJ investigators had never pushed to see became (after much courtroom fighting) available for investigation, including videotapes of BATF raid headquarters before the first day's shoot-out, an audiotape made in the BATF van that coordinated radio communications, 911 tapes showing that the Davidians had called for help, videotapes of internal FBI briefings, aerial photographs, meeting notes, and more.

McNulty leveraged his information in a meeting with Assistant U.S. Attorney Bill Johnston, who had prosecuted the surviving Davidians but was an honest man who took his work seriously. Johnston revealed that the feds had rented a warehouse filled with Waco-related evidence controlled not by the federal agencies, but by the Texas Rangers—a detail that had allowed the agencies to claim they had turned over all the evidence in their control, while actually keeping massive amounts of information hidden. McNulty arranged to visit the warehouse.

What he found staggered his imagination. By the Rangers' own measure, *twelve tons* of material were logged into two large rooms—videotapes, audiotapes, documents, and materials recovered from the fire—guns, clothing, gas masks, soil samples . . . all that remained of a building that had housed over a hundred people. No one outside the government had seen this evidence since the fire, and only a few people were even aware that the tons of evidence existed.

This was the Waco tragedy's King Tut's tomb, an enormous time capsule sealed in April 1993. Mike's treasures were not made of gold but of aluminum. He found photos of metal cylinders recovered after the fire that had been logged in as silencers—but the U.S. Army markings on these "silencers" showed them to be military-issue CS tear gas projectiles for the 40 mm grenade launchers the FBI had been using.

Mike was holding hard evidence that implicated the FBI in a string of lies—many told under oath. Tear gas projectiles fall into two main classes. One class is non-pyrotechnic and safe for use against buildings. The other class is pyrotechnic; these expel the tear gas (actually a fine dust) by a burning gunpowder-like fuel. Pyrotechnic rounds are not for use against buildings since they will start fires. To fire pyrotechnic rounds into a dry wooden building full of women and children would be considered criminal negligence, if not premeditated murder. The FBI and Attorney General Janet Reno had repeatedly sworn that on the day of the fire the FBI had fired no pyrotechnic rounds.[19] But the military rounds that the FBI had retrieved from Mount Carmel were pyrotechnic.

McNulty's efforts succeeded where multiple Congressional investigations had fallen flat. As a result of his persistence, we can finally set the record straight regarding the deadly confrontation outside Waco. We'll start with the core question.

COULD BATF HAVE ARRESTED DAVID KORESH PEACEFULLY?

The official Treasury Department investigation concluded that BATF had properly ruled out a peaceful arrest because Koresh never left Mount Carmel. BATF had, weeks before its raid, installed several undercover agents in the "undercover house" across the street from the Davidian residence, with instructions to keep an eye out for Koresh. The official 1993 Treasury investigation determined that the undercover house agents "never saw Koresh leave the Compound . . . and they never took the additional measures necessary to find out."[20]

It is obvious that BATF had withheld critical information from the Treasury Department investigators. The FOIA lawsuits also turned up evidence that clearly showed that BATF agents in the undercover house knew what David Koresh looked like and that he left Mount Carmel.

They knew this because he *had* left it. To go shooting. *With them.*

A BATF Report of Investigation authored by Special Agent Davy Aguilera nine days before the BATF raid reveals that, tasked with investigating the Davidians' firearms, the agents in the undercover house took a direct approach:

SYNOPSIS OF SURVEILLANCE—FEBRUARY 19, 1993; FRIDAY

On February 19, 1993, Special Agents Robert Rodriguez and Jeffrey Brzozoski in an undercover capacity, went to the Davidian Compound and met with Leader David Koresh and two other male members for the purpose of shooting the AR-15 rifles. When both agents arrived at the compound they were asked to enter the compound and wait for David Koresh. When David Koresh arrived, he examined the two AR-15 rifles very carefully. . . . After examining the firearms, Special Agents Rodriguez and Brzozoski followed David Koresh and the two males through the inside of the compound towards the back. . . . Before the shooting started David Koresh went back inside the compound and brought some .223 caliber rounds for the agents to shoot. . . . After shooting the rifles, Special Agent Rodriguez allowed David Koresh and the two males to shoot Rodriguez's .38 Super pistol. . . .[21]

The agents had no trouble getting David Koresh to leave Mount Carmel; they simply asked him to go shooting. Koresh was unarmed until one agent loaned him a gun. If this was not a good time to make the arrest, it would have been simple to arrange a repeat performance.

The Report of Investigation went up the chain of command, with the Assistant Resident Agent in Charge, the Austin Office, and someone acting for the Special Agent in Charge for Houston signing off on it. That Koresh could easily be brought to leave Mount Carmel was no secret within BATF.

If David Koresh could have been brought in so easily, why did BATF go with a plan that required shipping in seventy-six agents plus support personnel and laying hands on three military helicopters? Why prefer the expensive and complicated to the cheap and simple? That brings us to a number of deeper questions.

WHAT WAS THE REASON FOR THE RAID?

BATF was (and is) a troubled agency. For decades, it held a comfortable if sometimes dubious existence as an IRS division tasked with suppressing moonshiners. As moonshining died out in the 1970s, killed by the high cost of sugar, the agency transitioned to enforcing the then-new Gun Control Act of 1968. For a time, the agency prospered in its new role, largely prosecuting gun collectors and licensed dealers, safe targets that allowed for impressive statistics on the number of arrests made and guns seized. Agents could visit a gun show, sucker five collectors into technical violations, arrest them, and confiscate hundreds of guns in a single day.[22]

That sort of activity had a political price. In 1986, Congress reformed the Gun Control Act to require proof of illicit intent for most violations and to narrow the power to confiscate. BATF's arrests and seizures fell even as its budgetary demands increased. By 1993, its firearms enforcement operations were spending $369 million annually to produce barely more than fifteen thousand gun seizures—or about $18,650 per gun seized.[23]

Bill Clinton had pledged to promote more federal gun control measures, so when he was elected President in 1992, BATF might have felt a little more hopeful. But the new Administration also came to town with pledges to reinvent government and do away with inefficient agencies—a description that seemed to fit an agency that spent $18,650 for each cheap pistol it took off the street. Outside Washington, "reinventing government" sounded like one more campaign slogan. Inside the Beltway, it was cause for panic. In 1993, the *Washington Post* ran 248 articles mentioning the new Administration's proposals, with headlines like "To Slim Down the Federal Goliath" (January 16); "Doing More with Less: Time to Tame the Federal Behemoth" (January 31); "Texas Brand of Belt-Tightening Could Be Model for The Nation" (February 16).

A dramatic Waco raid was BATF's answer, a bureaucratic insurance policy: helicopters racing in as a diversion, scores of agents pouring from concealment in horse trailers, and press conferences with officials standing behind tables laden with seized guns. Journalist Carol Vinzant discovered as follows:

> In the jargon of at least one ATF office, the Waco raid was what is known as a ZBO ("Zee Big One"), a press-drawing stunt that when shown to Congress at budget time justifies more funding. One of the largest deployments in bureau history, the attack on the Branch Davidian compound was, in the eyes of some of the agents, the ultimate ZBO.[24]

On February 28, BATF had established a "raid headquarters" in a building a few miles from Mount Carmel. A videotape shot by an agent inside raid headquarters shows agents laughing and taking memento photos of one another. One is reading the newspaper comics. The PR team seems to have the only focused people in the room, standing behind long tables boasting rows of word processors, photocopiers, and fax machines, ready to spread the word coast-to-coast.

But one thing is missing from their preparations: ammunition. Agent Mayfield later testified he had carried only thirty rounds of pistol ammunition[25]—that is to say, enough cartridges to fill the magazine in his gun and probably one other. Agent Champion testified he did a bit better: three magazines.[26] Agent Dan Curtis, who carried an AR-15 rifle, had only twenty rounds—the contents of one small magazine.[27] The agents were equipped for a show-and-tell, not for a fight. For all BATF's portrayal of the Davidians as heavily armed fanatics, the Bureau regarded actual resistance as inconceivable. The battle cry that would begin the raid really was ironically accurate: "It's showtime!"

The military is authorized to provide equipment and its operators to law enforcement agencies. The military must be reimbursed for its costs, unless the law enforcement operation is antidrug, in which event the aid must be given for free. The BATF and FBI took liberal advantage of this, falsely claiming that Waco was part of the War on Drugs. Years later, the Army realized it had been swindled and forced BATF to reimburse it for $6,857, and the FBI to cough up over $199,000 (the FBI had kept, among other things, nine night-vision scopes, priced at $5,000 apiece).[28]

WHO FIRED FIRST?

Both the Davidians and the BATF witnesses agreed that as the horse trailers halted in front of Mount Carmel, David Koresh left the safety of the building, ran out, and began calling to the agents. There is general agreement that he attempted to defuse the confrontation with a comment like "Be careful, there are women and children here."[29] Only after gunshots rang out did he turn to run back into the building.

Koresh's rushing toward the agents strongly suggests that he did not expect a battle—he was leaving cover and running right into everyone's field of fire. Survivor David Thibodeau said that Koresh had earlier told the Davidians: "They're coming, but I want to talk it out with these people, so don't anybody do anything stupid. We want to talk to these people, want to work it out."[30] Koresh's conduct is consistent with these admonitions.

Add to this the fact that the Davidians said the right side of the double doors had bullet holes that proved BATF shot first, and that the right door mysteriously vanished from a crime scene controlled by the government; the evidence for BATF opening fire in the front of the building seems quite strong.

DID THE DAVIDIANS DELUGE THE BATF AGENTS WITH MACHINE-GUN FIRE?

One photo made as the gunfight began shows three agents standing or kneeling before the front door, guns at the ready or perhaps already firing, and without benefit of any cover whatsoever—hardly a posture they would have taken if facing a hail of bullets coming outward through the door.[31]

By the time of the Davidians' criminal trial, the agents had had time to assemble a most impressive story: BATF claimed that its agents were raked by a veritable battery of Davidian machine guns, firing from multiple positions. Agent Jim Curtis claimed to have heard five-shot bursts from a .50-caliber heavy machine gun in the center of the building,[32] and also firing from M16s on the left.[33] Agent Bill Buford stated under oath that he heard a Browning Automatic Rifle (a World War II vintage light machine gun, .30-06 caliber) or perhaps an M60 (Vietnam-era belt-fed machine gun, 7.62 mm NATO caliber).[34] Agent Gerry Petrelli testified that he had heard full-automatic fire from multiple M16s and AK-47s, plus .30- or .50-caliber belt-fed machine guns.[35] M16s, AK-47s, Browning Automatic

Rifles, M60s, .50-caliber machine guns—by that measure, the Davidians could have stocked a National Guard armory with fully automatic weapons. Based on this testimony, many of the surviving Davidians were sentenced to long prison terms for having used machine guns in a violent offense. With the results of the FOIA suit we now know that the Davidians were sentenced based on perjury.

BATF had positioned a van filled with radio equipment and operators near Mount Carmel. The "radio van" was charged with coordinating radio traffic during the raid. It contained an audio recorder connected to an "open mic" that picked up all sound in the van, including the gunshots from the battle at Mount Carmel and the voices of the radio van operators.

During the FOIA suits, BATF fought hard to keep the resulting tapes a secret, first claiming falsely (and under oath) that the tapes were full of "secret agent identifiers," which the court found were just agents' last names or badge numbers. The agency followed with other claims; only after the court rejected those did the agency reluctantly turn over the tapes.

The released tapes provided an excellent record of the gun battle in front of Mount Carmel. Plenty of gunfire was audible, ordinary gunfire, not machine guns. About twelve minutes into the fight, two bursts of full automatic fire, about five to ten shots each, are audible. The first burst comes as such a surprise that one of the radio van operators cries out in shock "F__king machine gun!"

Shortly thereafter, a voice on the radio asks the snipers, "Can you shoot tower two?"—the central tower. Forty seconds after the first machine gun burst, a garbled transmission is received, and the same radio van operator voice rejoices, "Hey, hey, we got the machine gun!"

A recent event has confirmed this conclusion. Fifteen years after the gunfight, BATF Agent Wendel Frost published his account of the day, *ATF Sierra One Waco*, which disclosed that he had been the sniper who carried out the command to shoot. Watching through a telescope sight, he had seen and shot two people who were using fully automatic guns—a man in a white shirt firing a MAC-10 submachine gun and a man in a black shirt firing a converted AR-15.[36] Agent Frost's account tallies perfectly with the radio van tape: exactly two Davidians fired fully automatic firearms, one burst each, and they died in the shoot-out.[37] The testimony to being raked by fire from multiple machine gun nests does not hold up when compared with actual evidence. None of the surviving Davidians could have fired a machine gun on February 28, 1993.

WERE THE DAVIDIANS BLOODTHIRSTY ANTI-GOVERNMENT RADICALS?

Also obtained in the Freedom of Information Act suits were audiotapes from the sheriff's 911 line. These enabled reconstructions of the firefight from the standpoint of the people inside Mount Carmel. Once the firing started, the Davidians did a remarkable thing: they called 911. Davidian Wayne Martin was a lawyer with a Harvard degree, and only a few seconds into the shooting he called 911 and reached Lt. Larry Lynch of the Sheriff's Department. The 911 tapes show that Martin begged, "There are seventy-five men around our building and they're shooting at us at Mount Carmel. Tell them there are children and women in here and to call it off!" As BATF bullets pierce the wall around him, Martin has to take cover, but he turns the speakerphone on, so all sounds within Mount Carmel can be heard. The rapidity of the gunshots declines after three minutes, only to temporarily pick up ten minutes later and then again taper off. Martin continues to cry out, "Want a cease-fire."

Lt. Lynch cannot reach BATF, because no one had given him a phone number or radio frequency. Inside Mount Carmel, Wayne Martin continues to shout, "Tell them to cease fire" and "want a cease-fire." By twenty minutes in, the firing has virtually ceased; when a few shots are heard, a Davidian can be heard crying out, "That's not us, that's them." Finally, half an hour after the raid began, Lt. Lynch is able to contact BATF by asking a Texas State Technical College policeman to drive over to the raid headquarters and stay in radio contact. Lynch begins working out a cease-fire so BATF can recover its wounded.

That was not the only surprise on the 911 tapes. Around forty-five minutes after the first shots, *David Koresh himself* calls 911, asking, "What'd you guys go and do that for? Now there's a bunch of men dead, a bunch of you guys dead, and that's *your* fault." He adds: "We're not trying to be bad guys." On the other 911 line, Wayne Martin is asking the dispatcher, "Please arrest these people. They came on our property and started shooting at us." A cease-fire is worked out, an ambulance arrives for an especially badly wounded agent, and the other agents withdraw.

By the end of the gunfight, the under-supplied BATF agents are running out of ammunition, with no way to retreat across a flat, open field. Had the Davidians intended an antigovernment bloodbath, they needed only to continue the fight.

The understanding is reinforced by an even more remarkable tape made sometime on February 28 after the gunfight. David Koresh had been badly wounded—a bullet entered his groin, blew a two-inch hole through the side of his pelvic bone, and exited from his side.[38] He is talking over a telephone to a BATF supervisor, Jim Cavanaugh. In terrible pain, Koresh might be expected to be angry; instead his tone is friendly. He tells Cavanaugh, "I wish you knew the Seven Seals." He mentions BATF undercover agent Robert Rodriguez, adding, "I really liked that guy, too. I've always loved law enforcement, because y'all guys risk your lives every day, you know." Koresh talks of his wound. Cavanaugh asks, "Anything else hurting?" and Koresh replies, "Just my feelings."

Koresh rambles on, asking, "Why did you start it? Why?" and then answers his own question with "You figured we were the bad guys, and now you know we aren't." Later, Koresh would assure Cavanaugh, "We are commanded by Scripture to abide by the laws of the land in every degree, so long as those laws don't 100 percent conflict with the law of God."

If there is one thing the 911 tapes can rule out, it is that David Koresh and the Davidians were government-hating cop killers. No wonder a memorial to the four dead BATF agents rests on the Davidians' church lawn.

WAS THE CS GAS ASSAULT INEVITABLE?

The inability of FBI negotiators to talk the Davidians into surrendering laid the groundwork for the CS gas assault. That failure had several causes, but one was predominant: no one in the FBI could grasp the Davidians' central motivation. The Davidians took their religion *very* seriously and believed that they were at a critical point in Christian, and world, history. Their religion centered upon the Book of Revelation, and the opening of the seven seals by the otherwise unidentified person described as "the Lamb." Most Christian religions assume that Jesus Christ is the Lamb, but reading Revelation in conjunction with the Book of Daniel, the Davidians concluded that the Lamb would be a mortal, a prophet. In Revelation, the seven seals divide up the final days into periods, and the Lamb's opening of each seal marks the transition from one period into another. Since the events are cloaked in symbolism (the bad guys are "Babylon," for instance), the interpretation is no simple thing.

The Davidians believed they stood at a critical moment of history—why else had an army of tanks and aircraft descended upon a church in the Texas countryside?—but which moment was it? What part of the seven seals were they experiencing, and what did God want them to do? Until that could be resolved, they could not act.

Their consensus appears to have been that they were toward the end of the fifth seal, which speaks of persecutions of the faithful, and close to the opening of the sixth, which is when things begin to heat up, beginning with a massive earthquake and the sun becoming "black as sackcloth of hair" while the moon becomes "as blood."

As the sixth seal progresses, four angels seal the foreheads of 144,000 of the faithful; these are presumably the same 144,000 who appear with the Lamb on Mount Sion or Zion in the Holy Land.[39] But that number, for the Davidians, led to a problem. The Davidians felt they were the persons who would be sealed, but as of spring 1993 they numbered barely a hundred rather than 144,000, and they were trapped about ten thousand miles away from Mount Zion. Was their interpretation in error, or had God left a loophole somewhere?

Two religious scholars, Phillip Arnold of the Reunion Institute and James Tabor of the University of North Carolina, had studied eschatological religions, ones that focus upon the end of the physical world. They had heard about the Waco standoff and set out to study the Davidian religion. They quickly concluded they could solve the impasse: the problem was that the FBI had no idea of how to address the Davidians' concerns. The FBI ignored their offers of aid, but early in March, Arnold appeared on a local radio program to explain their understandings. The Davidians obviously listened, because they sent out a note asking to talk directly with Arnold. The FBI refused, but the two theologians persisted on their own.

On April 1, Arnold and Tabor appeared on another radio program, one the Davidians were known to favor. Their solution to the paradox facing the Davidians was essentially: (1) David Koresh must give himself up to be judged, thereby proving he is indeed the Lamb; (2) the worldwide publicity resulting from the Davidians' trial would offer hopes of generating the required 144,000 converts; (3) the Lamb could create a "little book" (referenced in Revelation 10:8) to summarize his understanding of the seven seals and thus win the converts.[40] Arnold and Tabor's interpretation would enable the Davidians to fit a surrender into their religious worldview.

Shortly after the broadcast, the Davidians began to celebrate their Passover, during which they refrained from communications. Upon its ending, on April 14, David Koresh sent out a detailed letter. It began: "I am presently being permitted to document, in structured form, the decoded messages of the Seven Seals. Upon completion of this task, I will be free of my 'waiting period.' I hope to finish this as soon as possible and to stand before man to answer any and all questions regarding my actions."[41] He added that "as soon as I can see that people like Jim Tabor and Phil Arnold have a copy, I will come out and then you can do your thing with this beast."[42] FBI bugs planted inside Mount Carmel began to relay sounds of rejoicing and of people anticipating their departure.[43] Two days later, Koresh told an FBI negotiator over the telephone that he would come out as soon as the "little book" was finished. The negotiator asked for clarification, and Koresh responded, "I'll be in custody in the jailhouse. You can come down there and feed me bananas if you want."[44]

The impasse had been solved, but it was not a solution that the FBI-HRT's action-directed members favored. Their viewpoint was laid out by Christopher Whitcomb, an HRT sniper, in his book *Cold Zero*.[45] To Whitcomb, the negotiators were wimps who frustrated the desires of the Hostage Rescue Team operators:

> A virtual war had been brewing between negotiators and tactical personnel. Fifty of the best-trained tactical operators in the world sat idly by, day after monotonous, agonizing day, waiting for something to happen. Nothing happened. . . . For the warriors among us, talk had become tiresome.[46]

But now the impasse looked like it would resolve peacefully. The HRT had a simple solution. When Attorney General Reno repeatedly asked whether there was hope for a peaceful end, FBI representatives told her there was no such hope, and the letter's existence went unmentioned.[47] Three days after Koresh told the FBI negotiator that he was coming out, the FBI-HRT hit Mount Carmel with tanks and tear gas.

To the FBI-HRT, the command to gas represented not a last alternative, but a long-awaited opportunity. As Whitcomb put it, "After nearly two months of mind-numbing frustration, Headquarters was finally handing us the reins."[48] In his mind, "On April 19, 1993, David Koresh was coming out of that compound, one way or the other. None of us there gave a rat's damn about how."[49]

How Did the April 19 Fire Start?

As discussed above, there are two types of CS "tear gas" projectiles. The earliest type is the "pyrotechnic" projectile: it uses a burning gunpowder-like mixture to expel the CS. These projectiles commonly are marked with warnings not to use them against buildings because they can start fires. The later type of projectile, trade named the "Ferret," is a plastic case filled with CS dissolved in the solvent methylene chloride. Upon impact, the plastic bursts, the mixture splatters, and the solvent evaporates, leaving the CS powder in the air.

The government, as might be expected, claimed that the Davidians must have started the fire; the CS projectiles that it shot in could not have ignited anything, since it had only fired Ferret rounds. Attorney General Reno so testified before Congress, as did one of the Davidians' prosecutors, Ray Jahn. When the FBI acknowledged that it had made infrared videotapes from an aircraft on the day of the fire, it claimed under oath that the videotapes began at 10:42 a.m.

The FBI later had to admit that the tapes began when the gassing operation did, more than four hours earlier. Why conceal the earlier infrared tapes? Clouds blocked any view of the ground, so there were no images worth viewing. But there was a soundtrack, and it recorded events in the cockpit, including overheard radio traffic. That radio traffic included HRT's on-scene commander, shortly after 8:00 a.m., authorizing the use of military pyrotechnic CS gas rounds against an underground structure. *During the Congressional hearings, that on-scene commander sat behind Ms. Reno, in silence, as she testified that no such thing ever happened.*

The FBI had an easy response to any criticism over *that* use of pyrotechnic rounds. Those rounds could not have caused the fire: they were shot four hours before the fire broke out—and into an underground structure that never caught fire. Why take big risks—setting up your boss, the Attorney General, for a perjury charge, lying under oath, hiding a videotape—to conceal the use of pyrotechnics that could not have played a role in the fire? It makes no sense—unless that was not the only use of such dangerous projectiles. Davidian Clive Doyle had experienced the CS gassing, not in the underground structure, but on the first floor of Mount Carmel. In 1995, he described the gassing to a Congressional committee:

> When I first heard they were going to inject gas . . . in my uneducated understanding, I'm thinking of Hollywood where a grenade is thrown into a room and somebody runs over, picks it up, and throws it out of the window if you don't want it. I mentioned that to somebody and they said, well, *you can't pick them up, they're hot.*
>
> And I said, well, maybe we could use a glove. We never got to see them. They whizzed past your head so fast that, as I say, it was like a rocket. The only time you could see them at all is *when they hit a wall and stuck in the sheetrock and the hissing and so on.*[50] [Emphasis supplied]

Doyle did not realize the importance of what he had said, and neither did the Congressional committee. Ferret rounds don't heat up or hiss; but pyrotechnics do.

If government-launched pyrotechnic projectiles did start a fire, they had been aimed at the most dangerous location for igniting one. On April 19, powerful winds were sweeping Mount Carmel, coming in from the right (southeast) side. Survivor Clive Doyle was on the first floor, right side, when he heard the pyrotechnic rounds making hissing noises. The winds would drive a fire started at the right side down the length of Mount Carmel.

A few minutes before fire breaks out, the FBI's airborne infrared video shows something happening on the right side at a second-floor window. A bright white (i.e., hot) elongated object suddenly appears next to the window, consistent with a pyrotechnic round becoming stuck in the window sash. Within minutes, the infrared camera records hot gases bursting through the window and driving *into* the oncoming wind. The most likely explanation is that a fire has begun inside the room and that its internal door is closed. The flames and expanding hot gases cannot escape into the rest of the building and must vent into the wind.

A few minutes later, the venting stops. The fire has eaten through the door, a flashover has occurred, and the powerful winds are blasting the firestorm down the second-story hallway. FBI photographs taken from the ground confirm that the second story was an inferno before fire began on the first story. The Davidians on the lower floor may have had little warning of a fire before the burning upper story collapsed on them. Clive Doyle testified that "the whole area that we were in just turned pitch-black, and almost immediately it was like you could feel heat over your head and on both sides, and I found myself down on the floor rolling around trying to protect myself from the heat."[51]

But the greatest death rate was among the women caught in the vault. The vault was the concrete room in the center of the first floor, where the mothers and children had gone for shelter—and where every one of them perished. At 11:43, a quarter hour before the fire, a tank rammed its way up to the opening to the vault, and sprayed in a full load, ten gallons, of liquid CS. Why? During the 1995 House hearings, FBI Agent Byron Sage tried to portray the Davidian mothers as callous, but in so doing he let slip the FBI's own callous reason for gassing a building occupied by children: "I am telling you, I've been through CS gas a number of times and I would move heaven and earth to get my children out of that type of environment. That's why it was introduced, Congressman, to initiate an environment which would cause those people to come out safely, not even orderly."[52]

But most of that "liquid CS," about 98 percent of it by weight, is not CS but the solvent that carries it, methylene chloride (MeCl). MeCl vapor functions as an anesthetic, producing disorientation, giddiness, and eventually coma and death. Dow Chemical, one of the manufacturers of MeCl, warns that it is intoxicating at 500–1,000 parts per million (or 0.05 percent to 0.1 percent of air) and causes death by cardiac arrest at 10,000 parts per million (or 1 percent of air).[53] Still more dangerously, MeCl is metabolized in the body into carbon monoxide. These traits have led to its ban as paint remover after several deaths due to carbon monoxide poisoning.[54]

Dr. Eric Larson, formerly a Dow chemist, estimated the discharge of one bottle of MeCl into the vault would have made its occupants comatose and unable to escape a fire, and two bottles (the actual amount used) would have raised the MeCl concentration to lethal levels.[55]

The autopsies showed that nine persons in the vault died of asphyxiation without signs of smoke inhalation—they died before the fire began. The rest were likely comatose. When the fire did begin, the occupants of Mount Carmel faced another complication: burning CS releases deadly cyanide gas, and by that point Mount Carmel was saturated with CS powder. At autopsy, more than half the Davidians' bodies had measurable cyanide levels, and at least one had a lethal concentration.[56] (Burning plastic also releases cyanide, a major factor in aircraft fires, but a study of Dallas residential fires found that cyanide gas was only detectable in 12 percent of them, and never reached near-lethal levels.[57])

In short, Davidians trying to escape the blaze faced a multitude of obstacles, all created by the government. They had to fight their way past wreckage, were probably blinded by the CS, were made groggy or comatose by the MeCl, and had been breathing smoke made deadlier by cyanide gas.

Some of the Davidians brought suit under the Federal Tort Claims Act. The District Court ruled: "Claims relating to the planning of the raid, the standoff, or the final assault . . . are barred by the discretionary function exception because they involve the permissible exercise of law enforcement policy judgment."[58]

WHERE WERE THE FIRE ENGINES?

The final reason why the fire was so lethal: the FBI wanted it that way. No fire engines. The nearest fire department—with a total of one full-time employee and twelve volunteers—who must be summoned to the station before trucks can roll—is in Bellmead, ten miles from Mount Carmel. The fire department would later inform CNN that while the FBI had alerted them on other days when action seemed likely, they were never alerted to stand by on April 19.

Then there is an interesting series of conversations between the FBI Tactical Operations Center ("TOC"), Dick Rogers, the HRT commander

("HR-1"), and Jeff Jamar, Special Agent in Charge and overall commander ("SA-1"), as captured on the audio feed of the orbiting aircraft's FLIR camera:

> [Rogers speaking] 12:31:00 HR-1 to Forward TOC, if you have any fire engines, get them out here NOW.
> [TOC speaking] 12:31:42 We'll have the fire trucks sent to the T [road intersection, about a mile from Mount Carmel] for instructions.
> [Rogers speaking] HR-1. I want the fire trucks up here at the scene!

In his deposition testimony in the Davidians' wrongful death cases, Jamar stated that he detained the engines until Rogers indicated it was safe for them to proceed. Yet Rogers had indicated that he wanted them "at the scene."

There follows an ominous exchange between Jamar and Rogers—an exchange that clearly indicates that some FBI officials *did* envision that burning the adult Davidians alive was a good idea:

> [Jamar speaking] SA-1 to HR-1.
> [Rogers speaking] Go ahead, SA-1.
> [Jamar speaking] Our people focused on the bus area for the kids, is that what we're doing?
> [Rogers speaking] That's what we're trying to do.
> [Jamar speaking] No one else, I hope.

Rogers, the HRT leader, is silent for a few seconds, and then responds in a tone of frustration: "What's the ETA [estimated time of arrival] on the fire engines, SA-1?"

At this point, according to the Justice Department Report, the fire engines had already been held for several minutes at the FBI roadblocks, perhaps a mile from Mount Carmel. Jamar replies, "They will be there momentarily."

But they aren't. At 12:36 p.m., HRT commander Rogers shouts angrily, so angrily, in fact, that his voice overloads the microphone: "IF YOU HAVE FIRE ENGINES DOWN THERE, PULL THEM UP HERE IMMEDIATELY!"

Instead of a reply, a minute later another voice appears: "No fire engines at the T [a road junction]." The fire engines were still sitting at the outer FBI checkpoint, despite the HRT leader's repeated requests to allow them to pass immediately to the scene, his frustrated protests, and his superior's assurance that they were on the way.

The decision had been made. The Davidians, including those who had never fired on anyone, were cop killers who deserved death. At nearly 12:40 p.m., an aircraft crewman finally observes that two fire engines were approaching. At that point, Mount Carmel had already collapsed in flames; nine persons, some seriously burned, had managed to escape through the flames. No one else would be leaving it alive.

WHO WAS HELD ACCOUNTABLE?

The Davidians paid the highest price. Their next generation was virtually annihilated in the flames of April 19:

Chanel Andrade, 1	Abigail Martinez, 11
Shari Doyle, 18	Audrey Martinez, 13
Bobbie Lane Koresh, 2	Crystal Martinez, 3
Cyrus Koresh, 8	Isaiah Martinez, 4
Star Koresh, 6	Joseph Martinez, 8
Dayland Gent, 3	Melissa Morrison, 6
Page Gent, 1	Mayanah Schneider, 2
Chica Jones, 2	Aisha Gyrfas Summers, 17,
Little One Jones, 2	and unborn child
Serenity Jones, 4	Startle Summers, 1
Unborn child of Nicole Gent Little	Hollywood Sylvia, 1
Anita Martin, 18	Rachel Sylvia, 12
Lisa Martin, 13	Michelle Jones Thibodeau, 18
Sheila Martin, Jr., 15	

The handful of surviving Davidians likewise paid a huge price. A jury (hearing perjured testimony about multiple machine guns) convicted nine for aiding and abetting (i.e., helping others commit) voluntary manslaughter (homicide after extreme provocation) and of using a firearm in such an offense. Kathryn Schroeder, who testified for the government, was sentenced to two years. The court came down hard on the rest. Renos Avraam, Brad Branch, Jamie Castillo, Livingston Fagan, and Kevin Whitecliff were sentenced to the maximum of forty years each[59] for use of machine guns in a federal crime (although only two such guns were ever heard from and both operators almost surely died). The Supreme Court ultimately reduced the forty-year terms to fifteen years. Paul Fatta received fifteen years, Graeme Craddock ten years, and Ruth Riddle received five years.

On the government side, Attorney General Janet Reno formally accepted full responsibility for Waco—then, rather than resigning, she became the longest serving Attorney General in 150 years.

BATF did initiate proceedings to fire the two supervisors most responsible for the first day's gunfight. Agents Phillip Chojnacki and Charles Sarabyn stood charged with gross errors in judgment, lying to investigators, tampering with the evidence, and "attempting to wrongfully shift responsibility to a subordinate for failure to properly supervise the raid."[60] But their attorneys suggested that certain facts would become public if their clients were fired—in particular that "Some people 'way up' said some things after that weren't true, and that goes right down to the decision to go, and they were part of it."[61] The blackmail threat had immediate results. The termination proceedings were dismissed; the BATF supervisors were reinstated and given full back pay. The agency purged all mention of the disciplinary proceedings from their personnel files and paid their attorneys' fees.[62]

Only one government employee paid a serious price. Janet Reno eventually appointed Republican Senator and minister John Danforth as an independent counsel to investigate the Waco matter. Danforth hired staff, mostly present or retired federal attorneys, who were far from "independent" in their outlook. (The author was present when attorneys for the Davidians, and USDOJ attorneys for the government, arrived at the independent counsel's offices. The Davidians' attorneys were told to wait outside since the offices were a secure area. The USDOJ attorneys were immediately invited in.)

Danforth limited his study to the day the compound was destroyed, leaving out the BATF and FBI lead-up to the final attack, yet he still took fourteen months and spent $17 million. The investigation report documented a number of cover-ups and some outright perjuries; then spent the remainder of the report explaining why Danforth refused to prosecute those responsible.[63]

There was one exception, Assistant U.S. Attorney Bill Johnston, the man who let Mike McNulty see the warehouse full of evidence, and who thereafter wrote a letter to Janet Reno informing her that pyrotechnic tear gas projectiles had been used. Danforth's people found that he had withheld *one page of notes* from a grand jury and eventually forced him to plead guilty to a felony charge.[64]

> The Supreme Court has long ruled that the government may not prosecute a person while concealing evidence that tends to prove their innocence. But in a 2001 affidavit, a former FBI agent stated that the agency had "zero files," known for their numbering, that were kept secret from prosecutors so that they wouldn't have to disclose them.[65]
>
> Independent Counsel John Danforth's Waco report noted at one point that an FBI attorney had "placed a number on the Hickey memorandum which would result in its being placed in an FBI litigation file that would not be disclosed to the Department of Justice."[66] Apparently, neither FBI attorney, nor the Independent Counsel, nor the Deputy Attorney General to whom the report was given thought this was unusual.

While Danforth's team let everyone else walk, they pursued Johnston with a vengeance, seeking prison time rather than probation, issuing grand jury subpoenas to people who contributed to his defense fund, and trying to have him disbarred.[67] The judge gave Johnston probation and the Texas Bar Association refused to disbar him, but his finances and career suffered for his serious and dangerous crime—allowing the public to know the truth. Johnston had committed the bureaucrat's ultimate sin: he had embarrassed his agency, the USDOJ, by exposing its cover-up. That Senator Danforth was a Republican and Attorney General Reno and the Clinton White House were Democrats reveals much about the unity of the ruling class and its separation from the average taxpayer. Even with nearly a hundred Americans dead, the instinct of the ruling class was that "the right hand washes the left." With Danforth's investigation, the government's whitewashing reached new levels: he spent $17 million to cover up for a cover-up.

Smoke rising from the destruction at Texas City. (University of Houston)

The 3,200-pound anchor of the *Grandcamp*, near where it fell to earth 1.6 miles from the ship's explosion. (Courtesy of David Greif)

Buildings near the *Grandcamp* were simply obliterated. (University of Houston)

A parking lot a half mile from the *Grandcamp* shows the power of the explosion's shock wave, which even at that range could cave in the side of an automobile. (University of Houston)

Troops watch one of the Buster-Jangle detonations from six miles away. Shortly after the 31-kiloton detonation, these "Atomic Veterans" were marched to ground zero. (Department of Defense)

"Dirty Harry." A powerful warhead detonated on a tower; its fireball sucked up and irradiated large quantities of soil, generating exceptionally heavy fallout. (AEC)

Knothole-Badger test, 1953. A 23-kiloton warhead detonated on a tower. (Wikipedia)

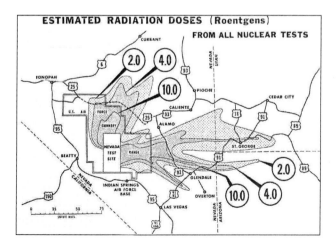

Even as it was assuring downwinders that there was no fallout worth worrying about, the AEC was generating maps showing significant radiation doses. (Wikipedia)

On May 16, 1997, the last survivors of the Tuskegee
Syphilis Study received a formal apology from President Bill
Clinton. (William Jefferson Clinton Presidential Library)

The FBI sniper who killed Vicki Weaver drew this sketch of his sight picture at
the moment he fired. It is not to scale—the window on the door was smaller and
higher up than shown here. Kevin Harris is rushing toward the door. Most criti-
cally, the tops of two heads are visible in the window. The sniper could see persons
behind the door even as he shot through it.

Outside their new church outside Waco, the Branch Davidians have memorials to the BATF agents killed in the assault, and to the victims of Oklahoma City.

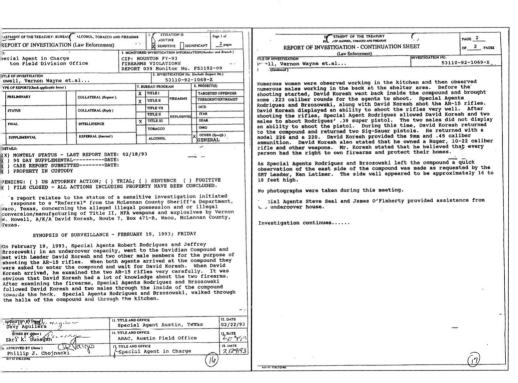

Supposedly, the February 28, 1993, raid was necessary because Koresh never left Mount Carmel. BATF had undercover agents observing the Davidians from a nearby house. On February 19, 1993, the agents went shooting . . . with David Koresh.

Koresh was unarmed until Agent Rodriguez loaned him a pistol.

In the April 19 assault, FBI armored vehicles demolished large parts of Mount Carmel. This is a view from the rear of what was known as the gym.

An aerial photograph shows the destruction to the front, as one of the armored vehicles rams into the building.

At 12:07 p.m., Mount Carmel began to burn.

Firefighters were held up at the FBI roadblock, until the flames had entirely consumed the building. The HRT commander was angrily radioing the on-scene commander for firefighters at the time.

After the fire died down, some of the FBI Hostage Rescue Team had trophy pictures taken.

Not all of the Fast and Furious guns made it to Mexico. One was used in this shooting in Phoenix, Arizona. (Phoenix Police Department)

A police videocam captured the second when an ad-hoc SWAT team shot into Jose Guerena's house in Tucson. One of the SWAT team's members tripped and accidentally fired his gun. In the confusion, the team emptied their magazines at Guerena, who died after being shot twenty-two times. (Tucson Police Department)

CHAPTER 6

LOOKING FOR TERROR IN ALL THE WRONG PLACES

I want an answer from a named FBI group chief for the record on these questions, several of which I have been asking since a week and a half ago. . . . If this guy is let go, two years from now he will be talking to a control tower while aiming a 747 at the White House.
— Unnamed CIA agent, speaking of Zacarias Moussaoui, 9/11's "twentieth hijacker," 2001[1]

Whatever has happened to this—someday someone will die—and wall or not—the public will not understand why we were not more effective and throwing every resource we had at certain "problems." Let's hope the National Security Law Unit will stand behind their decisions then, especially since the biggest threat to us now, UBL [Usama bin Laden] is getting the most "protection."
— Unnamed FBI agent, quoted by the 9/11 Commission, 2001[2]

During the year 2000 and beyond, The Turner Diaries *will be an inspiration for right-wing terrorist groups because it predicts both a revolutionary takeover of the government and a race war. . . . To understand many religious extremists, it is crucial to know the origin of the Book of Revelation . . .*
— FBI publication, *Project Megiddo, an FBI Strategic Assessment of the Potential for Domestic Terrorism,* 1999

THE ROAD TO 9/11 WAS LONG and wandering; it began more than a decade before aircraft hit the Twin Towers and the Pentagon, at a time when the terrorist organization al-Qaeda was about five years old. The distinguishing features of its early growth were repeated attacks upon Americans and feeble responses by the U.S. government.

FEBRUARY 1993: TRUCK BOMB EXPLODES IN THE WORLD TRADE CENTER, SIX KILLED

A decade before the attack on the World Trade Center, terrorists made an unsuccessful attempt to destroy it with explosives. Just after noon on February 26, 1993, a truck bomb laden with half a ton of home-brewed urea nitrate explosive was detonated in the parking garage beneath the north tower; its creators hoped to topple that tower into the south tower and kill thousands. The explosion penetrated five stories of the garage, killing six and injuring more than a thousand people.

The government's immediate response was unimpressive. President Clinton began his next radio address with "Good morning. Before I talk with you about our economic program this morning, I want to say a word to the good people of New York and all Americans who've been so deeply affected by the tragedy that struck Manhattan yesterday." He devoted twelve sentences to the subject before going into his economic proposals.[3]

OCTOBER 1993: SOMALIA, EIGHTEEN AMERICANS KILLED

While the events in Somalia were irregular warfare rather than terrorism, terrorists were involved and the outcome played a role in the evolution of anti-American terror. Whatever had passed for government in Somalia had vanished by 1992, with the countryside falling under the control of bands of feuding clans. Famine followed in the wake of the breakdown. The United Nations committed mostly American military forces to ensure the delivery of food and other humanitarian aid.

"Mission creep" set in, and soon protecting the food deliveries became a much more extensive project of "nation building." The UN persuaded itself that outside forces would somehow unite the warring Somali clans and would create a modern liberal democracy out of this less-than-promising political material.

The most powerful of the clans, led by one Mohamed Aidid, resisted the plan, and soon the UN/U.S. forces were implementing a plan to capture Aidid by helicopter assault. The now-famous terrorist Osama bin Laden was aiding Aidid's men and, had in particular, sent an advisor who had worked out how the ubiquitous RPG-7 antitank missile launcher could be used against helicopters once they stopped to hover.[4]

The outcome was well documented in the book and movie *Blackhawk Down*: Aidid's men noted that Americans launched every raid in the same way, with elite troops rappelling down from hovering helicopters. They laid an ambush, giving the Americans a false tip that Aidid would attend a meeting at a certain location in the capital, Mogadishu.

A Blackhawk helicopter, hovering while its combat team rappelled down to the objective, was downed by an RPG-7 hit. A Combat Search and Rescue team descended to rescue and protect the survivors. Another helicopter was downed and a third was damaged by RPG rockets. Armed mobs overran some of the defenders before relief forces broke through after an eleven-hour battle. Twenty-one UN troops, including eighteen Americans soldiers, were killed and seventy-three Americans were wounded. The scene was a disaster of poor intelligence and brave men.

Four days later, President Clinton announced all American troops would be withdrawn from Somalia by the end of March, some five months away. Relative stability would come after Aidid was killed in combat and succeeded by his son, Hussein Farrah Aidid, a U.S. marine and veteran of Operation Desert Storm.[5]

Bin Laden thought he found a lesson in the outcome of the brief fight. As he would later write:

> It cleared from Muslim minds the myth of superpowers. After leaving Afghanistan the Muslim fighters headed for Somalia and prepared themselves carefully for a long war, thinking the Americans were like the Russians. Our boys were surprised by the low morale of the American soldier, and they realized for the first time that the American soldier was just a paper tiger, and after a few blows ran in defeat.[6]

JUNE 1996: KHOBAR TOWERS BOMBING KILLS NINETEEN

Still the Clinton Administration acted as if all were normal. On June 25, 1996, terrorists detonated a truck bomb—variously estimated at containing five thousand or twenty-five thousand pounds of high explosive—outside the Khobar Towers, a military housing complex in Dharan, Saudi Arabia.

The Towers were occupied by American airmen enforcing the "no fly zone" in southern Iraq. Nineteen Americans died and 372 were injured.

President Clinton announced to the nation:

> The cowards who committed this murderous act must not go unpunished. Within a few hours, an FBI team will be on its way to Saudi Arabia to assist in the investigation. . . . We're grateful for the professionalism shown by the Saudi authorities and their reaction to this emergency. We are ready to work with them to make sure those responsible are brought to justice.
>
> Let me say again: We will pursue this. America takes care of our own. Those who did it must not go unpunished.[7]

Impressive words, but no action followed. To this day, there is some dispute over whether the terrorists came from the Iran-backed Hezbollah organization or Osama bin Laden's al-Qaeda. At the time, American sources blamed the Iranian group, so the government's reaction to Iran will serve as a measure of its determination.

FBI Director Louis Freeh headed the FBI investigative team. Saudi authorities informed him that they had four Hezbollah suspects in custody; FBI could question them, but protocol required that the President or a close surrogate contact Saudi Crown Prince Abdullah and request access. The FBI Director turned to Sandy Berger, the Assistant to the President on National Security Affairs, who was one of the key players in the Clinton Administration. A decade later, Freeh wrote of what followed:

> So for 30 months, I wrote and rewrote the same set of simple talking points for the president, Mr. Berger, and others to press the FBI's request to go inside a Saudi prison and interview the Khobar bombers. And for 30 months nothing happened. The Saudis reported back to us that the president and Mr. Berger would either fail to raise the matter with the crown prince or raise it without making any request. On one such occasion, our commander in chief instead hit up Prince Abdullah for a contribution to his library. Mr. Berger never once, in the course of the five-year

investigation which coincided with his tenure, even asked how the investigation was going.[8]

The indifference had a simple explanation:

While the investigation into the murder of nineteen Americans in an Iranian-backed operation was ongoing, the Clinton administration began a campaign to woo Tehran. It is difficult to warm relations with a regime at the same time as pursuing its connections to terror. So by 1998 the administration appeared prepared to forgive and forget Khobar Towers. . . . The administration softened the State Department warning about travel to Iran, waived sanctions against foreign oil firms doing business there, and removed it from the list of major exporters of illegal drugs.[9]

In the end, Freeh secured the intervention of former President George H. W. Bush, who persuaded the Saudis at least to allow the FBI to submit questions to be asked the prisoners and to observe the questioning. The results indicated that Iran had planned and executed the attack. When Freeh briefed the White House on the evidence, the main result was a meeting on how to spin the story in the media and on Capitol Hill: "It seemed we were there to manage the issue, not do a damn thing about it."[10] Five years after the bombing, a federal grand jury indicted thirteen persons, none of whom resided in the United States and none of whom have ever been arrested. The killers did indeed "go unpunished."

August 1998: al-Qaeda Bombs U.S. Embassies in Kenya and Tanzania, Killing Twelve

Truck bombs hit U.S. embassies in Nairobi, Kenya, and Dar es Salaam, Tanzania, on August 7, 1998. Describing the attacks as "abhorrent," President Clinton promised: "We will use all the means at our disposal to bring those responsible to justice, no matter what or how long it takes."[11]

Two weeks later, Tomahawk cruise missiles struck a factory in Sudan and an alleged al-Qaeda training camp in Afghanistan. The factory was vaguely suspected of making nerve gas. The factory had been included because the White House desired to hit targets in two different countries since bin Laden had hit embassies in two different countries. Immediately after the raids, the White House announced: "Our forces targeted one of the most active terrorist bases in the world. It contained key elements of the Bin Laden network's infrastructure and has served as a training camp for literally thousands of terrorists from around the globe."[12]

Twenty-six persons were killed at the training camps, most of whom were probably of low rank. The crude structures that were knocked down were made of mud brick, planks, and stones; at a million dollars apiece, the eighty cruise missiles certainly cost more than any structural damage they inflicted. "'What you told bin Laden,' says Mike Rolince, former chief of the international terrorism division of the FBI, 'is that he could go in and level two embassies, and in response we're going to knock down a few huts.'"[13]

That overpriced "retribution" was followed by a still more desultory affair. Sudanese intelligence had become suspicious of two Pakistanis who entered the country after having traveled in places that were popular with Islamist terrorists—now the two wanted to rent an apartment facing the American Embassy in Sudan. Arrested and grilled, the two admitted they were paymasters for al-Qaeda cells in Sudan and had planned to attack the Embassy. Sudanese officials recorded the confessions, had them translated into English, and asked the FBI to send an agent to Sudan to get the interesting evidence.

After months of waiting for an FBI agent, Sudan sent the two terrorists back to Pakistan. Later, the FBI blamed the State Department for not approving the travel, and the State Department blamed the FBI.

OCTOBER 2000: AL-QAEDA BOMBS THE USS *COLE*: SEVENTEEN DEAD

On October 12, 2000, the Navy guided-missile destroyer USS *Cole* was being refueled in Yemen's Aden Harbor when terrorists detonated an explosive-filled boat alongside her. The blast blew a forty-by-sixty-foot hole in the American destroyer's side, killing seventeen sailors and injuring thirty-nine.

President Clinton announced, "If, as it now appears, this was an act of terrorism, it was a despicable and cowardly act. We will find out who was responsible and hold them accountable."[14] Yemeni authorities did arrest several individuals and sentenced two to death for their role; they later escaped from prison. A third was captured by the United States and sent to Guantanamo Bay, where he remains.

Bin Laden found the attack on the *Cole* quite useful. According to *The 9/11 Commission Report*:

> The attack on the USS *Cole* galvanized al Qaeda's recruitment efforts. Following the attack, Bin Laden instructed the media committee, then headed by Khalid Sheikh Mohammed, to produce a propaganda video that included a reenactment of the attack along with images of the al Qaeda training camps and training methods. . . . Portions were aired on Al Jazeera, CNN, and other television outlets. It was also disseminated among many young men in Saudi Arabia and Yemen, and caused many extremists to travel to Afghanistan for training and jihad. Al Qaeda members considered the video an effective tool in their struggle for preeminence among other Islamist and jihadist movements.[15]

THE GOVERNMENT FINALLY ACTS

By 2000, Osama bin Laden might have, with good reason, begun feeling frustrated. In addition to organizing multiple acts of terror that killed dozens of Americans, he had repeatedly declared war on the United States and been ignored.

One inconvenient exception had occurred in 1996, when bin Laden was living in Sudan, a country that was interested in getting itself removed from the American list of countries that supported terrorism. Sudanese officials offered to maintain surveillance on bin Laden or to arrest him and turn him over to any country that could prosecute him.[16] The offer was not purely altruistic; the rulers of Sudan had come to fear bin Laden and his following. Yet the United States refused both offers. Sandy Berger, then Deputy National Security Advisor, later explained, "The FBI did not believe we had enough evidence to indict bin Laden at that time, and therefore opposed bringing him to the United States."[17] Gerald Posner notes, "This is not surprising. The FBI had not even opened a file on bin Laden until October 1995, only months before Berger claims the administration relied on the Bureau's decision as to whether the U.S. should seek bin Laden."[18]

The FBI was not prepared to prosecute, and the Saudis, who were happy to keep him and other terrorists as far from themselves as possible, were uninterested. "In the end [U.S. officials] said, 'Just ask him to leave the country. Just don't let him go to Somalia,'" Gen. Elfatih Erwa, the Sudanese Minister of State for Defense, later told the *Washington Post*. "We said he will go to Afghanistan, and they said, 'Let him.'"[19]

Bin Laden did not go as an impoverished refugee. He chartered a C-130 Hercules military aircraft to transport himself, his wives and children, and 150 aides to their new home.

The government's approach was the worst of all possible alternatives. How could anyone think that bin Laden in Afghanistan with no one watching him was superior to bin Laden in Sudan, under surveillance by a country trying to ingratiate itself with the United States? Sudanese Gen. Erwa explained to the *Washington Post* that three Sudanese intelligence agencies were watching bin Laden. They had planted informants throughout his operations, had bugged his phone lines and fax machines, and kept detailed records on everyone who met with him.[20] In Sudan, bin Laden would be unable to lift a finger without it being known, and soon the United States would have intelligence detailing every aspect of his organization and every order that he gave.

Afghanistan was one of the worst places to have bin Laden; in 1996, the murderous Taliban was solidifying its control over the nation. Upon his arrival, bin Laden infused the Taliban with $3 million, plus thousands of Arab radicals that boosted Taliban numbers at a time when its atrocities were starting to damage recruiting among Afghans. Pakistani author Ahmed Rashid summed up bin Laden's role on Radio Free Europe:

> He provided funds to them. He provided thousands of fighters. There [are] some 3,000 Arabs fighting for the Taliban in Afghanistan. He was involved in many business deals with them in exporting, in consumer goods and smuggling, and also drug trafficking. And he's also become a kind of ideological mentor of theirs. . . . He wanted not only to have a sanctuary with the Taliban, but he wanted them to be his allies.[21]

AT LAST! THE GOVERNMENT (ALMOST) TARGETS BIN LADEN

The dangers posed by al-Qaeda and bin Laden were no secret. In 1995, the CIA had released a National Intelligence Estimate titled "The Foreign

Terrorist Threat in the United States"; in 1997, it issued another Estimate that warned: "Civil aviation remains a particularly attractive target for terrorist attacks." In 1998, it gave Bill Clinton a Presidential Daily Briefing report titled "Bin Ladin Preparing to Hijack U.S. Aircraft and Other Attacks."[22]

But an appropriately lethal response to bin Laden's attacks was hindered by a peculiar legal barrier. Back in 1975, CIA and FBI activities had been investigated by the Church Committee, a Senate committee chaired by Senator Frank Church. Its work was highly critical of CIA activities, including involvement in some homicides overseas.

In 1976, President Gerald Ford responded with Executive Order 11905, which forbade federal employees to "engage in, or conspire to engage in, political assassination." Two years later a similar command, Executive Order 12036, was issued by President Jimmy Carter: the principal difference was to remove the word "political" before "assassination."

Then in 1981, President Reagan signed Executive Order 12333, which had still broader restrictions. Part 2.11 provided, "No person employed by or acting on behalf of the United States Government shall engage in, or conspire to engage in, assassination." The ban covered not only federal employees but any person "acting on behalf of" the government. Part 2.12 reinforced this point: no federal agency could "request any person to undertake activities forbidden by this Order."

But none of these Executive Orders defined the word "assassination." No one seems to have thought that the sniper who shot and tried to kill Randy Weaver and Kevin Harris was attempting an "assassination," or that the Hostage Rescue Team leader who ordered his snipers to shoot any armed male on sight was ordering them to undertake an "assassination." Nor would anyone use that word to describe one soldier's shooting of an enemy soldier. Perhaps "assassination" applies only to lethal termination of foreign government officials? Or perhaps only to those above a certain pay grade? Whatever the definition, in practice, the government's understanding seems to have been that putting a bullet into Osama bin Laden would be a forbidden assassination, while putting one into Vicki Weaver was merely a justifiable homicide.

In 1998, President Clinton signed a document essentially authorizing killing bin Laden as long as the death was incidental to other pursuits—i.e., incidental to capturing him alive.[23] If in the course of making an "arrest" bin Laden resisted and had to be shot, that was permissible, but taking him out with a sniper shot or a Hellfire missile was not. In preparation for this "arrest," a federal grand jury was readied to issue the appropriate indictment.

Bin Laden was fighting a war, and our government was answering with a legal proceeding. The proceeding would be governed by the usual civilian rules: no killing the defendant unless it was purely incidental to his apprehension. Do not kill an associate who might be standing near him. Nor, when the cry was to "bring him to justice," did there seem to be much thought about how difficult it is to prove a case in a terrorism setting, given the restrictions on hearsay evidence and the requirement that evidence be authenticated before it can be admitted. Need to prove that bin Laden signed this document? You'll need a handwriting expert and samples of his handwriting that can be authenticated—that is, witnesses who saw him sign it or are familiar with his handwriting. A 100 percent "reliable source" says he heard someone equally reliable say he heard bin Laden admit it? Sorry, that's hearsay and a Confrontation Clause violation.[24]

In the meantime, however, there had been indigenous attempts to remove bin Laden from the land of the living. In Afghanistan, his Taliban was opposed by the loose alliance that came to be known as the Northern Front, and the Northern Front was very interested in taking bin Laden out. Years later, Haroun Amin, the Northern Front's Washington representative, told investigative journalist Richard Miniter about three attempts to kill bin Laden in 1999 and 2000:

> The first attempt was a bomb placed in the wall of a building which bin Laden's convoy was expected to pass in Kandahar, Afghanistan. The bomb had a cheap detonator and exploded seconds too late—destroying the vehicle behind bin Laden's—in 1999. When American intelligence officials learned about the assassination attempt, they were not happy. At the time, the Northern Alliance intelligence liaison was a Tajik named Amrullah Saleh. . . . Saleh received a lecture on the laws of war—and was sternly told not to do it again. . . .[25]

The lecture given Saleh may seem strange, but it was perfectly in accord with the applicable Executive Orders. No federal employee, nor a person acting on behalf of the federal government, could become involved in an "assassination" or request someone else to carry one out. Miniter's account continues:

> Despite American pressure, Northern Alliance commanders kept trying to kill bin Laden. It would have been reckless for them not to go after the arch-terrorist, whose arms, money, and legions of men were an essential asset to their enemy, the Taliban. Simply assassinating bin Laden could win the war for the Alliance. . . .

> The next two Northern Alliance attempts to take out bin Laden were simply not reported to the Americans. Why bother? The first was a daring nighttime assault on bin Laden's convoy in 2000. The second was an ambush in the canyons south of Mari-i-Sharif, also in 2000. "We killed a lot of their officers and men," Amin insists, acknowledging that with American arms and training they would likely have been still more successful.[26]

On the other hand, Richard Clarke, who served as the chief antiterrorism member of the National Security Council, gives an entirely different version of events. He argues that there *was* sufficient legal authorization to terminate bin Laden, but that the Central Intelligence Agency repeatedly went passive-aggressive, always finding some reason why it could not be done. Clarke's argument is that the Executive Orders banning assassinations had exceptions allowing killing of enemy commanders. (While the Orders actually lack such exceptions, Clarke has a point. When it comes to sidestepping the Orders, where there's a will, there is a way. The 1986 bombing of Muammar Gaddafi was, for example, explained as meant to blow up his house and only by coincidence Gaddafi himself.)[27] "I believe that those in CIA who claim the authorizations were insufficient or unclear are throwing up that claim as an excuse to cover the fact that they were pathetically unable to accomplish the mission," Clarke wrote in 2004.[28] One way or the other, whether the cause was adherence to legalisms or was bureaucratic inertia, the government's inaction played a large role in clearing the path to 9/11.[29]

January 2001 saw Bill Clinton returning to Little Rock and the inauguration of a new President, George W. Bush. We might expect the change to improve the focus upon terrorism, if only because the new Administration stressed foreign policy. Clinton's first CIA Director, James Woolsey, had served for two years and never once had a one-on-one meeting with the President.[30] Under Bush, the CIA Director was present at each daily briefing.[31]

While things may have seemed promising, the result was not an immediate, or even prompt, war on terror. During the spring and summer of 2001, President Bush had on several occasions asked his briefers whether any of the terrorist threats pointed to the United States, and on August 6 he received a Presidential Daily Brief titled "Bin Laden Determined to Strike in US."[32] But those who surrounded the new president had different priorities. When National Security Advisor Richard Clarke pressed for speedy and dramatic action on terror, he encountered one roadblock after another. Some Administration officials were focused on European crises and the break-up of the Soviet Union. Others were focused on Iraq and regarded Saddam Hussein as a greater threat than bin Laden and al-Qaeda (which he clearly was not).

Clarke gave it his best try. On matters of national security, the highest body was the National Security Council Principals Committee, composed of the Secretary of State, the Secretary of the Treasury, the Secretary of Defense, the Chief of Staff to the President, and the Assistant to the President for National Security Affairs (joined, when asked, by the Director of Central Intelligence, the Chairman of the Joint Chiefs of Staff, and a few others).[33] Below the Principals Committee was the Deputies Committee, composed of those officials' deputies.

Five days after the inauguration, Clarke sent a memorandum to Condoleezza Rice, then the President's National Security Advisor, stating "We *urgently* need such a Principals-level review on the al Qida network." (At this point in time, al Qida was Clarke's spelling of what is today usually rendered al-Qaeda). He noted the group "is not some narrow, little terrorist issue that needs to be included in broader regional policy" but, in his view, a central factor in Middle Eastern power equations:

> Al Qida affects centrally our policies on Pakistan, Afghanistan, Central Asia, North Africa, and the GCC [Gulf Cooperation Council]. Leaders in Jordan and Saudi Arabia see al Qida as a direct threat to them. The strength of the network of organizations limits the scope of support

friendly Arab regimes can give to a range of US policies, including Iraq policy and the Peace Process. We would make a major error if we under-estimated the challenge al Qida poses, or over-estimated the stability of the moderate, friendly regimes al Qida threatens.[34]

Clarke proposed prompt decisions by the Principals on a number of issues—should the United States aid the Northern Alliance and Uzbekistan, which were fighting against al-Qaeda? What messages should go to Pakistan and Taliban-run Afghanistan about sheltering al-Qaeda? How should the Administration respond to the previous attack on the USS *Cole*?

Clarke's proposal met roadblock after roadblock, and the Bush Admin-istration was acting in the same fashion as the Clinton Administration . . . but Bush had less time. Rice initially informed Clarke that the Principals would not consider it until the matter had been "framed" by the Depu-ties. The Deputies in turn did not meet for three months. When they did, Deputy Defense Secretary Paul Wolfowitz wanted the emphasis to be Iraq, not al-Qaeda. In the end, the Deputies decided that responses to al-Qaeda, American-Afghan relations, and American-Pakistani relations formed a cluster that must be decided together and required further study.[35] The issue was first considered at a Principals' meeting on September 4, 2001. Clarke was tasked with drafting a "broad policy document," a National Security Presidential Directive.[36]

Exactly one week later, al-Qaeda hijackers took over four aircraft and commenced their attacks. The highest levels of government were not the only ones to miss the ball.

THE FBI TAKES A NAP

During the years leading up to 9/11, the highest levels of the FBI appear to have seen foreign terrorism as a career backwater, filled with concerns over profiling and such; its resources and hopes for agency expansion were poured into domestic terrorism. Professor Robert H. Churchill has identified the period as involving the "second brown scare," as distinct from the earlier red scares (where, as the saying went, it seemed there was a Communist under every bed) and the first brown scare (where the Communist was replaced by a brown-shirted Fascist). In the second brown scare, Fascists and Communists gave way to militia members.[37]

During this time FBI headquarters produced a report, *Project Megiddo*, described as a "strategic assessment of the potential for domestic terrorism in the United States undertaken in anticipation of our response to the arrival of the new millennium."[38] The report indicated that the Y2K computer bug, expected to hit all Windows computers in the year 2000,[39] might lead to the United States being destroyed from within by the Christian Identity movement, by "cult-related violence," or even (my personal favorite) the Black Hebrew Israelites, a group that maintains that African Americans are the true descendants of the Israelites and have not shown a disposition to destroy any government, large or small.

The contrast with the Bureau's treatment of foreign terrorism is sharp. A 1999 General Accounting Office report found that the Bureau lacked a comprehensive risk and threat assessment—a basic strategic document—for foreign terrorism.[40] The FBI agreed to prepare one but had other priorities. In September 2002, the Department of Justice Inspector General reported the following:

> The FBI has never performed a comprehensive written assessment of the risk of the terrorist threat facing the United States. Such an assessment would be useful not only to define the nature, likelihood, and severity of the threat but also to identify intelligence gaps that needed to be addressed. . . .
>
> By September 2001, the FBI had developed a draft of a Terrorist Threat Report that described terrorist organizations and State sponsors but did not assess the threat and risk of an attack on the United States. In addition, based on our review of the draft, the FBI's draft Terrorist Threat Report does not conform to the FBI's assessment guidance, other available guidance on preparing threat and risk assessments, or the FBI's representations as to how it would respond to the GAO's recommendations. Among the report's many omissions are assessments of the training, skill level, resources, sophistication, specific capabilities, intent, likelihood of attack, and potential targets of terrorist groups. Further, the draft report does not discuss the methods that terrorists might use.[41]

And this a full year after 9/11!

FBI FIELD OFFICES SEE TERRORIST PATTERNS

In the last months before the 9/11 attacks, two FBI Field Offices alerted their headquarters to similar patterns of events that suggested a future terrorist attack using passenger jets, and absolutely nothing happened.

In summer 2001, Agent Kenneth Williams, stationed in the FBI's Phoenix Field Office, noticed a highly suspicious pattern. Williams had found several Middle Easterners were enrolled for flying instruction at Embry-Riddle Aeronautical University in Arizona; at least one of the students was known to associate with a person described as a veteran jihadist.

On July 10, Williams emailed his findings to FBI headquarters and to its New York City office. The synopsis read: "Usama bin Laden and Al-Muhjiroun [another Islamist radical] supporters attending civil aviation universities/colleges in Arizona." None of the dozen FBI supervisors and headquarters staffers who saw the memo took action.[42]

In the wake of the 9/11 attacks two months later, the Justice Department's Office of the Inspector General sought the reason why Agent Williams's email had been ignored. The report was lengthy,[43] but essentially found that most of the addressees (or their subordinates who screened it) had considered it an "FYI" rather than a request for action.

A month after the Phoenix email, and four weeks before 9/11, the government had another chance. FBI agents in Minneapolis noticed Zacarias Moussaoui, a French national who had entered the United States six months earlier, had developed an interest in learning how to fly Boeing 747s. As the 9/11 Commission would later note, "He said he did not intend to become a commercial pilot but wanted the training as an 'ego boosting thing.' Moussaoui stood out because, with little knowledge of flying, he wanted to learn how to 'take off and land' a Boeing 747."[44]

An FBI agent found that Moussaoui had $32,000 in a bank account. When questioned, he had no explanation for that asset, and he "became extremely agitated" when asked about his religious views. The agent concluded that he was an Islamist extremist and that his flight training had something to do with his plans. A bit of investigation showed that he had overstayed his visa and was thus liable to arrest at any point. The FBI agent considered that an ounce of prevention was worth a pound of cure and had Immigration and Naturalization Service (INS) arrest him. It was a wise move: Moussaoui was part of the 9/11 plot and became known as "the twentieth hijacker."

If he was indeed a terrorist, his luggage and his laptop computer probably contained information relevant to a plot or plots. But although the
INS had his luggage and files, searching them required a search warrant,
which required proof of probable cause—commonly defined as "strong suspicions"—that it contained evidence of a crime, past or planned. Absent
probable cause and the warrant, searching Moussaoui's luggage and laptop
would violate his rights.

But to move from the theoretical to the real: to search Moussaoui's computer without probable cause or a warrant would mean that any evidence
found could not be admitted in a court of law, *against Moussaoui*. If an
allegedly illegal search and seizure occurs, only the person searched can
object; it is their rights that were violated. If anyone but Moussaoui was
implicated by the contents of his computer, these others would have no legal
"standing" to complain; *their* constitutional rights had not been infringed.

The FBI declined to think outside the legal box but continued to investigate. A few days later the case agent, Coleen Rowley, received word from
French intelligence that Moussaoui had recruited men for a unit of Islamist
rebels fighting against the Russians in Chechnya, a group that had blown
up a hospital.[45] Agent Rowley thought the Bureau clearly had probable
cause at that point.

What followed was typical of what happens when someone tries to move
quickly and decisively in a complex bureaucracy. Rule 41 of the Federal
Rules of Criminal Procedure says a search warrant may be issued at "the
request of a federal law enforcement officer or an attorney for the government." Although agents thus have the legal power to apply directly to the
court for search warrants, FBI protocol required an agent to ask a prosecutor
to make the application. In a case like Moussaoui's, the chain of command
was quite complex. The FBI agents would have to ask FBI headquarters to
seek the approval of the U.S. Department of Justice's Office of Intelligence
Policy Review (OIPR) before the agents were permitted to ask the local
U.S. Attorney's Office to apply for a search warrant.[46] The agents made the
request, but the OIPR denied they had probable cause and refused to allow
them to request the U.S. Attorney to apply to the court. Indeed, the OIPR
refused permission even *after* the 9/11 attacks, claiming Moussaoui's quest
for flight training and the attacks were unrelated.[47]

The internal opposition to further investigating Moussaoui suggests that its basis was less a matter of reasoned objections than of sheer bureaucratic pigheadedness. Agent Rowley later wrote the Acting Director of the FBI:

> [A]t one point, the Supervisory Special Agent at FBIHQ posited that the French information could be worthless because it only identified Zacarias Moussaoui by name and he, the SSA, didn't know how many people by that name existed in France. A Minneapolis agent attempted to surmount that problem by quickly phoning the FBI's legal Attache (Legat) in Paris, France, so that a check could be made of the French telephone directories. Although the Legat in France did not have access to all of the French telephone directories, he was able to quickly ascertain that there was only one listed in the Paris directory. It is not known if this sufficiently answered the question, for the SSA continued to find new reasons to stall.[48]

The route through headquarters and the local U.S. Attorney appeared to be blocked solidly. Rowley knew of one alternative: to apply for a search warrant in the Foreign Intelligence Surveillance Court, which has broad powers to authorize searches, provided the target individual was sufficiently linked to a foreign power (i.e., was a spy or saboteur, or something similar). Obtaining one of these warrants involved a complex process: the application must first be made to the National Security Law Unit in FBI's General Counsel's Office. If approved, it would send the request up to the USDOJ which might apply to the special court.

But in the National Security Law Unit, the request got tied up in a different dispute: Moussaoui had been in a unit of Islamic rebels in Chechnya, but was such a body of rebels a foreign power? This question was key to bringing the case within the jurisdiction of the Foreign Intelligence Surveillance Court.

The debate continued even as the hijackers' airplanes hit the Twin Towers and the Pentagon.

THE CONSEQUENCES

So far as is publicly known, no one responsible for the failures that led up to 9/11 suffered any measurable consequence. Those of very high rank were too big to fail. The middle rank had merely followed agency custom in the "we've always done it this way" mentality.

In the wake of 9/11, the argument was made, quite predictably, that the bureaucracy needed more power, more money, and more ability to gather information. That the agencies *already had* the key information—that al-Qaeda was going to attack airliners, that named suspicious Middle Eastern persons were obtaining training at flight schools—was ignored. "More" must equal "better," to the point where USDOJ operatives began using their Patriot Act powers to seek information on who had checked out certain library books.[49] (A survey of 1,020 public libraries found that over 8 percent had had their checkout records searched. What they were searched for is unknown, since the Patriot Act forbids the libraries to reveal that information.[50]) But in intelligence work, more is not always better. In radio, there is the concept of the "sound to noise ratio."[51] A signal can be unintelligible, not because it is too weak, per se, but because it is swamped by too much noise. The same principle applies to the gathering of intelligence. Vacuuming in information about library books and the like involves processing a lot of "noise," which may obscure the "signal" (e.g., FBI agents in the field reporting that suspicious foreigners are learning how to fly passenger jets).

It is also predictable that the bureaucracy took a passive-aggressive approach to two measures that would have made civilian aircraft into difficult targets. One involved placing armed Air Marshals among the passengers, and the other involved arming the pilots.

The Department of Homeland Security (DHS) undermined the undercover Air Marshals program for years by imposing a dress code and sign-in requirements. Male Air Marshals had to wear suits, ties, and dress shoes, and be clean-shaven with hair properly trimmed.[52] As if that did not make them sufficiently conspicuous, for a time they had to pre-board and sign a logbook before entering the aircraft, assuring that any hijacker within eyesight would know whether the flight had an Air Marshal, and if so, who he was. Dave Adams, a DHS spokesman, tried to explain the rationale for the practice. "In order to gain respect in a situation, you must be attired to gain respect," he told the *New York Times*, adding that if the Marshals dressed informally "they probably would not gain the respect of passengers if a situation were to occur."[53] (A more likely explanation is that DHS saw the Air Marshals as security theater rather than security. To DHS, having passengers *think* the agency was protecting them was more important than actually protecting the passengers.) For a time, the Marshals had to play hide-and-seek with supervisors, sent out to catch any who were not conforming to the agency's sartorial standards.[54] DHS finally relaxed its dress code in 2006.

The other obvious counter to hijacking allowed pilots and cockpit crew to carry firearms. Although the crew was already trusted with the passengers' lives, TSA resisted proposals to arm pilots until Congress forced the issue.[55] Then TSA announced that certifying pilots would require five days of training, given only at a facility in Artesia, New Mexico, and the pilots would have to pay for their own travel.

If that were not enough, TSA mandated that the pilots' guns be carried in a strange, lockable holster that had the lock so situated that while the pistol was being holstered the locking mechanism could easily press the pistol's trigger and fire the gun, which happened to one U.S. Airways pilot in 2008.[56]

The most fundamental function of a government is to provide security against external threats, and in twenty-first-century America, the most serious external threat is terrorism. We are left with the paradox that the same government that reacted so ruthlessly against the Weaver family and against the Davidians proved utterly unable to act decisively when faced with a real threat.

The Davidian situation in particular illustrates the paradox. In the spring of 1993, the government sent two M1 tanks, four armored combat engineering vehicles, and a number of Bradley armored personnel carriers into action at Waco to assault a building held by two dozen untrained men and fifty women and children. In fall of 1993, American military commanders in Somalia reported that they needed armor support, particularly M1 tanks—and were turned down, out of the fear that that would be seen as an "escalation" of our presence there.[57] The result was the "Blackhawk Down" incident and eighteen dead American soldiers.[58]

CHAPTER 7

ARIZONA:
OPERATION FAST AND FURIOUS
ARMS THE DRUG CARTELS

———————

*Attorney General Eric Holder said that putting the [assault weapon] ban
back in place would not only be a positive move by the United States, it would
help cut down on the flow of guns going across the border into Mexico, which
is struggling with heavy violence among drug cartels along the border.*
                                             —ABC News, February 25, 2009[1]

*Our inability to prevent weapons from being illegally smuggled across the
border to arm these criminals causes the deaths of police officers, soldiers, and
civilians.*
                                 —Secretary of State Hillary Clinton in Mexico City,
                                                                   March 25, 2009[2]

*We're walking guns. How many guns have we flooded the border with? How
much of the crime down there are we responsible for? We are just as culpable
as if we had sold them ourselves. We're never going to get anywhere with this
case. . . . We haven't learned anything. The only thing that's changed from the
very beginning is the number of guns we've let walk.*
                                   —BATF Agent John Dodson, to the BATF agent
                                        in charge of Operation Fast and Furious[3]

BORDER WORK IS DANGEROUS, WHICH IS why the Border Patrol has had
more agents killed in the line of duty than any other federal agency. For
especially risky work, Border Patrol has its tactical unit, BORTAC, agents

specially selected, conditioned, and trained to handle exceptionally dangerous encounters.

On December 14, 2014, the BORTAC team's target for the night was a "rip crew," a Mexican gang that operated north of the border and robbed drug smugglers in the desert night. If the drug cartels were dangerous, men who set out to rob the cartels' smugglers were even more so. This rip crew had been operating for around a year and were suspects in several murders.

The rip crew were professionals by now. They stashed their guns during the day. If apprehended, they would seem like one more group of ordinary illegal entrants to be scooped up and returned to Mexico. When they wanted to strike, they retrieved their hidden guns, semiautomatic AK-47s, and were ready to steal and, if they met with resistance, to kill. Two nights earlier, they'd had a brush with the BORTAC team. One of the rip crew was captured, but the other five got away.

This night they had retrieved their arms and were on the hunt again, moving up Peck Canyon in southern Arizona, about a dozen miles inside the border. The half moon gave enough light for them to spot victims.

Six BORTAC members were waiting, two in an advanced position scouting and handling radio contact. Four more were positioned on a small hill within the canyon. A ground sensor had alerted them to approaching footsteps. Soon five men could be seen carrying rifles at the ready. The rip crew on the prowl.

The four agents on the hill waited until the rip crew was in front of them, then one agent called out, "Police, drop your weapons" in Spanish.

The rip crew opened up with their AK-47s, pumping shots at the dimly visible agents. The agents initially responded as policy required, with shotguns firing nonlethal "bean bags," meant to stun rather than to kill. Eventually Agent Keller got a rifle shot in that dropped one of the robbers; the rest fled into the night.

Echoes of the gunshots had barely died away when the BORTAC team heard Agent Brian Terry shout, "I'm hit!" Agent William Castano went to his aid and Terry told him, "I can't feel my legs. I'm paralyzed." The bigger problem was not visible in the darkness. The AK-47 bullet had punctured Terry's aorta, the body's biggest artery, and he was bleeding out. He died on that little hill.[4]

The effects of that murder would be heard all the way to Washington, where Cabinet officials and agency heads would publicly wash their hands of any connection to the crime. The reason for their anxious disavowals is simple: the rip crew's guns had been obtained through an FBI informant and sold with the connivance of the U.S. Department of Justice (USDOJ) and the Bureau of Alcohol, Tobacco and Firearms (BATF). Agent Terry would not be the only person killed by guns sold to border criminals in Operation Fast and Furious, the government's covert gun-running program. Fast and Furious saw government agents blessing the sale of more than two thousand guns to cartels and other criminal groups, while falsely assuring gun dealers that they were helping a secret government program meant to destroy these cartels.

Does that seem insane? If so, consider that Fast and Furious was not the first attempt, by a government agency, to give guns to the cartels.

PRELUDE: OPERATION WIDE RECEIVER

The first government gun-running operation (like many BATF cases) originated when a licensed gun dealer called the agency to report a suspicious purchaser. In 2006, Arizona gun dealer Mike Detty sold six AR-15 receivers (the receiver is the core part of a firearm and is legally regulated as the firearm) to a purchaser who wanted to buy twenty more. Detty could not see any legitimate reason why the person would want that many receivers: he must be "up to something illegal and . . . just not bright enough to be less obvious about it."[5]

Detty called a BATF agent whom he knew well and explained his suspicions. Whenever a gun dealer sells a gun, he and the buyer must fill out BATF's Form 4473, recording the buyer's name, address, driver's license number, physical description, and usually his social security number. Detty thus had a perfect set of identifiers for the suspect. He faxed the 4473 to BATF.

The suspect buyer called Detty and arranged to buy twenty more receivers at a gun show. For that show, Detty had a supposed salesman at his table. The salesman was actually a BATF agent, as were most of the customers standing around his table watching the sale.

After a few more sales, a new buyer appeared and told Detty that he would be replacing the original buyer. He explained that his unnamed employer had found his predecessor unreliable; he did not say what had happened to him, but Detty guessed that it was unpleasant. The new buyer bought more than $10,000 of receivers and later placed more purchases in large quantities. The dealer informed BATF of each sale, and during one transaction an agent was able to attach a radio tracking device to the buyer's car.[6]

Detty's sales, monitored and encouraged by BATF, were given the title Operation Wide Receiver. The program would provide 410 firearms to drug cartels or other illegal buyers in Mexico; more than 10 percent would be traced to Mexican crime scenes.[7] William Newell, the Special Agent in Charge (SAC) of the Phoenix Field Office, would later say that he had concerns about using a licensed dealer as an informant. Apparently, he had no qualms about the overall plan to run guns to the cartels.

Sometimes we have to wonder which side a government agency is on. In 2005, a federal Child Protective Services agency convinced the mother of a three-year-old to take a juvenile into her house, hiding the fact that the juvenile had a serious record as a child molester. He molested her daughter, and the mother sued, but the Eighth Circuit held that the agency's action was protected by the discretionary function exception; keeping things secret was "a policy decision" because the agency had to balance the molester's confidentiality against the dangers of "placing a known sexual abuser in a home filled with children."[8]

One thing was missing from the BATF operation. Obviously, once the guns crossed the border they would have to be tracked, if at all, by Mexican authorities. The agency's liaison with Mexican law enforcement was through BATF's Mexico City Office, also known as MCO. The gun sales began in early March 2006. No one asked the BATF MCO to coordinate with Mexico until April 2007.[9] Even then coordination does not seem to have been much of a priority: the agent in charge of the MCO handed the duty off to one of their local employees, who, he later discovered, had done nothing about it.[10] The result was that once the guns crossed the border, they went right to the cartels with no Mexican authority able to interfere or investigate.

The legal effects of Wide Receiver were desultory at best: a few low-level offenders, the persons who bought directly from Detty, were indicted, and it took years just to get that far. A review of the operation by the Justice Department's Office of Inspector General (OIG) reported that much of the delay came because the local federal prosecutors, the U.S. Attorney's Office, declined to prosecute the offenders who bought from Detty. The reason a prosecutor gave in a 2008 internal memo was "I don't like the case. I think it is wrong for us to allow 100s of guns to go into Mexico to drug people knowing where they are going."[11]

Mike Detty, the gun dealer who was at the heart of the case, got a somewhat different version. A local federal prosecutor told him, "I never prosecuted that case because the ATF lied to me. . . . I was led to believe that there was ongoing cooperation with the Mexicans on this case. When I found out they were lying to me, I wasn't going to devote any more time or work to that case."[12] A few years later, BATF persuaded USDOJ head-quarters to take the case, which eventually led to indictments against the buyers.

SEEKING A MOTIVE

An obvious question arises: Why would a federal agency encourage gun-running to the drug cartels? Why would it aid some of the most vicious criminal organizations on the planet and make them a gift of more than four hundred American firearms? Mike Detty, the firearms dealer whose reports had begun the operation, later asked a federal prosecutor for an explanation:

> "Dan, what do you really think was going on with Wide Receiver? I mean nothing makes sense to me."
> "Anytime you have an operation like this you have to ask yourself; what is the end gain. Was it to take out a cartel?"
> "That's what they told me," I said.
> "How? By what mechanism? How do you shut down a cartel when all of their assets are in another country?"
> "I wondered about that."
> "Was it to find out what cartels these guns were going to? Thanks to you they had that information within the first couple of buys. Was it to track the guns to see where the cartels are operating? That's ridiculous—we already have that intelligence."
> I looked up from my work. He made it all sound so simple.

[The prosecutor] said, "I can only think of one reason that Newell would allow American guns to continue to cross the border and show up at Mexican crime scenes." He cocked an eyebrow for emphasis.

At last I understood the ugly truth. . . . In my opinion, the reason that guns were allowed to cross the border in Wide Receiver as well as Fast and Furious was to have American guns show up at Mexican crime scenes. . . . There never was a plan to take down a cartel.[13]

That is a possibility: the emergence of the American-guns-are-going-to-Mexico theme was quite profitable for BATF. As the Congressional Research Service later explained,

For the past two fiscal years, FY2009 and FY2010, Congress has provided ATF with program increases to address illegal gun trafficking from the United States to Mexico under an initiative known as "Project Gunrunner." For FY2008, Congress also provided ATF with a program increase for domestic gun trafficking, but the focus of this program increase was also largely on the Southwest border. As a result, for those three fiscal years, Congress has provided over $49 million in program increases to address gun trafficking.[14]

To be fair, it is also possible that BATF leadership thought that somehow they actually could damage the drug cartels by running guns to them. If so, the result, four hundred guns run to the cartels in exchange for prosecuting a few low-level straw men, would have ended any such expectations.

Operation Wide Receiver was a success in one sense: BATF managed to keep it secret. There was no press coverage until years later, when the Obama Administration—under criticism for a much larger gun-running operation—used Wide Receiver to argue that the same thing had happened under the George W. Bush Administration.

Operation Wide Receiver had one other significance. When USDOJ headquarters prosecutors took the case, they became worried that exposure of the BATF gun-running might embarrass the government and took pains to alert a number of officials, among them Lanny Breuer, Assistant Attorney General for Criminal Division, and William Hoover, BATF's

Acting Deputy Director.[15] The highest levels of the USDOJ and BATF thus knew that allowing official gun-running would do no good against the cartels—but also knew that such gun-running could be covered up.

IF AT FIRST, YOU DON'T SUCCEED: OPERATION FAST AND FURIOUS

Operation Fast and Furious began, as had Wide Receiver, with an Arizona firearms dealer calling BATF to report a suspicious purchaser. In this case, the dealer suspected a "straw-man sale," where one person fills out the required paperwork and passes the criminal records background check with the intent to transfer the firearm to another person, who actually put up the money.[16] (The form that the buyer must fill out asks whether the purchaser is the real buyer of the firearm and giving a false answer is a federal felony.)

The dealer's call came at an auspicious political moment, in January 2009, just as Barack Obama was inaugurated as the forty-fourth President of the United States; two weeks later Eric Holder was sworn in as his Attorney General. Mr. Obama was a lifelong gun control advocate.[17]

The new Obama Administration wasted no time deciding that gun restrictions were to be given a high priority and that these restrictions could be promoted by arguments that American guns were being illegally taken into Mexico. The new President, Attorney General, and Secretary of State (Hillary Clinton) all began to raise the issue of U.S. guns flowing into Mexico. A month after the inauguration, the *Washington Times* reported:

> Mr. Obama said he wants to renew a ban on some semiautomatic weapons but that it is not likely to pass Congress. Instead, he called for the Senate to ratify a decade-old hemisphere-wide treaty that would require nations to mark all weapons produced in the country and track them to make sure no weapons were exported to countries where they were banned.

> "I will not pretend that this is Mexico's responsibility alone. The demand for these drugs in the United States is what's helping keep these cartels in business," Mr. Obama said at a joint news conference with Mr. Calderon. "This war is being waged with guns purchased not here, but in the United States. More than 90 percent of the guns recovered in Mexico come from the United States, many from gun shops that line our shared border.[18]

There were political changes in Arizona, as well. In September 2009, Dennis Burke became the Obama U.S. Attorney for Arizona. Burke had been a political hanger-on, beginning his career as a staffer to Senator Dennis DeConcini. Burke had a political firearms agenda. He drafted and lobbied for the first "assault rifle" bill, and DeConcini attributed its passage to Burke's work. "A lot of it was not my eloquence on the bill," DeConcini would later say, "it was stuff that Dennis had done."[19]

Burke was rewarded with the post of Senior Policy Analyst in the Clinton White House, where he seems to have continued this focus on firearms restrictions. The internal document titled "Domestic Policy Council Accomplishments and Plans, December 1996" listed him as the point man on "Crime Initiatives," including the assault weapons ban.[20] Another internal document faxed to Burke from the Treasury Department reports that the number of licensed firearms dealers had declined by half[21]—the Clinton Administration was anxious to put licensed dealers out of business, and he was involved in the plan.

Back in Arizona, Burke attached himself to Arizona Attorney General Janet Napolitano, becoming her Chief Deputy Attorney General. When Napolitano became Governor, Burke was her Chief of Staff; when she was tapped to head the Department of Homeland Security, he came along as her Senior Advisor. As a U.S. Attorney, Burke finally had an independent command. As a U.S. Attorney, Burke would serve this agenda and further his own career by deciding whether to prosecute or refuse to prosecute all federal cases arising in Arizona.

In short, 2009 saw the ingredients for a "perfect storm" brewing along the Arizona–Mexico border:

- A new Administration that saw American guns going to Mexican drug cartels as an issue that could advance its gun control policy priorities;
- A new U.S. Attorney in Arizona who would be very sympathetic to that approach;
- An Arizona BATF office that happened to have experience, through Operation Wide Receiver, with allowing guns to flow to Mexico quietly; and

- A firearms dealer's report of illegal buyers, a situation that offered opportunities to renew the government-endorsed running of guns across the border.

Bingo! Linking American guns to cartel-related violence in Mexico could justify a push for more gun control. Of course, the operation would also lead to many deaths on both sides of the border.

BATF continued to receive reports of straw-man sales from the cooperating firearms dealer. In September 2009, the firearms dealer reported suspicious purchases by a Uriel Patino and a Jacob Chambers. By November, Patino purchased 77 guns and Chambers bought 102. The majority of them were new semiautomatic AK-47s—making it clear that Patino and Chambers were not gun collectors.[22]

In the Phoenix BATF Field Office, agents were organized into "Groups," and Special Agent in Charge Newell had announced a new unit, Group VII. Group VII was to be devoted to border issues, and headed by Agent David Voth. The Field Office continued to watch as straw men bought up large quantities of guns and sent them to the cartels. Soon the dealer was reporting more straw men—a Joshua Moore bought sixty-seven guns over the same time period, and a Jamie Avila showed up with Patino, then branched out on his own as a straw man.

Any gun found at a crime scene can be run through the BATF National Tracing Center (NTC) in West Virginia. The NTC will trace the gun to its manufacturer, then to its distributor, then to the licensed dealer who sold it, and report the results to the law enforcement agency that requested the trace.

Since the dealer who sold the gun must be contacted as part of the trace, a dealer knows whenever a gun he has sold is being traced. BATF agents put a "block" on that trace, which meant the NTC would not trace the gun nor report to the law enforcement agency that asked for the trace. Instead NTC would notify the BATF agent who requested the block, letting him or her know which law enforcement agency requested the trace. There were two advantages to blocking traces.

First, BATF agents had assured the cooperating firearm dealers that the sold guns would be intercepted before they got to the drug cartels. Blocked traces ensured that the dealer who sold the gun would not be contacted and would never know that the gun had been recovered by a police agency. If the dealers had received multiple calls trying to trace the guns, they would have been alerted that BATF was letting the guns pass to the cartels. As it was, the dealers got zero requests to trace these guns, suggesting that BATF was indeed keeping the guns away from criminal hands.

Second, when the BATF agent was tipped off that the requesting police agency had the firearm, the agent could ask that agency to turn over the gun because it was part of a BATF case. BATF could thus inflate its gun seizure statistics by claiming credit for guns that were seized by other agencies. For example, in July 2010, Agent Voth filed a Significant Incident Report describing how the Peoria, Arizona, police had arrested a Kenneth Thompson for hit-and-run and state gun charges after he fled from a traffic stop and crashed his car. The police found twenty semiauto AK-47s, purchased earlier in the day by a different person, obviously as a straw man for Thompson. BATF accepted the AKs from the Peoria police; the report ends, "This recovery adds to the total of ninety-six firearms recovered in the last twenty-four days by Group VII agents . . ."[23] The agents had done nothing but pick up the rifles from the Peoria police.

Late in November, BATF SAC Newell emailed U.S. Attorney Burke informing him that a number of Fast and Furious guns had been recovered by the Mexican Army. Significantly, Newell added: "We are advising ICE [Immigrations and Customs Enforcement] to stand down on their current proactice activity in Arizona in order not to compromise our case."[24] BATF had turned a blind eye to firearm transfers to the cartels, but now BATF and the U.S. Attorney were *protecting* the drug cartels' shipments against the legitimate enforcement mission of another federal agency. By the end of November, BATF knew that the straw men had purchased, and presumably shipped to the cartels, 341 firearms at the cost of $190,000. Yet, as the OIG would later note, "The investigative plan did not include seizing guns or approaching subjects. There also was no discussion about taking any action to try to limit the substantial purchasing activity by the subjects of the investigation."[25] In December, the frenzied buying continued. On six occasions, licensed dealers gave BATF advance notice of a planned purchase by straw men. BATF made no arrests. Its agents simply watched the sales go down and tried, without success, to follow the straw man as he drove away. From the OIG Report:

ATF also learned in December 2009 and January 2010 of additional recoveries of firearms tied to Operation Fast and Furious subjects in Mexico and the United States. For example, on December 9, 2009, one day after the Douglas seizure of firearms which had been purchased earlier in the day by Steward, the Mexican Army recovered 900 pounds of cocaine, 132 pounds of methamphetamine, $2 million in U.S. currency, and 48 firearms (46 AK-47 style rifles) in Mexicali, Mexico, a town approximately 240 miles southwest of Phoenix. Twenty of the recovered firearms had been purchased by Operation Fast and Furious subjects Chambers [and] Moore, between October 21 and November 19, 2009. According to an ATF report, Mexican authorities believed the firearms were destined for the Sinaloa Cartel to help replenish the loss of hundreds of firearms to the Mexican government and to sustain the drug cartel's fight with a rival cartel. ATF and the U.S. Attorney's Office took no action with regard to the straw purchasers of the 20 firearms recovered in Mexico. ATF records indicate that Chambers purchased another 10 firearms on December 11 and Moore purchased another 21 firearms in March 2010, including two .50 caliber rifles.[26]

This was followed in January by a seizure of Fast and Furious guns by the El Paso Police Department. Searching a drug "stash house," they found forty-two AK-47s that were being stored until they could be shipped across the border. When the El Paso Police tried to trace the guns, the blocked trace tipped off the BATF agents. BATF picked up the rifles and reported them as its own seizure. It took no further action.

SAC Newell announced the seizure in an email to BATF headquarters. The email's contents were breathtaking in their audacity and their mendacity: "[W]e are working this 'fast and furious,' the good news being we got another 42 off the street and can keep our case going. Hopefully the big bosses realize that we are doing everything possible to prevent guns going to Mexico while at the same time trying to put together a phenomenal case."[27]

FIREARMS DEALERS ASK—AND THE FEDS LIE

By January 2010, the original cooperating firearms dealer was beginning to worry. When he had cooperated with BATF investigations, arrests had always been made in one or two months. Three months later, the straw men were purchasing ten or twenty guns at a time and no arrests had been made.

He requested a meeting with BATF and was reassured that his cooperation was valuable, indeed "unprecedented," and they wanted him to continue to sell to the straw men.[28]

The second licensed dealer, the Scottsdale Gun Club, had also begun cooperating, and in April 2010, its owner emailed BATF, noting, "We just want to make sure we are cooperating with ATF and not viewed as selling to bad guys."[29] Agent Voth, head of Group VII, assured him, "If it helps put you at ease, we (ATF) are continually monitoring these suspects using a variety of investigative techniques which I cannot go into detail. . . ." The email closed with the assurance, "Your continued cooperation with our office has greatly aided the investigation so far."[30]

More months went by with no arrests. In June, the Scottsdale Gun Club's owner again emailed BATF:

> I wanted to make sure that none of the firearms that were sold per our conversation with you and various ATF agents could or would ever end up south of the border or in the hands of the bad guys. I guess I am looking for a bit of reassurance that the guns are not getting south or in the wrong hands. . . . I want to help ATF with its investigation but not at the risk of agents (sic) safety because I have some very close friends that are US Border Patrol agents in southern AZ as well as my concern for all the agents (sic) safety that protect our country.[31]

The owner requested a meeting with BATF. He later informed the OIG that he had told Agent Voth that his company "would not assist ATF unless the owner was assured that the firearms sold to subjects in the investigation would not be allowed to enter Mexico or fall into the hands of individuals that could use them against law enforcement. The owner said Voth assured him that the investigation would be conducted in a manner to prevent that."[32]

BATF has an enforcement and a regulatory side: the regulatory side can audit dealers' records (which, since each sale requires more than forty entries, are rarely perfect), revoke their licenses, and impose civil fines. When some dealers became reluctant despite the assurances, persuasion and even coercion were used. One dealer was told that it was his duty to help BATF battle the cartels.[33] Another dealer required pressure. BATF enforcement agents told the reluctant dealer: "We're not from the regulatory side of the house, but we do have lunch with those guys."[34] The dealer took the hint and continued with the suspicious sales.

THE MOST VIOLENT MONTH

In December 2009, Agent John Dodson reported for duty in the Phoenix Field Station. Dodson was an experienced law enforcement officer who had worked with military intelligence, local law enforcement, and the DEA before signing on with the BATF.

Dodson was confused. He'd been told that he was being brought in on a major and complicated case, one that might even qualify for wiretapping authority, a hallmark of a *very* complex federal case. But Fast and Furious seemed simple and routine. With the help of licensed dealers, BATF had already identified the straw-man buyers. Standard procedure would be to confront some of the lower-echelon suspects and offer them the choice of becoming informants or going to prison. They'd identify the persons for whom they'd bought the guns, and BATF would confront those and repeat the process on them, until everyone who could be rounded up had been, and the gun ring or rings had been eliminated.

Dodson was finding that Fast and Furious existed somewhere outside this simple reality. The BATF office received a phone call from a cooperating dealer that a known straw man, whose purchases had been traced to Mexican and American crime scenes, had just walked into his shop looking for guns. The dealer promised to stall him as long as he could.

Dodson and other agents raced to stake out the shop's parking lot. They saw the straw man exiting the shop with fifteen semiautomatic AKs, requiring three trips to his car to load them all. BATF already had plenty of evidence; it was time to make the arrest. "It didn't get much easier than this," Dodson later reflected.[35]

He radioed the case agent to ask when they would make the bust. She replied there would be no arrest, the straw man was probably taking them to the suspected stash house and they were to follow him. Dodson thought, *they must want to take down the stash house with a search warrant,* and radioed, "We'll keep eyes on the house and make sure the guns don't leave. Who's writing the paper [search warrant and its affidavit] and what kind of turnabout time are we looking at?"

The reply: "No paper. Just follow him to the house and come on back to the office."[36]

Over the next few months, Dodson saw the process repeated. Get a tip from a gun dealer, race to the scene, watch the straw man leave with the guns, and return to the BATF office. Sometimes the suspects left with so many guns they had to borrow a cart or dolly and wheel them out. The BATF agents sat in their car, watched the transfer, and returned to the office.

The agency by now knew all there was to know about the straw men (they had to identify themselves in detail on the Forms 4473 and show the dealer a picture ID) and the person for whom they were buying guns, one Manuel Celis-Acosta. He was hardly a high-ranking figure—in all likelihood he wasn't even a member of a cartel; he just sold them guns. The cartel members stayed in Mexico and let Celis-Acosta deliver the guns to them. So Celis-Acosta was as high as BATF was likely to get.

Finally, a rare opportunity came: a DEA wiretap picked up that Celis-Acosta would be traveling to El Paso, where, for once, some transporters for a cartel would meet him on U.S. soil and receive thirty-two semiautomatic AK-47s. DEA relayed the report—and BATF refused to act. The case agent in charge of the operation claimed that the Christmas holidays were approaching and the Phoenix Field Station would be too shorthanded to make the bust.[37]

"IF YOU ARE GOING TO MAKE AN OMELET, YOU NEED TO SCRAMBLE SOME EGGS"

Within BATF's Phoenix office, a division arose on how to view Fast and Furious. While some agents acquiesced, others found that letting the guns go to Mexico, letting them be "walked," was contrary to all their training and experience. Agent Larry Alt objected strongly to the plan and later told investigators, "You can't allow thousands of guns to go south of the border without an expectation that they are going to be recovered eventually in crimes and people are going to die."[38]

Agent Dodson found himself "outraged and disgusted": "I cannot see anyone who has one iota of concern for human life being okay with this."[39]

BATF management, in contrast, seemed to rejoice every time a Fast and Furious gun was recovered at a crime scene in Mexico. On April 2, 2010, Group VII's supervisor, Agent Voth, sent an email to its members, noting that the previous month had seen "958 killed in March 2010 (most violent month since 2005)" and adding, "Our subjects purchased 359 firearms during the month of March alone, to include numerous Barrett .50 caliber rifles. I believe we are righteous in our plan to dismantle this entire organization and to rush into arrest any one person without taking into account the entire scope of the conspiracy would be ill-advised . . ."[40]

Agent Dodson later told Congressional investigators how the BATF management viewed the toll the guns would likely wreak in the hands of border criminals:

> Q. [S]omebody in management . . . used the terminology "scramble some eggs."
>
> A. Yes, sir.
>
> Q. If you are going to make an omelet you have got to scramble some eggs. Do you remember the context of that?
>
> A. Yes, sir. It was—there was a prevailing attitude amongst the group and outside of the group in the ATF chain of command, and that was the attitude. . . . I had heard that . . . sentiment from Special Agent [redacted], Special Agent [redacted], and Special Agent Voth. And the time referenced in the interview was, I want to say, in May as the GRIT team or gunrunner initiative team was coming out. I was having a conversation with Special Agent [redacted] about the case in which the conversation ended with me asking her are you prepared to go to a border agent's funeral over this or a Cochise County deputy's over this, because that's going to happen. And the sentiment that was given back to me by both her [and] the group supervisor [Voth], was that . . . if you are going to make an omelet, you need to scramble some eggs.[41]

Agent Voth emailed Group VII members that he was concerned that "there may be a schism developing within the group" and calling a meeting. He added, "Whether you care or not, people of rank and authority are paying close attention to this case . . ." In other words: get into line; our bosses want this and are watching us.

The email made it obvious on which side of the divide Supervisor Voth was to be found:

I will be damned if this case is going to suffer due to petty arguing, rumors, or other adolescent behavior. I don't know what all the issues are but we are all adults, we are all professionals, and we have an exciting opportunity to use the biggest tool in our law enforcement tool box. If you don't think this is fun you're in the wrong line of work, period! . . . Maybe the Maricopa County Jail is hiring detention officers and you can get paid $30,000 (instead of $100,000) to serve meals to inmates all day.[42]

At the meeting, Voth called in the Assistant Special Agent in Charge, second in command of the Field Station, to deliver the lecture. He told the agents that the U.S. Attorney was on board and that Burke and an Assistant U.S. Attorney had advised that Fast and Furious was completely legal.[43]

WHY?

What reason could two agencies, BATF and the U.S. Attorney's Office, have for facilitating the shipment of guns and grenades to the drug cartels? The agencies' "official explanation" of the motive brings to mind Shakespeare's phrase "a tale told by an idiot, full of sound and fury, signifying nothing."

During Congressional hearings that followed the exposure of Fast and Furious, Rep. Trey Gowdy questioned BATF Special Agent in Charge Newell as to the purpose:

> Mr. Gowdy. I want to ask you about the greater investigation, because I have read now four different times you have said "disrupt, dismantle, destroy [the cartels]."
> Mr. Newell. Yes, sir.
> Mr. Gowdy. How are you going to extradite drug kingpins from Mexico?
> Mr. Newell. We don't have plans do that, no, sir.

Gowdy kept trying—so how *did* you plan to arrest the cartel leaders? Newell's response: "We hoped that the Mexican officials would, in fact, prosecute them for that."[44]

Newell thought that the Mexican officials, who (1) were being kept in the dark about the gun-running, and (2) had not been able to prosecute the drug cartel leaders for possessing and selling drugs, would be able to arrest the drug cartel leaders on gun charges?

At the time of Fast and Furious, Newell was in charge of all BATF operations in Arizona and New Mexico, and had previously handled those in Colorado, Montana, Wyoming, and Utah as well.[45] He had also served in BATF headquarters as Chief of the Major Case Branch and as Chief of Staff to the Assistant Director.[46] That doesn't seem like the career path of a person incapable of grasping these simple concepts or the even simpler concept that sending guns and grenades to Mexican drug cartels was not a good idea.

That leaves us with one other possibility. What if the object of running American guns to Mexican drug cartels was simply to ensure that Mexican drug cartels obtained lots of American guns? It could be foreseen that the cartels would use them in crime, Mexican police would seize many, and the result would be Mexican cartel guns, particularly "assault rifles," would be traced to American firearms dealers.

U.S. Attorney Burke—the person who, while working for Senator DeConcini, had drafted the first "assault gun ban"—is key here. He understood the impact of what he was setting up: a public relations extravaganza that would support the Obama Administration's push for gun control. At one point, Burke emailed a friend: "Some of these weapons bought by these clowns in Arizona have been directly traced to murders of elected officials in Mexico by the cartels, so Katie-bar-the-door when we unveil this baby."[47]

Burke was plainly building up to that publicity splash. In September 2010, the *Arizona Republic*, Phoenix's largest newspaper, reported:

Arizona's status as a guns-and-drug hub for the rest of the country has created an industry that brings tons of marijuana, cocaine and meth-amphetamine into the United States and sends cash and guns back to Mexico, according to federal agents.

In a three-month span, more than 80 ATF agents linked 141 guns from crime scenes in Mexico to buyers in Arizona and made 66 arrests.

"We have a huge problem here," Dennis Burke, U.S. attorney for Arizona, said Friday as he stood near a table piled high with dozens of high-powered weapons seized during the operation.

"We have now become the gun locker of the Mexican drug cartels," Burke said.[48]

Four of Burke's emails, written very late in Fast and Furious, detail his end-game plans, capped by a press conference featuring the Attorney General, and how those plans fell apart after the murder of Border Patrol Agent Brian Terry:

- On the afternoon of December 14, Burke emailed three subordinates: "AG's office is now expressing interest in the AG coming out for it. Will you send me 4 or 5 lines about it so I can brief Monty on it—esp time window. Thx." "Monty" was Monte Wilkinson, Attorney General Eric Holder's Deputy Chief of Staff.
- At 2:14 a.m. the next morning—a few hours after Brian Terry's murder, but before Burke knew of it—Burke emailed Monte Wilkinson: "I did get your vm. We have a major gun trafficking case connected to Mexico we are taking down in January. 20+ defendants. Will call today to explain in detail."
- At 7:00 p.m. Burke emailed Wilkinson: "The guns found in the desert near the murder[ed] BP officer connect back to the investigation we were going to talk about—they were AK-47s purchased at a Phoenix gun store."
- On December 21 Burke emailed Wilkinson with the obvious: "I would not recommend that the AG announce this case. I can explain in detail at your convenience."[49]

Envisioning Fast and Furious as a political and public relations gambit would explain why BATF supervisors were elated at reports of cartel violence and "walked" American guns being linked to it. BATF supervisor Voth was described as becoming "giddy" at reading reports of escalating violence.[50] Agent Dodson, one of the whistleblowers, told Congressional investigators, "Whenever he [Voth] would get a trace report back . . . he was jovial, if not giddy, but just delighted to hear about that, hey, 20 of our guns were recovered with 350 pounds of dope in Mexico last night."[51]

It's hard to see why anyone would rejoice over such news, unless the entire purpose of the operation was to generate such traces, in hopes of advancing the agency's objectives: obtain more power and resources to combat this growing problem of American guns being tied to Mexican crime scenes.

THE WHISTLE IS BLOWN AT LAST

Things began to unravel on December 13, 2010. By law, firearms trace results are confidential, but somehow the *Washington Post* laid hands on the traces from Mexico and ran an article naming the gun dealers with the most traces.[52] Two days later a follow-up article appeared:

> As an unprecedented number of American guns flows to the murderous drug cartels across the border, the identity of U.S. dealers that sell guns seized at Mexican crime scenes remains confidential under a law passed by Congress in 2003. A year-long investigation by *The Washington Post* has cracked that secrecy and uncovered the names of the top 12 U.S. dealers of guns traced to Mexico in the last two years.[53]

The articles named the twelve most-traced dealers. Of the three Arizona dealers named, two were Fast and Furious dealers and the third was the Operation Wide Receiver dealer. All three had begun by reporting suspicious sales to BATF, and all had continued with fishy sales only because the agency encouraged them to do so, claiming that this would help their investigation.

The second article appeared the morning of Brian Terry's murder and quoted Special Agent in Charge Bill Newell in a remarkable bit of hypocrisy:

> The lack of charges against dealers is not unusual, in part because it's difficult to prove a straw purchase took place.

> "If you're a gun dealer and you see a 21- or 22-year-old young lady walk in and plop down $15,000 in cash to buy 20 AK-47s, you might want to ask yourself what she needs them for," said Newell, the ATF special agent in charge in Phoenix. "If she says, 'Christmas presents,' technically the dealer doesn't have to ask for more."[54]

Newell's arrogance was breathtaking. He knew what was really happening. Dealers were doing the right thing, asking a lot of questions and keeping Newell's office tipped off to their suspicions. Agent Dodson read the article, heard of Brian Terry's murder, and knew that the killers' guns had come through straw-man sales to Jamie Avila. Dodson contacted the FBI agents working on Terry's murder investigation to discover that BATF had not told the FBI about the origin of the murder weapons.

Then Dodson discovered that BATF had arrested Avila but had not charged him in connection with the semiautomatic AK-47 Terry murder weapons. Avila had been making straw-man gun buys for two years, but federal prosecutors only charged him with three handgun transactions. Dodson concluded that BATF and the U.S. Attorney's Office were engaged in a cover-up.[55]

Dodson decided it was time to put his career on the line and expose the governmental gun-running. But how? The reporter he called was too busy to listen; the voice mail to BATF's Chief Counsel's office was never returned. The OIG, officially charged with preventing fraud, waste, and abuse, told him to email his statement. The email bounced back twice.

Not too many years ago, Dodson's effort to get the truth out would have been completely stymied. But this is the twenty-first century. The Internet site CleanUpATF.org had been organized by BATF agents frustrated by their corrupt and incompetent superiors. Dodson turned to it and quickly made some discoveries. An anonymous post written by "1desertrat" read:

> Word is that curious George Gillett the Phoenix ASAC stepped on it again. Allegedly he has approved more than 500 AR-15 type rifles from Tucson and Phoenix cases to be "walked" to Mexico. Appears that ATF may be one of the largest suppliers of assault rifles to the Mexican cartels! One of these rifles is rumored to have been linked to the recent killing of a Border Patrol Officer in Nogales, AZ. Can anyone confirm this information?[56]

Dodson also found a link to an article written by gun blogger David Codrea, alleging that BATF had let guns walk and that those guns might be linked to the killing of Agent Brian Terry. Codrea was posting articles on the issue to the *Examiner* and so was another gun blogger, the late Mike Vanderboegh, using his site at sipseystreetirregulars.blogspot.com. Both had long been posting about CleanUpATF.org as well. On December 28, 2010, Vanderboegh's blog reported CleanUpATF.org's postings relating to Agent Terry's murder and BATF's allowing the guns involved to "walk." Six days later, Codrea reported that "while speculation was introduced on CleanUpATF.org that one of the 'walked' guns may have been involved in the death of a Border Patrol officer, at this point I have nothing to validate this. I have been informed some journalists are working on following up on what's been described to me as 'discrepancies' in that story, but can't predict the outcome we should expect."

Reading Codrea and Vanderboegh's posts, Dodson concluded that "whoever was talking to them was giving them accurate information, although it didn't seem like firsthand stuff."[57] Still, the two were doing investigative journalism when the mainstream media was not.

Dodson used an anonymous Gmail account to contact David Codrea and eventually to obtain his telephone number. Codrea, in turn, put him in contact with the staff of Senator Chuck Grassley of Iowa, the Republican who has been dubbed the patron saint of whistleblowers. Grassley had written the Whistleblower Protection Act of 1989 and received the National Whistleblower Center's Lifetime Achievement Award. He was the ranking minority member of the Senate Judiciary Committee's Subcommittee on Oversight, Agency Action, Federal Rights, and Federal Courts, the appropriate committee for a Congressional investigation. A major scandal was about to break, one that would lead to criminal charges against an Attorney General . . . and the key to breaking it had been an honest agent, two gun bloggers, and a website.

THE COVER-UP COLLAPSES

BATF leadership had acted predictably in the wake of Border Patrol Agent Brian Terry's murder. They arrested nineteen straw men and other suspects, held a press conference, and triumphantly announced that they had taken down a major gun-smuggling network. Never mind that these were all the low-level figures that they'd refused to round up a year before. One reporter had heard the rumors about guns being allowed to leave the United States, and asked SAC William Newell whether he'd allowed guns to be "walked" to Mexico. Newell snapped, "Hell, no!"[58]

As ranking minority member of the Subcommittee on Oversight, Grassley wrote BATF's Acting Director, Kenneth Melson, to ask pointed questions:

> It is my understanding that ATF is continually conducting operations along the southwestern United States border to thwart illegal firearms trafficking. I am specifically writing you concerning an ATF operation called "Project Gunrunner." There are serious concerns that ATF may have become careless, if not negligent, in implementing the Gunrunner strategy.
>
> Members of the Judiciary Committee have received numerous allegations that the ATF sanctioned the sale of hundreds of assault weapons to suspected straw purchasers, who then allegedly transported these weapons throughout the southwestern border area and into Mexico. According to the allegations, one of these individuals purchased three assault rifles with cash in Glendale, Arizona, on January 16, 2010. Two of these weapons were then used in a firefight on December 14, 2010 against U.S. Customs and Border Protection (CBP) agents, killing CBP Agent Brian Terry. These extremely serious allegations were accompanied by detailed documentation which appears to lend credibility to the claims and partially corroborates them.
>
> On Tuesday, according to press reports, the ATF arrested 17 suspects in a Project Gunrunner bust. William Newell, the Special Agent in Charge of the ATF's Phoenix Field Office was quoted as saying "We strongly believed that we took down the entire organization from top to bottom that operated out of the Phoenix area." However, if the 17 individuals were merely straw purchasers of what the ATF had been previously aware before Agent Terry's death, then that raises a host of serious questions that the ATF needs to address immediately.[59]

Grassley requested a briefing for his staff within the week. He did not get a briefing. Instead, on February 4, 2011, a written response from Ronald Weich, Assistant Attorney General for Criminal Division, used bold language for a bureaucrat:

At the outset, the allegation described in your January 27 letter—that ATF "sanctioned" or otherwise knowingly allowed the sale of assault weapons to a straw purchaser who then transported them into Mexico— is false. ATF makes every effort to interdict weapons that have been purchased illegally and prevent their transportation to Mexico.

The defendants named in the indictments referenced in your January 27 letter include leaders of a sophisticated gun trafficking organization. One of the goals of the investigation that led to those indictments is to dismantle the entire trafficking organization, not merely to arrest straw purchasers.[60]

Both statements were clearly false, outrageously false. Not that AAG Weich was himself being deceptive—in Washington, no high-ranking bureaucrat writes his own letters. Such letters are always a group effort; many times, the top dog adds nothing but his signature. In this case, Weich's office relied upon Dennis Burke, the U.S. Attorney, to inform them and draft major portions of the response. Burke's input took the form of an unbelievable display of arrogance and deception. Burke emailed USDOJ headquarters: "Grassley's assertions regarding the Arizona investigation and the weapons recovered at the murder scene are based on categorical falsehoods. I worry that ATF will take 8 months to answer this when they should be refuting its underlying accusations right now."

He also claimed the gun used to kill Agent Brian Terry was sold before Fast and Furious began—another lie.[61] Burke dug in with another email:

I am so personally outraged by Senator Grassley's falsehoods. It is one of the lowest acts I have ever seen in politics.

What is so offensive about this whole project is that Grassley's staff, acting as willing stooges for the Gun Lobby, have attempted to distract from the incredible success in dismantling a gun trafficking operation (while also changing an acceptable culture of straw purchasing) by not uttering one word of rightful praise and thanks to ATF—but, instead, lobbing this reckless, despicable, accusation that ATF is complicit in the murder of a fellow federal law enforcement officer. . . .

I sat there during the press conference on this case wondering how the Gun Lobby would counter the American public's exposure to the legality of people buying 20-30 AK-47s during one purchase [with] no reporting requirement. Well, they figured out [their] counter. Never crossed my [mind?] they would stoop this low . . .[62]

Even for a political appointee, the arrogance and self-delusion were impressive. But whom the gods would destroy, they first drive mad. Six months later, Burke resigned as U.S. Attorney. A bureaucrat can lie to the public, or kill a few of them, but Burke had embarrassed his superiors, and that put him beyond the pale.

In the meantime, Agent Dodson had kicked over a hornet's nest in the Phoenix Field Division. Just before Senator Grassley's letter went out, whistleblowing Agent John Dodson had a meeting with BATF's Assistant Special Agent in Charge George Gillett. In the meeting, Dodson explained that he'd been contacted by Congressional staffers. Gillett ordered him to write down everything that had been said. Dodson began the task, then asked for a second meeting, in which he detailed what he'd been asked and what he'd said. Gillett listened in horror as Dodson recounted the truth; then Gillett panicked. In Dodson's words:

Gillett was stunned. Usually cocky and arrogant, I could see his cool escaping him fast. "Now, I ask you, do you want me to put that in a memo? On official government letterhead?"

Gillett was red in the face when he answered, "No! Now I'm ordering you to sit, right now, and you're going to write me a memo saying how you came in here and lied to me the first time and how now you're coming in here with a different story!"

When Dodson refused, Gillett screamed, "And now you're refusing to obey a direct order and you're gonna put that in there, too."[63]

Gillett's reaction is more understandable if one understands institutional psychosis: the true bureaucrat moves into a manner of alternate agency reality, where anything can be true if the group decides it is. In this case, if

Phoenix BATF decided guns had not been walked, then guns had not been walked. The final proof of this alternate reality would come when Dodson accepted it, and put it in an official writing.

Dodson was not the only agent willing to talk about the burgeoning scandal. Vince Cefalu, a special agent based in California, had previously rocked the BATF boat by objecting to using illegal wiretaps. His punishment was to forfeit his assignment for undercover infiltration of white supremacist and other illegal groups, and instead sit in an office with no duties beyond occasionally adding gasoline to other agents' cars.[64] Trying to bore the average bureaucrat into retirement is like trying to drown a fish, but good law enforcement agents are a different breed.

Cefalu began to speak out on Fast and Furious and how it was the product of BATF's institutional practices. He pointed out to journalist Elisabeth Meinecke:

In the 18 months leading up to Fast and Furious, Special Agent in Charge Bill Newell's actions required that the agency had to pay out over a million dollars in settlements which should have led to his removal for the related conduct, had it ever been investigated and documented. Special Agent in Charge George Gillette had been disciplined multiple times, and his subordinates had logged dozens of complaints related to his incompetence and mismanagement. Had ATF dealt with them at the time, the Fast and Furious program would never have been undertaken. However, by attacking those who exposed corruption, ATF was able to keep their golden boys in place. This process was repeated all over the country. . . .

[M]illions of taxpayer dollars and countless hours of manpower have been expended by my agency to attack and discredit me and other whistleblowers.[65]

As the affair grew, the whistleblowers gained a new ally: Rep. Darrell Issa (R-CA), Chair of the House Committee on Oversight and Government Reform, which has broad power to investigate federal agency misconduct. Rep. Issa was a valuable ally because at that point in time Republicans controlled the House but not the Senate; Sen. Grassley was ranking minority member of his committee, but Rep. Issa was chairman of his. Issa thus had the power to issue subpoenas, schedule hearings, and generate reports. Issa and his staff began to do just those things.

BATF leadership "lawyered up," out of necessity with USDOJ lawyers. This was risky: under high pressure, USDOJ leadership can be counted upon to boldly order a banzai charge, so long as the charge can be carried out by their client agency while they themselves stay somewhere safe. The lawyers ordered BATF's Acting Director Kenneth Melson to stay silent and to defy Congressional subpoenas for documents.

Melson began to worry—if held in contempt of Congress for his defiance, Melson himself would be the one prosecuted, not the empty suits at USDOJ who gave him the marching orders. He obtained copies of the Fast and Furious file and took them home to read. He would later testify: "I remember sitting at my kitchen table reading the ROIs [reports of investigations.] . . . I had pulled out all Patino's [one of the straw men] . . . my stomach being in knots reading the number of times he went in and the amount of guns that he bought."[66]

He emailed USDOJ officials a stark warning that their public positions were belied by the files and the hard facts.[67] It says something about the size and irresponsibility of the federal establishment that while assuring Congress for months that nothing irregular had happened, neither the agency head nor the Assistant Attorney General had read the actual evidence.

Then came newspaper articles suggesting that Melson might be fired. Melson realized he might be caught in the perfect USDOJ gambit: order him to stay silent, let him draw all the criticism, then announce that the bumbling agency head who caused the problem has been fired.

Melson struck first. He retained a private lawyer, who negotiated with Issa's staff. Then, on the Fourth of July, when federal employees would be off duty and unlikely to accidentally spot him, Melson went to Capitol Hill. He proceeded to spill his guts to Grassley's and Issa's staffers, beginning with how USDOJ had ordered him to stonewall the Congressional investigations and to defy their subpoenas.[68]

"It was very frustrating to all of us," Melson told the Congressional investigators. "It appears thoroughly to us that the department is really trying to figure out a way to push the information away from their political appointees at the department."[69]

The Congressional investigations turned up one more startling fact. The entire purpose of Operation Fast and Furious had supposedly been to pass over the straw-man buyers (whose identities already were known) and the person to whom they passed the guns (ditto), and instead to identify the higher-ups in the chain of illicit transfers. But, the investigation discovered, "the higher-ups" were two Mexican nationals who turned out to be paid FBI informants who sometimes used FBI money to buy the guns. They drew FBI salaries for informing on the cartels, and on the side, engaged guns-for-drugs transactions for an extra profit.[70]

Agent Dodson sums it up:

> Take the government out of this equation and nothing gets done. No guns get ordered by the FBI's assets; no guns get purchased, because there is no FBI money to pay for them; no guns get sold, because ATF is not coercing dealers to sell them; and no guns get trafficked, because ATF is not using the guise of a "big case" to allow it all to happen. And Border Patrol agent named Brian Terry makes it home to Michigan for Christmas because there are no armed bad guys in Peck Canyon, Arizona, that night.[71]

THE FINAL IMPACT

Ultimately, 2,040 firearms were transferred to the cartels, mostly to the Sinaloa drug cartel. At last count, 389 had been recovered in the United States and 276 in Mexico, the latter mostly at crime scenes.[72] The current count of deaths inflicted by cartel gunmen in Mexico using Fast and Furious guns is sixty-nine, including a police chief and two policemen.[73] How many American crimes the Fast and Furious guns figure in is unknown, but in 2011 alone these guns were used in eleven deadly offenses.[74]

WHO WAS HELD ACCOUNTABLE?

The list of who was held accountable is short, considering that BATF and the U.S. Attorney's Office had committed acts of war (arming of insurgents) against an allied republic, and caused or contributed to the murders of at least sixty-nine Mexican citizens and an American law enforcement officer.

Dennis Burke, as noted, resigned as U.S. Attorney. He cofounded a firm named Global Security and Innovative Strategies. For withholding documents, Attorney General Eric Holder was held in contempt of Congress.[75] Since he declined to prosecute himself, little came of the citation.

Within BATF, Special Agent in Charge William Newell received a demotion, as did Special Agent Voth. Someone at Justice headquarters must have had a warped sense of humor, because Newell was also appointed to head BATF's Mexico City Office. He and Voth ultimately received promotions to BATF headquarters. Hope MacAllister, the Lead Case Agent (essentially the nonsupervisory agent with lead responsibility on the case), received a fourteen-day suspension.[76]

This nominal discipline—the demotions did not mean less pay[77]—was imposed by BATF Deputy Director Thomas Brandon. In March 2015, Brandon was appointed Acting Director of the BATF.[78]

THE WHISTLEBLOWERS

Special Agent Dodson stayed with BATF, but Phoenix Field Station agents were told that associating with him would be bad for their careers. Ostracized, he took an assignment on the East Coast.

BATF accused Special Agent Vince Cefalu of misconduct. "This was followed by six official reprimands, two suspensions, and attempts to demonstrate that Cefalu was not fit for duty. He was told he needed to undergo a psychiatric evaluation. Cefalu was transferred five times and given two 'termination proposals.'"[79] Finally, BATF fired him. He sued the agency, and won $85,000 and reinstatement. He retired after thirty years of service.[80]

* * *

Operation Fast and Furious established that the bureaucracy was indeed utterly out of control. Agencies had, prior to this, killed American citizens and walked away, but Fast and Furious established that they could commit acts of war against other nations without suffering any serious consequences. A private citizen who set out to arm the most violent criminals in Mexico would, quite justifiably, have been jailed for a lengthy term, if not for life. But the federal employees who sent two thousand guns to the cartels, resulting in quite a few homicides,[81] did not even face firing.

CHAPTER 8

THE MILITARIZATION OF POLICE: TANKS, BAYONETS, AND GRENADE LAUNCHERS

Everything was done right, except it was the wrong apartment.
>   —A Boston police source, after a SWAT raid killed
>   a seventy-five-year-old retired minister[1]

If I'd been here and heard that [the SWAT raid on his house] going on, I probably would have taken my pistol and shot through the door. I'd probably be dead. And some of the officers would probably be dead, too.
>   —Tyrone Echols, Mayor of Venice, Illinois[2]

THE INVENTION OF THE LAW ENFORCEMENT SWAT concept traces to the late Daryl Gates, the controversial head of the Los Angeles Police Department[3] who seemed to think there was no such thing as excessive force and once told the Senate Judiciary Committee that casual drug users should be "taken out and shot."[4] Gates's brainchild was a civilian police unit that was given special training and military weaponry, and was intended to be used in high-speed storming of hostage and other barricade situations. The unit was initially to be termed the Special Weapons Assault Team until it was pointed out that "assault" in a police unit's name would be bad public relations. The unit's name instead became the Special Weapons and Tactics unit, SWAT.[5]

At the state and local level, the concept of SWAT units quickly spread, probably aided by the understanding that getting paid to practice with machine guns, armored vehicles, and high-tech instruments was an attractive job description. Even small-town forces soon had SWAT teams—the "militarizing of Mayberry" some termed it.[6] John Fund, writing in *National Review*, noted: "By 2005, at least 80 percent of towns with a population between 25,000 and 50,000 people had their own SWAT team."[7]

Few would complain if this approach were used only where it was originally intended: against dangerous criminals in barricade situations, where there was no alternative to the sudden use of overwhelming force. But such uses are rare, and thus mission creep has become the rule. As John Fund continues, "the number of raids conducted by local police SWAT teams has gone from 3,000 a year in the 1980s to over 50,000 a year today."[8]

Such SWAT deployments in routine searches and law enforcement often bear tragic results.

MAY 5, 2011, TUCSON, ARIZONA

Jose Guerena was sound asleep; the Marine veteran had finished working his graveyard shift in the copper mines a couple of hours before. He awakened to the sound of explosions and the terrified screams of his wife, Vanessa, that there were people in the yard with guns.

"Take the boy and get in the closet, get in the closet," he called as he grabbed his AR-15, emerging from his bedroom in time to see his front door smashed open and a crowd of armed men standing outside. One began to enter.

The strangers were an ad-hoc SWAT team of officers from four agencies. They had a search warrant for the Guerena house but no arrest warrants. They suspected that some of Guerena's relatives were dealing in marijuana and that he might have some evidence.

The team's briefing had included assurances that "this family has a history of violence to include kidnapping and homicide." The briefer neglected to say that the history consisted of Guerena's *relatives* having been crime *victims*.

Guerena stood with his AR-15's safety set to "safe," as he tried to make sense of the situation. Armed men in dark-green outfits and helmets smashing his door and entering his house?

The officer in the lead, seeing that Guerena had a rifle, halted and began to step backward. He tripped over the man behind him and fell. He had his finger on the trigger, and his gun fired.

The rest of the team heard the shot and saw him fall. Reflexively, they assumed that Guerena had shot the fallen man and went into an "empty your magazines" drill. Those who were outside packed into the doorway to add their firepower. Four men fired seventy-one shots in a matter of seconds; twenty-two hit Guerena.

Vanessa left the closet and tried to talk to her husband, who did not respond. She called 911 as their son pleaded, "Mom, what's happened to my dad?"

The 911 call was futile; the SWAT team had retreated and did not know if Guerena was alive or dead. They held the ambulance at bay for more than an hour while they brought in a bomb-deactivation robot and sent it in to locate his body. The search revealed nothing illegal, and they retrieved Guerena's rifle with its safety still on.[9]

JANUARY 25, 1994, STOCKTON, CALIFORNIA

At 2:00 a.m., retiree Manuel Medina Ramirez was awakened by armed men breaking down his door. He drew his bedside pistol and fired at the invaders. One fell, but the other police opened fire on Ramirez, who died at a local hospital. The intruder who fell was Officer Arthur Parga. He too died, leaving behind a pregnant wife and five-year-old son.

The motive for a violent raid: Ramirez had let a friend use his (Ramirez's) address to obtain a driver's license. When the friend was arrested with five pounds of marijuana, police had assumed that the address shown on the license was a drug stash house.[10] A search of the house found no drugs.

MARCH 25, 1994, BOSTON, MASSACHUSETTS

Rev. Accelyne Williams, a seventy-five-year-old retired Methodist minister, died of a heart attack after thirteen heavily armed police used sledgehammers to break into his apartment, then broke down his bedroom door, wrestled him to the floor, and handcuffed him.

A reportedly intoxicated informant had told police the apartment was full of drugs and guns. The search found nothing illegal.[11]

AUGUST 2, 2008, BERWYN HEIGHTS, MARYLAND

Cheye Calvo, Mayor of Berwyn Heights, recalled his experience:

I remember thinking, as I knelt at gunpoint with my hands bound on my living room floor, that there had been a terrible, terrible mistake.

An errant Prince George's County SWAT team had just forced its way into our home, shot dead our two black Labradors, Payton and Chase, and started ransacking our belongings as part of what would become a four-hour ordeal. . . .

I remain captured by the broader implications of the incident. Namely, that my initial take was wrong: It was no accident but rather business as usual that brought the police to—and through—our front door.[12]

Prince George's County Sheriff's deputies had kicked down the Mayor's door, shot his dogs, and held the Mayor and his mother-in-law at gunpoint. The reason for the search: a marijuana sales ring had come up with a novel way to move its product. They would ship the pot via FedEx to innocent persons, and a confederate who delivered for FedEx would skim off the packages and keep them. Police had intercepted a box of pot addressed to the Mayor.[13]

MAY 16, 2010, DETROIT, MICHIGAN

Detroit's Police Special Response Team raided seven-year-old Aiyana Stanley Jones's grandmother's house looking for a male suspect, who in fact lived in a different apartment. The team was accompanied by a film crew for the A&E series *The First 48*, recording the raid for the television show. The team opened by throwing a flash-bang grenade (a beer can–sized firecracker designed to give a blinding flash and stunning concussion). It landed near and burned Aiyana; a member of the raid party then accidentally shot her to death.[14]

Danger and adrenalin do not make for safe gun handling. In 1989, police mistook the sound of exploding flash-bangs for gunfire and fatally shot twenty-year-old Dexter Herbert. The same year saw police sergeant Mark Murphy shot in the head by a fellow officer during a SWAT raid, and Irvington, New York, police officer Keith Neumann was killed by "friendly fire" during a search that recovered an eighth of an ounce of cocaine. In a 2000 drug raid, the SWAT team ordered three children to lie on the floor, and for unknown reasons kept their guns aimed at them. An officer accidentally fired his shotgun, killing eleven-year-old Alberto Sepulveda.[15]

MARCH 10, 2011, PHOENIX, ARIZONA

Sheriff Joe Arpaio had obtained five armored vehicles from the military. He let actor Steven Seagal command an enormous self-propelled 155 mm howitzer (which looks like a tank on steroids)—and take it on a SWAT raid against the home of Jesus Sanchez Llovera. Seagal crashed it through the wall surrounding the house. The SWAT team went in, bashed in the door of the house, and arrested Llovera. The criminal charge that required such a raid? Organizing cockfights. Llovera ultimately pled guilty to a misdemeanor.[16]

In 2011, after waiting four hours for treatment in a Veterans Administration hospital, a sixty-five-year-old vet decided to go to a different hospital. A nurse informed him he was "not authorized" to leave, and when he insisted, she called in the VA police. (Yes, the VA has its own police.) They tackled him, threw him down, and pinned him with a knee in his back and a boot on his neck. The latter caused a split in a neck artery, which killed him. A doctor informed his wife that he had fallen and suffered a stroke, and reported his death as natural.[17]

JANUARY 28, 2012, FITCHBURG, MASSACHUSETTS

Judy Sanchez was awakened by a pounding on her apartment door. Then a chain saw began cutting through the door, and armed men entered, shouting, "FBI, get down!" She lay down and they proceeded to search her apartment while her three-year-old daughter cried in terror for her. After half an hour, one agent noticed that the search warrant was for apartment 2F, but they had sawed their way into apartment 2R. They instructed Sanchez on how her landlord could get reimbursement for a new door and left.[18]

MAY 28, 2014, CORNELIA, GEORGIA

Police obtained a search warrant claiming that a reliable informant told them he'd bought a small quantity of meth from Wanis Thonetheva. The

SWAT team sent to execute the search warrant threw in a flash-bang grenade. The grenade landed in the crib of an eighteen-month-old child, blew off the child's nose, and inflicted third-degree burns. A team member was later charged with lying to obtain the search warrant: the tip had not come from a reliable informant but from someone she barely knew.[19]

* * *

These are not rare, isolated cases. There is a simple indication that such fouled-up SWAT raids occur with frequency. Performing a Google search for "botched swat raid" will turn up 1,390 hits (and 58,000 if the words are not put in quotation marks).

How did we get to a situation where we tolerate outright attacks on American citizens on American soil—and indulge them until they are almost commonplace? One study of seventy-nine SWAT deployments in Massachusetts found that only ten involved barricaded and nonsuicidal subjects. The remaining seven-eighths involved drug searches, routine patrol, or—oddly—responses to suicide threats.[20]

Another study of eight hundred SWAT deployments nationwide found that that only 7 percent involved barricade, hostage, or active shooter situations; 62 percent were drug searches, two-thirds of which involved use of battering rams or other forced entry.[21] Search warrants that not long ago would have been served by uniformed officers and a knock on the door are now being served by black-clad teams with battering rams and assault rifles. Investigative journalist Radley Balko, in his book *Rise of the Warrior Cop: The Militarization of America's Police Forces*, calculates that the average annual number of SWAT team deployments rose from thirteen per team in 1986 to fifty-five in 1995, a rise of 423 percent in nine years.[22]

Of still greater concern is that nearly half of departments have used SWAT in crime *prevention*—that is, not to apprehend lawbreakers, but to try to intimidate the locals into following the law.[23] A representative of an unnamed "highly acclaimed" police department explained to researchers:

> We're into saturation patrols in hot spots. We do a lot of our work with the SWAT unit because they have bigger guns. We send out two, two-to-four men cars, we look for minor violations and do jump-outs, either

on people on the street or automobiles. After we jump-out, the second car provides peripheral cover with an ostentatious display of weaponry. We're sending a clear message: if the shootings don't stop, we'll shoot someone.[24]

Quite an original approach to preventing shootings!

FEDERAL AGENCIES GO SWAT

The FBI was the first federal agency to form a SWAT unit, and by the 1990s, each of its fifty-six Field Offices had its own team. Other agencies rapidly followed suit. The Marshals Service had its Special Operations Group; the Bureau of Alcohol, Tobacco and Firearms had a Special Response Team; and so on. By the late 1990s, if an agency still did not have its own paramilitary unit, it simply didn't rate.

> Between 1996 and 2008, the number of federal nonmilitary employees authorized to carry guns increased from 74,000 to 120,000.[25] By 2016, the number had expanded to 200,000. Federal law enforcement officers now outnumber the United States Marine Corps.[26] This expansion is all the more remarkable when we reflect that serious violent crime—murder, rape, robbery, assault—is primarily a state and local concern; only rarely do these offenses violate federal law.

Even agencies that were not charged with apprehending violent criminals began arming as if they were pursuing terrorists or drug cartels. Soon journalists were wondering:

Why does the U.S. Department of Agriculture (USDA) need submachine guns? The agency's Office of Inspector General (OIG) is seeking .40 Caliber semiautomatic submachine guns.

Earlier this year, the US Postal Service listed a similar notice on its website, soliciting proposals for assorted small arms ammunition. And the Social Security Administration put in a request for 174,000 rounds of hollow-point bullets, shortly after the USDA requested 320,000 rounds about a year ago. The National Oceanic and Atmospheric Administration, which oversees the National Weather Service, also requested 46,000 rounds.

The ammunitions purchases are to supply dozens of federal agencies which, in the years since 9/11, have acquired Special Weapons and Tactics (SWAT) teams to enforce the inflating definition of their missions. The Department of Agriculture, the Railroad Retirement Board, the Office of Personnel Management, the Labor Department, the National Aeronautics and Space Administration, the Department of Health and Human Services, the Food and Drug Administration, and the US Fish and Wildlife Service are just some of the federal agencies that have their own SWAT units.[27]

Why does every federal agency need a SWAT team? For the same reason that every government building needs to be hypersecure: agency prestige. To lack tight building security would be to admit that no terrorist would waste explosives on the Council on Environmental Quality, the Bureau of Indian Affairs, or the Pension Benefit Guarantee Corporation. By the same token, to have no SWAT team is to admit that the offenders your agency pursues aren't particularly nasty characters.

> The federal Byrne grant program exacerbates the problem of militarized policing. The program awards grant monies based on matters such as numbers of drug-related arrests and numbers of drug seizures. As Radley Balko notes, "The grants reward police departments for making lots of . . . arrests (i.e., low-level drug offenders), and lots of seizures (regardless of size) and for serving lots of warrants. . . . Whether any of that actually reduces crime or makes the community safer is irrelevant . . ."[28]

FEDERAL AID ENCOURAGES THE MILITARIZATION OF LOCAL POLICE

Much of this militarization of law enforcement is the product of a 1994 federal program that was consciously designed to encourage such militarization. Under that program, the Justice Department and the Pentagon were jointly given $37.5 million to promote law enforcement use of military weapons. One purpose of the program was to open new markets for defense contractors, whose industry was declining after the collapse of the Soviet Union.[29] Where President Dwight D. Eisenhower once warned of the "military-industrial complex" and of its "potential for the disastrous rise of misplaced power,"[30] we might today have the same concern over an apparent military-industrial-law enforcement complex.

In 2014, a black teenager, Michael Brown, was killed by a police officer in Ferguson, Missouri. The result was rioting, and police responded with armored vehicles and other military equipment. The public for the first time began to hear of the federal "1033 Program." The program is established by section 1033 of the 1997 National Defense Authorization Act[31] and authorizes the Defense Department to transfer military items to federal and local law enforcement, provided that the items are "excess" to the needs of the Defense Department and "suitable for use by the agencies in law enforcement activities, including counter-drug and counter-terrorism activities." Weaponry—firearms, tanks, etc.—cannot be transferred legally so it is regarded as loaned property.[32] No fewer than eleven thousand state and local agencies are registered to use the program, and about eight thousand of them are active users.[33]

The 1033 Program, one might say, exists to put the "war" in the "War on Drugs." The Defense Department appears to have taken a rather relaxed stance on the question of what is "excess" and "suitable for use . . . in law enforcement activities."

This is no small program and one has to wonder if it makes the world a safer place. In 2013 alone, the Pentagon transferred *half a billion dollars' worth* of equipment to law enforcement agencies.[34] A broader study of transfers between 2006 and mid-2014 found that the Defense Department had passed out:

- 50 airplanes, including 27 cargo transport aircraft
- 79,288 assault rifles
- 11,959 bayonets
- 479 bomb detonator robots
- 3,972 combat knives
- 205 grenade launchers
- 422 helicopters

- $124 million worth of night-vision equipment, including night-vision sniper scopes.[35]

Los Angeles area law enforcement alone received 3,452 firearms. Quite a few MRAPs (mine-resistant ambush-protected vehicles) were passed out as well, sticker price $733,000 each. It is unclear why *any* domestic law enforcement agency would need M16s that fire twelve to fifteen rounds per second or bayonets, let alone mine-resistant ambush-protected armored vehicles.

Federal programs such as the Byrne grants distort local police decision making. Investigative journalist Radley Balko cites the case of a small police department where the sex crimes unit had to struggle for financing, but the SWAT team and drug units were "always flush with money."[36]

The recipients of the arms were as remarkable as the program:

The 67 police officers of Johnston, Rhode Island, (population 29,000) got ten tactical trucks and 35 assault rifles. Or the security guards of the University of Arkansas for Medical Sciences signed up for eight rifles and four shotguns, and the campus police at Florida International received 50 M-16 rifles and a mine-resistant vehicle (MRAP).

Are things so bad along the banks of the Missouri River that the town of Yankton (population 14,500) really needs a robot, a grenade launcher, 14 reflex sights, and a pair of riot guns from the U.S. military?

But the town of Mitchell (population 15,500) is listed with $733,000 worth of equipment. The sheriff of Codington County (population 27,500) with $415,400. And when we reach the South Dakota Highway Patrol, headed by Colonel Craig Price, things get wildly out of hand: $2.7 million worth of full-tracked carriers, armored trucks, grenade launchers, and other equipment. Robots, riot guns, night sights, a military helicopter: the Highway Patrol has you covered if war breaks out in the Bad Lands and the Black Hills.[37]

Navajo County, Arizona, experienced zero murders and one armed robbery in 2014, but was given one MRAP vehicle, three other armored vehicles, and twenty-four assault rifles. Wasatch County, Utah, which experienced no murders and no robberies, received an MRAP and fifteen M16s. Where there actually was some crime to be found, the equipment totals were quite impressive. Five counties in the Los Angeles urban area (Los Angeles, Riverside, Santa Barbara, San Bernadino, and Ventura) sought and received 4,854 night-vision devices; 3,851 M16s; 27 helicopters; 7 armored vehicles; and 5 grenade launchers.[38]

> The 1033 Program is actually but a part of the whole picture. The Department of Homeland Security has been issuing grants to local law enforcement to finance their militarization, a program that today "dwarfs the 1033 program."[39] In 2011, it was estimated that over the past decade DHS had issued no less than $34 billion in grants for this purpose, which underwrote the purchase of everything from assault rifles to armored vehicles.[40]

SCHOOLS GET MILITARY EQUIPMENT

The *Chronicle of Higher Education* found that many university police departments were joining the law enforcement arms race; 124 colleges and universities obtained material through the 1033 Program. Half had acquired M16s, fully automatic assault rifles. Arizona State University had the most, seventy, while the University of Maryland and Florida International University had fifty each.[41]

Even K-12 school security wanted to be able to rock-and-roll with M16s:

> Texas and California top the list of states in which school districts are known to have received weapons, with 10 districts in Texas having received a total of 82 M-16 and M-14 rifles, 25 automatic pistols and 45,000 rounds of ammunition, and the Los Angeles Unified School District (LAUSD) receiving 61 M-16 rifles, three grenade launchers and an MRAP.[42]

Gone are the days when elementary school teachers kept classroom order with deadly rulers—today they can draw M16s and grenade launchers from the school armory!

LAW ENFORCEMENT MILITARIZATION: THE LARGER PICTURE

Ever since the concept of professional policing arose in the nineteenth century, the American approach has been to draw a clear line between military and police functions, training, and thinking. This was a practical separation: the military is fundamentally aimed at the enemy with an objective to break things and kill people; the police are aimed at erring citizens with an objective to bring them into compliance with the law. Over the past few decades the two functions have moved toward a merger. The military function is seen as bringing the enemy (the word itself has vanished from our discourse, now they are "insurgents" or "fighters") to "justice." The police function, in contrast, is increasingly seen as obtaining compliance by intimidation and overt use of force. The confusion of the two functions is neither practical nor politically healthy and leads to a government that is more dangerous and intimidating to its own citizens than to its enemies.

The military function is one that is especially dangerous, and thus we have for centuries kept it under the tightest of controls. Or perhaps it would be more accurate to say that the military has kept itself under those controls. The military world is bound by concepts of honor, duty, obedience, and submission to civilian control. There is a considerable danger that civilian agencies may take on the military's weapons and tactics without acquiring these restraining factors.[43] We need look no farther than the tragedies at Waco and at Ruby Ridge to see the reality of this danger. To have the weapons of war carried by those who lack the military's restraining ethos is to create a dangerous imbalance between power and responsibility, and to make the United States a more dangerous place.

CHAPTER 9

THE DEPARTMENT OF VETERANS AFFAIRS KILLS VETERANS

To care for him who shall have borne the battle, and for his widow, and his orphan.
—Motto of the U.S. Department of Veterans Affairs (VA)

This report cannot capture the personal disappointment, frustration, and loss of faith of individual veterans and their family members with a health care system that often could not respond to their mental and physical health needs in a timely manner. Immediate and substantive changes are needed.
—Richard Griffin, Acting VA Inspector General, 2016[1]

IN 2009, GENERAL ERIC SHINSEKI BECAME our seventh Secretary for Veterans Affairs. By all accounts an outstanding officer, Shinseki had risen from Second Lieutenant to a four-star, serving two tours of duty in Vietnam and losing most of one foot to a land mine. A man who knew how to get things done, Shinseki retired as the Army's Chief of Staff, the most senior position in that branch of the military.

But some things were beyond the capability even of a man like Shinseki: reforming the VA was one of them. After five years as Secretary, Shinseki resigned, explaining:

I said when this situation began weeks to months ago that I thought the problem was limited and isolated, because I believed that. I no longer believe it. It is systemic. I can't explain the lack of integrity among some of the leaders of our health care facilities. It is something I rarely encountered during 38 years in uniform. I will not defend it because it is indefensible.[2]

At that point, remarkably, the VA hadn't yet hit rock bottom. The next year was considerably worse. In 2015, the agency set a record for medical malpractice settlements: $230 million.[3] Spending nearly a quarter of a *billion* dollars to settle one year's malpractice liability might be taken as a sign that things are not going well. But VA leadership may not care, since the payments never came out of the VA's budget. As discussed previously, any judgment against the government that exceeds $2,500 is paid from the Judgment Fund, a budget allocation administered by the Department of Justice. So budgets, spending, and bonuses went on as if there were no lawsuits—even the VA's attorneys' fees were paid outside the VA's budget. The taxpayer did not get off so easily, nor did the veterans and their families.

The core problem of the VA hospital system is a staggering lack of accountability. One case settled that year demonstrated just how far out of control things are. In the Lafayette, Louisiana, VA hospital, personnel originally told a family that a seventy-year-old veteran had injured himself in a fall, but the coroner ruled the case a homicide. The investigation found hospital employees who witnessed the burly 240-pound nursing assistant beating the veteran to death.

State prosecutors had the nursing assistant arrested and charged with manslaughter. The VA responded by suspending him, *with pay*, while charges were pending. (Suspension with pay is the functional equivalent of a paid vacation.) The criminal proceedings were prolonged; the "vacation" continued *for two years*. After the VA started receiving Congressional inquiries about employees suspended with pay, it reacted—by returning the nursing assistant to his work in the hospital![4]

Cases of hospital staff committing homicide on patients are rare. Simple negligence racks up a higher body count, especially when those who complain of unsafe conditions are the ones who get punished. Early in 2012, Sharon Helman was appointed head of the Phoenix VA hospital and went to tour her new domain. She received frank advice from one of the ER doctors, Dr. Katherine Mitchell, who later explained:

> There was a perfect storm in the ER and I was afraid a patient would die because I could not get to them, I did not have the resources. She came by and asked me how things were going. I answered her honestly and told her that unless we had additional staffing, unless we had additional

ancillary services and other resources, that the ER was too dangerous to continue and we should be shut down immediately.[5]

Among other things, while triage (determining the priority assigned to ER patients based on the urgency of their need for care)[6] is essential to an ER, not a single nurse in the Emergency Department had completed a comprehensive triage training regimen. Dr. Mitchell could identify more than a hundred cases of mistaken triage resulting in dangerous delays in care.[7]

One might expect a new director would react by thanking Dr. Mitchell and dealing with the problems she raised. Instead, Dr. Mitchell found herself pulled into a meeting with top administrators who told her that the only problem in the emergency room was her lack of communication skills.[8] Mitchell subsequently filed a complaint about conditions, whereupon the VA put her on administrative leave, further reducing the minimal staffing in that ER.

"Three days after the U.S. Veterans Affairs Inspector General issued a review that found systemic failures at the Pittsburgh VA led to a recent Legionnaires' outbreak that killed at least five veterans, the man who oversees the Pittsburgh system was in Washington, D.C., receiving the government's highest career award for civil servants that included a $62,895 bonus." *Pittsburgh Post-Gazette*, May 2, 2013.

But what goes around, eventually comes around—just often not in time for our veterans to benefit. Dr. Sam Foote was also a physician in the Phoenix VA. In 2013, he had filed a complaint with the Office of Inspector General (OIG), and his superiors engaged in retaliation. His caseloads were increased to the point where he accelerated his retirement date. In the meantime, he gathered evidence.[9]

A key part of the hospital's malfunctioning related to scheduling appointments. One of the VA's standards was that a patient requesting an appointment should be seen no more than fourteen days in the future. Most higher VA supervisors were in the federal Senior Executive Service, where earning bonuses is a major part of pay: 10 percent of the amount budgeted for their salaries is put in a fund to award bonuses based on performance. If a supervisor's operation couldn't give veterans appointments within fourteen days of request, the supervisor would be ineligible for a bonus.

The fact was that no patients were getting appointments in anything like fourteen days. Six months to a year was typical, and some veterans who needed specialists had to wait for nearly two years. (By way of comparison: a 2014 survey of doctors in fifteen major metropolitan areas found that the average wait time to see a specialist was 18.5 days.)[10]

The Phoenix VA supervisors were not about to give up their bonuses, and so they set out to cook the books. The VA system required appointments to be made through a computerized system that would track when the appointment was requested and the date assigned for the appointment. VA regulations forbade any other scheduling system, whether paper or computerized; that way its computerized system could report real wait times, with no one able to alter the data. But the supervisors instructed the scheduling personnel to keep unofficial calendars that would reflect the real date and time of appointments. Each appointment would only be entered into the official computer database fourteen days before its assigned date. All the veterans still waited six months to a year for an appointment, but the computer record showed that every patient got an appointment in fourteen days or less.

Dr. Foote took his early retirement and set out to expose the corruption. He contacted the VA's OIG, which is charged with preventing "fraud, waste, and abuse," as well as the Arizona Congressional delegation and national news media. The results were dramatic. A later OIG report noted the enormity of the problem:

> As of April 22, 2014, we identified about 1,400 veterans waiting to receive a scheduled primary care appointment who were appropriately included on the PVAHCS EWL [Phoenix VA's Electronic Wait List]. However, as our work progressed, we identified over 3,500 additional veterans, many of whom were on what we determined to be unofficial wait lists, waiting to be scheduled for appointments but not on PVAHCS's official EWL. These veterans were at risk of never obtaining their requested or necessary appointments. PVAHCS senior administrative and clinical leadership were aware of unofficial wait lists and that access delays existed. Timely resolution of these access problems had not been effectively addressed by PVAHCS senior administrative and clinical leadership.[11]

The OIG report found that falsified appointment records were not unique to Phoenix; since the story first appeared in the media, the OIG had "received approximately 225 allegations regarding PVAHCS and approximately 445 allegations regarding manipulated wait times at other VA medical facilities." The OIG concluded:

> Inappropriate scheduling practices are a nationwide systemic problem. We identified multiple types of scheduling practices in use that did not comply with VHA's scheduling policy. These practices became systemic because VHA did not hold senior headquarters and facility leadership responsible and accountable for implementing action plans that addressed compliance with scheduling procedures. In May 2013, the then-Deputy Under Secretary for Health for Operations Management waived the FY 2013 annual requirement for facility directors to certify compliance with the VHA scheduling directive, further reducing accountability over wait time data integrity and compliance with appropriate scheduling practices. Additionally, the breakdown of the ethics system within VHA contributed significantly to the questioning of the reliability of VHA's reported wait time data.[12]

This was merely the beginning. A year later, the OIG returned to investigate the Urology Department, which had functioned for four months with only one full-time and one part-time physician.[13] The report singled out ten cases where delays in urological treatment "significantly impacted" the patient's medical care. The first was a veteran with a history of prostate cancer; his February 2013 appointment was canceled by the hospital for unknown reasons. Ten months later, during a routine checkup, it was discovered that the disease had flared up and invaded his bones. Four months later he was dead. Another veteran began urinating blood clots, but it took two months for him to get an appointment, and then the records of that appointment were lost. He died ten days after his appointment.[14]

The Office of Special Counsel, which is tasked with protecting federal whistleblowers and investigating retaliation against them, investigated the VA and found:

In Federal Way, Washington, the manager of a VA clinic falsified government records, repeatedly overstating the amount of time she spent in face-to-face counseling sessions with veterans. Regional leaders were aware of the manager's misconduct, yet failed to take action to address it. The VA's Office of Medical Inspector (OMI) substantiated both sets of allegations, yet the manager and regional leaders received only a reprimand, the lowest form of available discipline.

The director of a VA outpatient clinic within the Martinsburg, West Virginia, VAMC [VA Medical Center, or hospital] system improperly monitored witness interviews through a video feed to a conference room during an OMI investigation of patient care problems. The manager also approached a witness after the employee provided testimony to OMI and was not candid when interviewed about his actions. The director's actions create a chilling effect on the willingness of employees to participate in OMI and other investigative processes that promote better care for veterans. Yet the director received only a written counseling.

Officials at the Beckley, West Virginia, VAMC attempted to meet cost-savings goals by requiring mental health providers to substitute prescriptions for veterans, requiring them to prescribe older, cheaper, and less effective antipsychotic medications. These actions violated VA policies, undermined effective treatment of veterans, and placed their health and safety at risk. To date, no one has been disciplined.

In Montgomery, Alabama, a staff pulmonologist copied and pasted prior provider notes for veterans, resulting in inaccurate recordings of patient health information and in violation of VA rules. The pulmonologist copied and pasted other physicians' earlier recordings, including the patients' chief complaint, physical examination findings, vital signs, diagnoses, and plans of care. An investigation confirmed that the pulmonologist copied and pasted 1,241 separate patient records. Yet the physician received only a reprimand.[15]

The Office of Special Counsel reports led to more investigations and more discoveries. The VA OIG found that the Los Angeles Regional

Office had shredded documents, including applications for care or for benefits, submitted by veterans that should have been placed in their files.[16] In New York, a Veterans Crisis Line, meant to provide suicide counseling and similar aid, let telephone calls go to voice mail, and then never returned the calls. Personnel manning the hotline did not even know there was a voice mail system and thus never checked it.[17] When the General Accounting Office turned its attention to the VA, it found that VA hospitals had exposed over 2,600 vets to blood-borne diseases, such as HIV and hepatitis, through mistakes that included putting the wrong parts in dialysis machines and failure to properly sanitize the equipment used for colonoscopies.[18]

A new VA facility in Colorado had an estimated cost of $600 million—and actually cost $1.7 billion—mostly due to "aesthetic" features of the building.[19] That kind of hospital budget overrun was the rule rather than the exception. A Government Accounting Office study of four VA hospitals under construction found that construction costs had increased by 80 to 144 percent during construction, and completion dates had been pushed back by one to six years.[20] This did not stop the VA from giving its construction chief $55,000 in performance bonuses.[21]

In 2010, a VA hospital in Missouri had to inform 1,800 veterans that they may have been exposed to hepatitis and HIV due to defective cleaning of dental instruments.[22]

BONUSES TO THE MISCREANTS

The VA supervisors most responsible for the messes seem to have been the ones most rewarded and protected. Take Rebecca Wiley, head of the VA Medical Center in Augusta, Georgia: "Rebecca Wiley received nearly $18,000 in bonuses while she served as the director of the Augusta and Columbia VA medical centers in Georgia from 2007 to 2013. During that time, mismanagement delayed 8,500 gastrointestinal appointments and nine veterans died while awaiting treatment . . ."[23]

Wiley ultimately agreed to retire—in exchange for $76,000 plus $10,500 in attorneys' fees.[24] She was not the only person rewarded for failure. A 2016 investigation by the *Arizona Republic* found that the VA had handed out

$177 million in bonuses the previous fiscal year. *USA Today* noted that the following were among those receiving bonuses:

- Dr. Darren Deering, former chief of staff of the Phoenix VA hospital, who was fired for "negligent performance of duties."
- Jack Hetrick, formerly the top VA official in Ohio, who had retired after receiving a notice of firing.
- Stella S. Fiotes, former executive director of VA's Office of Construction and Facilities Management, who was in charge of building the Colorado VA center with its billion-dollar overrun.[25]

> A 2013 investigation by the General Accounting Office found that the VA had paid thousands of dollars in bonuses: to a doctor who had been disciplined for practicing without a license (the VA noted that being licensed to practice medicine was not "a specific performance pay goal"), to an ER doctor who had refused to see ER patients, and to a surgeon whose privileges had been suspended after he abandoned the operating room midway through a surgery procedure.[26]

PUNISHMENT FOR THE WHISTLEBLOWERS

In 2015, the Office of Special Counsel, the agency tasked with protecting whistleblowers, found: "The VA has attempted to fire or suspend whistleblowers for minor indiscretions and, often, for activity directly related to the employee's whistleblowing." It cited a long string of examples: the first was a food services manager who was fired for eating some expired-date sandwiches rather than throwing them away; the last was a nurse suspended for fourteen days over having, a year before, charged another employee five dollars to notarize a document.[27]

> In 1996, a VA nurse botched connecting a veteran to a dialysis machine. She then stepped out to take a phone call while the machine "drained him of blood instead of cleansing it." The veteran died, and she was prosecuted. The VA noted she was "only" their third medical professional arrested in 18 months for killing a patient.[28]

And those were only the official punishments for having "snitched." Unofficial sanctions included ostracism and rumor-mongering. Two Phoenix whistleblowers, who were VA patients as well as VA employees, found that another employee had been illegally examining their medical files.[29] A Louisiana whistleblower who exposed secret wait lists found the VA was trying to get him prosecuted for having revealed confidential medical data—that is, the secret wait lists.[30]

It would be fair to say that the Office of Special Counsel found that protecting VA whistleblowers was a full-time job. It required a *team of full-time employees* to combat a culture rotten to the core: "In 2015, OSC received over 2,000 complaints from VA employees."[31] *In that year, investigating the VA comprised 40 percent of the OSC's entire, government-wide workload.*[32]

Reforms have not been made, so little is likely to change. In 2016, the Senate Committee on Veterans Affairs considered an omnibus bill to reform the VA and—among other things—make it easier to fire negligent employees and supervisors. The American Federation of Government Employees resisted the proposals, and in the end the bill was amended to quell the union's resistance.

> Even the accountability measures for senior executives are burdened with so many caveats they may have little effect. Senior executives stand to have their pensions diminished after resigning to avoid firing only if they are convicted of a felony, have exhausted appeals on the felony, the Office of Personnel Management (OPM) determines the felony was sufficiently related to their work, and the VA secretary chooses to avail themselves of the option.

> Even then, the disgraced director can appeal this decision to OPM.[33]

The measure did, at least, allow for somewhat accelerated firing of Senior Executive Service managers, and under those provisions Sharon Helman, head of the Phoenix VA, was given her walking papers. She appealed, as the statute required, to the Merit Systems Protection Board, which upheld her firing. She went to court—and Attorney General Loretta Lynch ruled that the statute was unconstitutional and refused to let her Justice Department attorneys defend it.[34] Since (with a few exceptions, none applicable here) the Justice Department has a monopoly on representing government agencies, the effect was to reinstate Helman as head of the Phoenix VA and to prevent any further firings under the 2016 reform legislation.

So, essentially, nothing could be done. Government-run hospitals can kill their patients with little in the way of personal accountability: punishment is meted out to those who try to keep patients alive, and bonuses are given to management who let them die. No wonder General Eric Shinseki resigned as agency head, after essentially proclaiming the VA's problems to be unsolvable.

I'd suggest he was partially right and partially wrong. The VA's problems may well be beyond solution. The question we should be asking is why that hopelessly fouled-up agency should be responsible for veterans' health care. The VA hospital system is largely a historical fluke. It has its origins in the nineteenth century when the government established what were essentially retirement homes for elderly veterans, rather than hospitals. (The Army's first, "Soldier's Home," north of Washington, D.C., was established by General Winfield Scott, with funds he had accumulated as a conqueror's "perks" during the Mexican War.[35])

Federal civilian employees and retirees, in contrast, are covered by a far more modern program that allows them to pick from a wide variety of health insurance companies offering a wide variety of coverage (in most states, eleven insurers are available to all federal employees, with more plans available to employees of certain agencies).[36] Costs are kept low by subsidies, and also by insurers' desire to bid for a market containing several million potential customers (2017 Virginia rates for a very good Blue Cross family plan are $254 per month, with a government subsidy adding another $505 to the insurer's revenue).[37] Abolishing the VA hospital system and enrolling military retirees into the system that covers civilian federal retirees seems an approach worthy of consideration. It makes no sense to have a retiree from the IRS or FBI, or for that matter, the VA itself, to have a health plan that allows a choice of private-sector caregivers, while military retirees must receive care from an irresponsible agency that suffers no penalty if it kills or maims them.

PUTTING A LEASH ON THE DEADLY BUREAUCRACY

The Government, as a defendant, can exert an unctuous persuasiveness, because it can clothe official carelessness with a public interest.
> —Supreme Court Justice Robert H. Jackson,
> dissenting in *Dalehite v. United States*, 1947[1]

Experience suggests that the discretionary function exception is probably the most important reason that the Tort Claims Act does not exceed several billion dollars in additions to the deficit each year.
> —Assistant Attorney General Stuart M. Gerson,
> testifying before a Congressional subcommittee, 1989[2]

PONDER, FOR A MOMENT, THE ASSISTANT Attorney General's words. The discretionary function exception can only save the government money to the extent that:

1. federal employees negligently harm taxpayers' persons and property; and
2. the government uses the exception to escape paying for the damage caused.

His statement thus translates to: *We, federal employees, negligently inflict several billion dollars of harm on Americans annually, and we should be allowed to walk away from it because of the cost.*

Billions of dollars annually? It's not unbelievable.

THE UNINTENDED LEVIATHAN

The federal government was envisioned as a miniscule establishment (see how often the authors of the Federalist Papers assured Americans that the prospective national government would be small and have quite limited powers). At the outset, the federal government was incredibly tiny: Secretary of State Thomas Jefferson, for example, presided over a headquarters consisting of four clerks, a translator, and a messenger.[3] Attorney General Edmund Randolph's operation was no larger: he was the federal government's only "headquarters attorney," obliged to privately practice law on the side to supplement his salary.[4]

The government's design matched its intended size. In a typical county government, voters elect about six executive officials, but with the federal government, we elect only the president and vice president. Electing just two officials was seen as sufficient to ensure accountability to the voters, given how few employees the president supervised and the fact that all were employed on a "hire and fire at will" basis. If a federal employee became a danger to the public, the president was likely to observe it or hear of it, and could boot the employee.

Today, of course, the federal government is one *very* big business. At around two million civilian employees and growing, the federal government is one of the nation's largest industries, twice the size of our automotive industry, for example.[5]

The government business is prosperous as well as huge: a quarter of its employees pull down over $100,000 a year, more than twice the national family median income, even before their considerable job benefits are added in.[6] In fact, of the nation's five highest-income counties, four are suburbs of Washington, D.C., (Silicon Valley isn't even close: California's Marin and Santa Clara Counties have median household incomes about 20 percent below these D.C. suburbs).[7]

The national government is also by far our largest landowner. Even leaving out Indian reservations, the feds hold 604 million acres, about 28 percent of the surface of the nation, and 47 percent of the land area of eleven coterminous western states.[8]

What would be the public, and Congressional, reaction if a corporation of this size, power, and prosperity were to demand legal immunity from lawsuits because having to compensate people injured by its negligence would cost it billions? The first reaction would probably be to question the sanity of the speaker, and the second would be outrage. If this imaginary corporation inflicts harm at that level, it certainly should be required to pay. Someone must pay for medical care, or suffer lost wages: better this negligent corporation pays than an innocent member of the public. Besides, if this corporation inflicts this much harm on us today, how much more will it inflict if given immunity from any responsibility?

> Phillip Garrido was twice convicted in federal court of kidnapping and rape; he admitted that using drugs gave him uncontrollable violent sexual impulses. When paroled, he quickly committed *seventy* drug-related parole violations, while his parole officers did nothing. He then kidnapped an eleven-year-old girl, held her captive in a shed and raped her for eighteen years, during which she was forced to deliver two children without medical assistance. The Ninth Circuit Court of Appeals ruled that the parole officers had no legal duty to protect her from such a monster: "While our hearts are with Ms. Dugard, the law is not."[9]

THE FEDERAL TORT CLAIMS ACT ACTUALLY ENCOURAGES AGENCIES TO ENDANGER US

But the Federal Tort Claims Act and its discretionary function exception go beyond immunizing government negligence. They actually create a perverse incentive for bureaucrats to make operations more dangerous. The best way for a government agency to reduce its legal risk is *by doing absolutely nothing about safety.* As an illustration, let's take a real case, *Myslakowski v. United States.*[10]

The U.S. Postal Service (USPS) had long engaged in auctioning off its used delivery vehicles (at the time, a modified, enclosed one-man Jeep, with the driver's seat on the right) to the public. In 1971, the USPS commissioned a safety study of the vehicles, which found that they had a propensity to roll over and that tendency increased with the weight of the load they carried. USPS deliveries were made carrying only the driver and some mail, so the risk was acceptable. But if used to carry multiple passengers, they would become dangerously unstable.

The public was never warned that vehicles the USPS was selling were not safe for carrying passengers. When a former USPS vehicle flipped carrying four passengers, one was killed and another seriously injured. A lawsuit was filed.

The trial court ruled against the government: the decision to sell the vehicles was protected by the discretionary function exception, since it was a policy decision as to how best turn government assets into money, but the failure to give a warning was not; there was no good policy reason to put the government's customers at risk. The Sixth Circuit Court of Appeals, however, reversed the decision and ruled for the government on all counts: every aspect of the sale, including failure to warn, was discretionary. (How was not warning customers a policy decision? The court reasoned that the government might choose to get a better price by not telling people it was selling a dangerous product!) Whether the USPS employee selling the Jeeps gave a safety warning or not, the USPS could not be sued so long as the USPS did not give the employee an order to warn people.

Now, let's change that scenario a little. Suppose that someone in the USPS hierarchy read the 1971 safety study, understood that the agency was selling vehicles that would become dangerous if used as passenger vehicles to people who were likely to use them as passenger vehicles, and ordered that buyers be warned. That would certainly be a wise and moral decision, but what are its legal effects?

In the absence of any safety warning policy, the government was immune from lawsuit whether the employee selling the vehicles warned the buyers or did not warn them; he had discretion there and the government was immune. But now, that employee has been ordered to give warnings. If he negligently fails to do so, he has violated an order he had no discretion to ignore, and so the government is liable. The government is only vulnerable to lawsuit if its managers and lower-level employees try to do the right thing! So long as they *completely neglect* safety and give no safety-related orders, the discretionary function exception protects everything. As one court noted, in dismissing a suit over a Forest Service swimming area, the injured person could have won "if there had been a lifeguard on duty who acted negligently," but since the Forest Service provided no lifeguard at all, the government won.[11]

It was common knowledge in the U.S. Postal Service that mailman Leslie Tucker was a child molester. As the Seventh Circuit Court of Appeals noted, "Tucker came to be called 'Lester the Molester' by his co-workers because of his notorious sexual abuse of the children who lived along his routes." USPS responded by giving him a desk job, then returning him to delivery duty, where he molested a seven-year-old girl. The Seventh Circuit ruled that the USPS could not be sued. In addition to its exception for "discretionary functions," the Federal Tort Claims Act also has an exception for assault and battery cases. The Seventh Circuit ruled that Congress thus had not consented to be sued for assault and battery; child molestation involved assault and battery, and thus the USPS had complete legal immunity to knowingly set child molesters loose on the public.[12]

Of course, some government employees do the right thing anyway, but the incentive is never to include safety in planning. Ignore safety, and the agency usually wins any lawsuit: it has been estimated that the discretionary function argument has a 76 percent success rate in court.[13] Ostensibly, the discretionary function exception has a limitation: it only protects decisions that relate to government "policy." But the courts have made this limit almost meaningless. After all, the Supreme Court has ruled that the government must only show that the decision was "susceptible to policy analysis,"[14] not that the decision really did involve policy decisions. That is, lawsuits are not allowable if the government attorneys can think up any way in which the agency *could have* based its negligence on policy grounds, on balancing one consideration against another, even if the agency actually never thought of the safety issue. Any reasonably inventive government attorney can make any government action or inaction into a potential policy decision; if nothing else, making things safe would have required spending some money, and that is a policy decision. Some real-world examples:

- Alleged negligence in rescuing an accident victim (delay and failure to provide a backboard for a spinal injury case) was ruled to be a policy decision since "Limited staff and financial resources requires an assessment of each situation as it arises, balancing the potential need for assistance with the resources available."[15]

- The decision to leave open hiking trails that were known to be dangerous in winter without posting a warning sign was held to be a policy decision since the Park Service could have been "unable to maintain all the trails in the park, cognizant that posting warning signs would inadvertently attract visitors to unmaintained trails, and unable to post signs throughout the park . . ."[16] (The government attorneys got very inventive here, arguing that the Park Service could have feared that posting warning signs would attract people to the dangerous trails.)
- An alleged negligent decision to design a government electrical system without a ground fault circuit interrupter (which reduces the risk of electrocutions) was a policy decision because it was a "discretionary decision at a planning level, similar in character to formulation of safety specifications."[17] (Imagine what it would be like if all builders could ignore building codes. The paradox here is that the government has staked out a libertarian paradise—for itself only.)
- The decision to build a government water canal without concrete lining was a policy decision because the "decision not to line fully the canal was rooted in economic policy judgments."[18]
- The decision to release water from a dam without warning a marina downstream (and indeed, after refusing to discuss the timing of the release with the marina's owner) was immune from lawsuit; the decision to not warn the owner "goes to the manner of exercise of a discretionary function."[19] (The discretionary function exception is so broad that there have been suggestions to rename the Federal Tort Claims Act the "Federal Negligent Operation of Motor Vehicles Act," on the basis that bad driving is the one human function clearly outside the exception.[20])

Thus, virtually any decision of a government employee, with the exception of steering an automobile, will be considered "discretionary" and protected from lawsuits for negligence, *provided that no one gives anyone orders about maintaining safety.* The federal government—our largest employer and biggest landowner—is free to harm the taxpayers who finance it and to walk away. The structure of the Federal Tort Claims Act goes beyond allowing unsafe agency behavior. It encourages it.

REFORMING THE FEDERAL TORT CLAIMS ACT

A fundamental change in the statutory system is long overdue; one could even say that Americans are literally dying for change. What follows here will be an outline for a set of amendments that will convert the Federal Tort Claims Act into something that does not encourage dangerous negligence and affords reasonable compensation to those harmed by the federal leviathan.

One thing should be understood at the outset. The federal government is not some small and helpless entity that must be protected against those who would take advantage of it. The federal government has *massive* advantages in any civil case. For any government agency, its Justice Department attorneys are, essentially, free, as is their support staff, and there is an essentially unlimited budget for interviews, overhead, research, and travel. The government lawyers know they will be paid biweekly whether they win or lose.

The plaintiff, the person or persons suing the government, is often quite poor: compare the people devastated by the Texas City explosion to the Defense Department, the Utah ranchers to the nuclear program, or the U.S. Department of Veterans Affairs to its patients. If the plaintiff is lucky, his attorney will work on a contingent fee basis and get paid a percentage of the win, if and when they win. If not, the attorney requires a hefty up-front retainer fee, and in either case the client or the attorney must pay experts out of their own pocket. To top that off, the Federal Tort Claims Act limits any contingency fee to 25 percent, well below attorneys' traditional 33 percent level.

In short, no sane attorney will take a case against the federal government unless he is almost certain of winning and the damages are in the hundreds of thousands of dollars. To a large extent, the legal system itself is self-regulating against frivolous lawsuits against the government.

The mineral fiber asbestos was once used for insulation—until it was discovered that its dust caused asbestosis, a serious and often fatal lung condition. When the federal government was sued for having sold large quantities of asbestos, the Third Circuit held that the discretionary function exception barred the suit: the harm resulted from "the implementation of the mandate to minimize costs to the government in the sale . . ."[21]

In other words, the government decided it would get a better price if people didn't know the stuff was dangerous.

The amendments I propose could be entitled the "Federal Accountability in Damages Act" (FADA) or any other similar simple title. A draft of such a statute may be found in the appendix to this book. In place of the discretionary function blanket exception in the Federal Tort Claims Act, FADA would introduce a four-level system for defining liability for governmental harms to person or property, dividing the litigation world into claims that are not allowed, those that require proof of intentional misconduct, those that require proof of reckless misconduct, and those that can be based on ordinary negligence. (In the real world, the last category would be by far the broadest.)

Level 1. No Lawsuits Allowed

The highest level of restriction, no lawsuits for damages allowed, would be reserved for events that must be spared from legal liability *even if* the person causing the event *actually intended* to inflict harm. That is, these are situations where it is imperative to preserve freedom of action unaffected by risk of suits for damages. Since lawsuits cannot be brought for these actions *even if the government decision maker was out to "get" someone*, the definitions should be kept strict and narrow. Logical inclusions would be:

- The enactment of legislation;
- The promulgation, or failure to promulgate, regulations and executive orders;
- Judicial decisions and processes;
- Failure to control or regulate a nongovernmental actor, other than a prisoner in confinement or person on supervised release (suit would be allowed if the government went beyond failing to control the nongovernmental actor and encouraged or aided him in his wrongdoing);
- Spending money and provision of services *per se* (carefully defined so as not to revive the discretionary function exception).

In short, no one can sue Congress for passing legislation, or the courts for enforcing it, or an agency for failing to regulate or restrain a member of the public. Further examples could be taken from the Federal Tort Claims Act exemptions listed in 28 U.S.C. §2680—lawsuits covered by admiralty law, military combat activities, etc.

Level 2. Lawsuits Allowed If the Government Actor Intended a Legal Wrong

For these claims, proof of negligence would not be enough; the government employee must have actually intended to commit a legal wrong. Candidates for inclusion:

- Wrongful prosecution, that is, conducting a prosecution where there was not even "probable cause" to believe a person had broken the law;
- Abuse of process, the use of legal process for improper purposes (e.g., filing a criminal prosecution in hopes of forcing a person to give up something valuable);
- Assault and Battery;
- Defamation.

The Federal Tort Claims Act now *entirely* prohibits lawsuits on many of these grounds, so long as the government employee was not a law enforcement agent (why should you be able to sue if an FBI agent beats you up, but not if a mailman does so? I have no idea. Ask Congress, they wrote the law). This was understandable at one point in time: if a federal employee wanted to sucker punch or slander a citizen, let the wronged person sue the employee, but not the government. The wrongdoer wasn't working on behalf of the government when he inflicted the harm; he was acting on his own, so sue him.

Then came the 1988 Westfall Act, in which Congress provided that— in any personal injury suit against a federal employee—the United States Department of Justice (USDOJ) might certify that the employee was acting within the scope of their official duties, in which event the case would be removed to federal court, the employee would be dismissed from the case, and the United States would be substituted as the defendant.[22] Since the government could not be sued for wrongful prosecution, abuse of process, or defamation, the practical effect was that neither the federal employees nor the government could be sued for those offenses. The requirement that USDOJ certify that the employee was acting within the scope of their employment was no protection. USDOJ issued such certifications for an EPA employee driving home from work while blind drunk,[23] an Army major who sexually harassed a university secretary,[24] and a government doctor who sexually groped his patients.[25] We might wonder how any of those offenses fall within a federal employee's scope of employment, but USDOJ was so zealous in protecting federal employees that it saw nothing wrong with so certifying.

Federal employees have the advantage over James Bond. Agent 007 was only licensed to kill. By virtue of the Westfall Act, federal employees (other than law enforcement officers) are licensed to kill, batter, maliciously prosecute, and defame. The Westfall Act needs to be overturned, and FADA does just that.

Level 3. Lawsuits Allowed If the Governmental Employee Acted Recklessly or with Gross Negligence

The law has a concept of recklessness, or gross negligence, which is something more than simple negligence: it essentially requires a person to consciously disregard the rights of other persons. The intention required is not "I intend to hurt someone"; it is more like "I don't care whether I hurt someone." The classic example is the drunk driver. He doesn't *intend* to crash into someone, but has consciously taken actions that greatly raise the risk that he will do so, and thus disregarded others' right to be free from collisions. FADA would require proof of government recklessness before suit could be filed over certain things. Good candidates for inclusion here would be the following:

- Failure to control a prisoner while on supervised release or to prevent his escape if confined;
- Failure to arrest a criminal offender, where it was foreseeable that the offender would harm others in the near future;
- Failure to enforce existing laws or regulations, under conditions where the failure to enforce foreseeably leads to personal injury.

Level 4. Lawsuits Allowed If Negligence Is Proven

In the law, negligence consists of failure to do what a reasonable person would have done to observe the rights of others. That standard would apply to all remaining governmental actions that inflict harm. It would thus cover the majority of government-inflicted harms.

Defenses

Liability would be restricted by certain designated defenses. For instance, claims for negligent design of roadways or buildings might be subject to a defense based on use of generally accepted engineering or safety standards.

Damages

The injured citizen may recover the value of his or her actual damages; punitive damages would not be allowed. The interest on those damages would run from the date of the injury rather than (as now is the case) the date of the judgment. The first $250,000 of damages would be paid from the agency or departmental budget, not from the Judgment Fund. (Granted, in the end it would come from the taxpayers' pockets, but in the short term the agency or department would feel the pain and be motivated to maximize the safety of its operations. Thus, this would reverse the Federal Tort Claims Act's existing perverse incentive that rewards unsafe agency practices.)

* * *

The purpose here is not to lay out a detailed system of government liability; it is simply to demonstrate that a fair and just system can be designed. Whatever its enacted form might take, the system would be capable of improvement in light of experience as the courts interpret it and Congress fine-tunes it by amendments. These changes to the Federal Tort Claims Act, standing alone, would do much to ensure that agencies respect the safety of the taxpayer. But further reforms are necessary.

REFORMING FEDERAL CRIMINAL PROCEDURE

Separate questions are posed when we examine federal criminal enforcement—where the government does the suing—with the objective of taking away a citizen's physical freedom. Federal criminal procedure is quite primitive when compared either to state criminal procedure or to federal civil procedure. In a federal civil case—for example, a lawsuit for damages—both sides are required to begin by disclosing certain things, such as likely witnesses and exhibits. Both can then require the other side to answer written questions (interrogatories), admit or deny specified matters, and produce copies of documents. Both sides are also entitled to take witnesses' testimony by deposition.

Federal *criminal* procedure contrasts sharply with this rational arrangement and is stacked in favor of the government. The prosecution is required to disclose only a few things: any statements by the defendant, any physical exhibits the prosecution intends to use at trial, and summaries of any expert testimony that it will use at trial.

Beyond this, the Supreme Court has imposed a requirement, the *Brady* rule—that the prosecution must reveal any evidence it possesses that tends to show the defendant is innocent. As we have seen above, federal prosecutors often flout this requirement, and, in any event, it requires the prosecution to guess what might be useful to the defense.

> The Supreme Court may have imposed the *Brady* rule, but prosecuting agencies often ignore it and hide evidence suggesting that the defendant is innocent. "There is an epidemic of *Brady* violations abroad in the land. Only judges can put a stop to it." The quote comes from Alex Kozinski, Chief Judge of the Ninth Circuit U.S. Court of Appeals, in a case where the Department of Justice did not disclose that its expert witness was in the process of being fired for incompetence. Judge Kozinski was dissenting; the majority upheld the conviction.[26]

Under our Bill of Rights, all serious federal prosecutions must begin by persuading a grand jury to indict the defendant after finding "probable cause" (basically, a strong suspicion) to believe that he broke the law. The rules relating to grand jury proceedings are hopelessly stacked in favor of the prosecution. They begin with a broad secrecy requirement: no one, including the grand jurors themselves, may "disclose a matter occurring before the grand jury." Then there are the exceptions—those events may be disclosed to "an attorney for the government" and anyone he designates.[27] So the prosecution may make use of grand jury proceedings, but the defense cannot. This can give the prosecution a considerable advantage: it knows what certain witnesses are going to say, while the defense must guess. A witness who testified before the grand jury knows that if he changes his story in a way that favors the defense, the prosecution will know and can file perjury charges, whereas if he changes his story in ways that favor the prosecution, the defense has no way to know this.

In *Jencks v. United States*,[28] the Supreme Court made an attempt to partially level the playing field, which Congress promptly undermined. The Court had long held that a trial court had an inherent power to order the government, if justice so required, to produce written reports filed by its witnesses. This doctrine had an obvious problem: the defense had to prove that it would be unjust to let the government withhold reports (for example, that the reports contradicted the witness's testimony), but it had to prove this without knowing what was in the reports! In *Jencks*, the Court imposed a new and much broader requirement, ruling that the government must produce *any* statements it possesses that were made by government agents or informants who were expected to testify for the prosecution. The defense had no obligation to first prove that keeping the reports secret would cause an injustice.

It was hardly an earthshaking change, but Congress went passive-aggressive and passed a statute (known as the Jencks Act)[29] to make using the disclosure as difficult as possible. The Jencks Act provided that a government witness's statements would only be obtained after the witness testified.[30] So the defense attorney gets the statement only in mid-trial, just as he or she is ready to begin cross-examination.

It is no coincidence that the Federal Rules of Criminal Procedure originated in the same time frame (1948) as that of the Federal Tort Claims Act (1946). In the late 1940s, after the New Deal and the Second World War, the federal government's reputation stood at its peak. Federal employees were civil servants, federal prosecutors were seen as crusaders for a righteous cause—people who could be counted upon to make honest and honorable choices. Seventy years later, we have learned that this is often not the case.

In federal civil cases, where all that is at issue is money, there are extensive processes to follow, known as disclosure and discovery, for each side to find out what evidence the other has. In federal criminal cases, where freedom and reputation are at stake, there is very little. It's time we changed this, and state legal regimes illustrate how this can be done. In California, the discovery process is mostly dictated by court rulings.

There, the defense can secure access to evidence and investigative reports if it can demonstrate a "plausible justification" for being allowed to inspect them; the courts retain a discretionary power to withhold documents if necessary.[31] In Arizona, the discovery process is established by court rule and is even more straightforward: the prosecution must disclose transcripts of the grand jury proceedings and copies of all police reports, and the prosecution and defense may tape interviews of witnesses (other than a crime victim). If the prosecution contends something must be kept secret (e.g., identity of a witness who would be subject to coercion), it can file a motion for that relief. Either of these approaches would be far better than that of the current federal system.

A clarification of the prosecution's duty to disclose information favorable to the defense (the *Brady* requirement) would fit in well with such requirements. As it is, prosecutors guess at what might favor the defense and have an incentive to be as narrow as possible in their guesswork. Federal district courts have experimented with rules that define this duty, of which the most extensive is that of the U.S. District Court for the District of Massachusetts. That court's rule clarifies that the duty to disclose extends not just to evidence that directly suggests the defendant is innocent, but also to matters such as what benefit is being given to any government witness, the criminal record of any such witness, and known crimes committed by any such witness.[32]

A THIRD MEASURE: CREATION OF AN OVERSIGHT AGENCY

Presently, there is very little real oversight of federal agencies. Congressional oversight exists but has limited value. An agency has but one focus, while legislators have many. An agency can afford to stall for time, calculating that a pesky legislator will eventually become distracted and move on to other things. Congressional committees have investigated most of the incidents documented in this book with no significant changes. The House held two weeks of hearings on the Waco tragedy and nothing changed. The House investigations into Fast and Furious went to the extent of holding the Attorney General in contempt and nothing changed.

The solution is to create an independent agency that is specifically tasked with ensuring public safety and investigating events that put that safety at risk.

One government agency overseeing another involves no paradox. Think of an agency as a living thing: its drives are to survive and to enhance its own power. We've already seen how the Atomic Energy Commission viewed nuclear testing, one of its agency priorities, as far more important than the health of a few thousand Americans.

An agency naturally attracts staff who sympathize with its purposes: the Park Service is predictably staffed by people who like the outdoors; the Drug Enforcement Agency attracts people who dislike illicit drugs and drug sellers.

The average bureaucrat has no particular loyalty to the government as a whole. In fact, agencies often have significant rivalries. The bureaucrat's loyalty is directed at his agency. He has no problem at all if his agency's work impedes that of another agency; he may even take malicious amusement at that prospect.

There have been many experiments in using one agency to control others, and these have been at least moderately successful. The concept of the Offices of Inspector General (OIG) is an example—an office within each Cabinet department, reporting to the Secretary and not to any agency within, and charged with detecting and acting on agency fraud, waste, or abuse. Another example is the Office of Special Counsel, charged with enforcing the protections for whistleblowers and a few other statutes and reporting directly to the President. As a third example, the U.S. Fish and Wildlife Service is charged with protecting endangered species against other agencies' activities and has no problem at all tinkering with their programs. Its most famous court case stopped the Tennessee Valley Authority from constructing Tellico Dam because it would supposedly render a small fish, the endangered snail darter, extinct,[33] until Congress overrode the ruling. (The case had an amusing if expensive outcome. It turned out that the snail darter was not endangered; there were undiscovered populations in many other rivers. But it also turned out that the dam was a complete boondoggle that cost more to build than it was worth.)

An independent agency reporting to a suitably high level of the bureaucracy (perhaps the Office of Management and Budget, the agency whose work would be most affected by damage awards, or to the President himself), charged with protecting Americans' lives and estates against other agencies' negligence and misconduct, would function to minimize the problems we have seen documented. It should have the capacity to investigate and report, to request criminal prosecution, and to file civil cases seeking injunctions. It should have its own legal staff and "sue or be sued" capabilities, as well as the power to issue subpoenas and take depositions. This would end the peculiar situation where federal agencies must show great respect for the lives of endangered chub fish or the furbish louse-wort,[34] but are unrestricted in their ability to write off human life as a "cost of doing business," where the environmental consequences of every agency action must be "given a hard look,"[35] but the human consequences need not be considered.

USING STATE GOVERNMENTS AS A COUNTERBALANCE TO THE FEDERAL LEVIATHAN

The brilliant individuals who created this nation were realists, that is to say, cynics. They did not expect that government would always attract the best and most public-minded of people. Rather, they acknowledged it would tend to attract ambitious citizens who longed for power and control. They faced this problem with their eyes open and strove to create a system that would function in spite of human nature.

One of their solutions was to put the ambitious in a state of rivalry. One level of this approach was the concept of separation of powers, where the three federal branches would offset one another. A second level was to pit state government and federal government against each other, each vying for the approval of the ultimate source of power, the people.

The Civil War Amendments, in particular the Fourteenth Amendment, gave the federal government the ability to counterbalance the powers of a state—the Department of Justice regularly investigates and prosecutes state officials who have violated constitutional rights. But the reverse is hardly true. Even where state officials make the effort, such as Idaho's response to the killing of Vicki Weaver, the results are invariably negative.

This could be redressed by legislation that spells out when a state has the power to prosecute a federal actor who breaches its laws. It is hard to see much drawback to providing, for instance, that a state may prosecute a federal employee whose actions violate constitutional rights as well as state law.

INTO THE FUTURE

This book opened with a citation from this Republic's foundational document, the Declaration of Independence. The Declaration complained of King George's officials that they "harass our people and eat out their substance," a rather mild indictment; any county building codes office does as much today. The Continental Congress could say nothing stronger; it could not say that royal officials had killed Americans with legal impunity, for the simple reason that neither George III nor his Parliament had done anything of the sort. They had, at most, provided for a change of venue if their officers were criminally prosecuted (of which provision the Declaration separately complained).

We may hope that, with the changes proposed here, our national government will become *at least as* responsible as the one our Founders rejected back in 1776, and we will become as secure and free as we were under the reign of George III.

APPENDIX

PROPOSED REFORM OF FEDERAL LAW

Be it enacted by the Senate and House of Representatives of the United States of America in Congress assembled, that:

Sec. 1. Short Title. This law may be cited as the Federal Accountability in Damages Act.

Sec. 2. Replacement of the Discretionary Function Exception. 28 U.S. Code §2680(a) is amended to read:

(a) Any claim arising out of the enactment, or failure to enact, legislation, the promulgation, or failure to promulgate, regulations or executive orders, the rendering, or failure to render, judicial decisions and orders, or the failure to control or regulate a nongovernmental actor. *Provided,* that claims arising out of grossly negligent failure to reasonably control a person who is incarcerated or on supervised release, or out of failure to enforce the law may be brought, where the failure to control or enforce foreseeably risks harming the public.

Sec. 3 Repeal of the Intentional Torts Exclusion. 28 U.S. Code §2680(h) is repealed.

Sec. 4. Agency Reimbursement of the Judgment Fund. 31 U.S. Code §1304 is amended by adding a new subsection (d), to read as follows:

Where a settlement or judgment against the United States is entered pursuant to 28 U.S.C. §2674, the agency whose employee or employees are responsible for the liability shall reimburse the Government for the first $250,000 of the amount paid by the Government.

Sec. 5. Disclosure in Criminal Proceedings.

(a) Rule 6(e)(3)(A), Federal Rules of Criminal Procedure, is amended by renumbering paragraph (iii) as paragraph (iv), deleting "or" from paragraph (ii), and inserting a new paragraph (iii), to read as follows: "the defendant or his attorney pursuant to Rule 16; or"

(b) Rule 16(a) and (b), Federal Rules of Criminal Procedure, are amended to read as follows:

(a) Government's Disclosure. Within 30 days after arraignment in a felony case, or at the first pretrial conference in a misdemeanor one, the Government shall make available to the defendant the following material and information within the Government's possession or control:

(1) The names and addresses of all persons whom the Government intends to call as witnesses in the case-in-chief together with all their relevant written or recorded statements;

(2) All statements of the defendant and of any person who will be tried with the defendant;

(3) (All then existing original and supplemental reports prepared by a law enforcement agency in connection with the particular offense with which the defendant is charged;

(4) The names and addresses of experts who have personally examined a defendant or any evidence in the particular case, together with the results of physical examinations and of scientific tests, experiments or comparisons that have been completed;

(5) A list of all papers, documents, photographs or tangible objects that the Government intends to use at trial or which were obtained from or purportedly belong to the defendant;

(6) A list of all prior felony convictions or prior bad acts of the defendant which the prosecutor intends to use at trial;

(7) All then existing material or information which tends to mitigate or negate the defendant's guilt as to the offense charged, or which would tend to reduce the defendant's punishment therefor;

(8) Whether there has been any electronic surveillance of any conversations to which the defendant was a party, or of the defendant's business or residence;

(9) Whether a search warrant has been executed in connection with the case;

(10) Whether the case has involved an informant, and, if so, the informant's identity, unless the United States will not call him to testify and disclosure would result in a substantial risk to the informant or to his operational effectiveness, unless constitutional considerations require his identification;

(11) A certified transcript of any grand jury proceedings.

(b) Defendant's Disclosure. Within 10 days of the Government's disclosure, the defendant shall disclose to the United States:

(1) all defenses as to which the defendant intends to introduce evidence at trial, including, but not limited to, alibi, insanity, self-defense, defense of others, entrapment, impotency, marriage, insufficiency of a prior conviction, mistaken identity, and good character. The notice shall specify for each listed defense the persons, including the defendant, whom the defendant intends to call as witnesses at trial in support of each listed defense;

(2) The names and addresses of all persons whom the defendant intends to call as witnesses, together with their relevant written or recorded statements;

(3) The names and addresses of experts whom the defendant intends to call at trial, together with the results of the defendant's physical examinations and of scientific tests, experiments or comparisons that have been completed; and

(4) A list of all papers, documents, photographs and other tangible objects that the defendant intends to use at trial.

Sec. 6. Liability for Actions Which Violate Both the Constitution and State Law.
Chapter 13 of part 1 of title 18, United States Code, is amended by adding at the end thereof a new section 250, to read as follows:

A State or its subdivision may bring criminal charges against an employee or agent of the United States for actions which (1) deprive a citizen of his or her rights under the Constitution of the United States and also (2) violate the State's criminal law.

ENDNOTES

INTRODUCTION

1. William Blackstone, *Commentaries on the Laws of England*, Book One, ch. 7 (1765).

2. Bernard Bailyn, *The Ideological Origins of the American Revolution*, p. 125 (1977).

3. *United States v. Clarke*, 33 U.S. 436, 444 (1834). The United States was commonly treated as a plural until after the Civil War. For example, the Thirteenth Amendment, ratified in 1865, provided that slavery shall not exist within "the United States, or any place subject to their jurisdiction." "Their," not "Its."

4. *The Siren*, 74 U.S. 152, 154 (1868).

5. 106 U.S. 196 (1882).

6. 106 U.S. at 220.

7. *Price v. United States*, 174 U.S. 373, 375–76 (1899).

8. *Larson v. Domestic & Foreign Commerce Corp.*, 337 U.S. 682 (1949). Since Congress had established the Court of Claims, with the power to award compensation for a governmental taking of property, the *Larson* ruling meant that *United States v. Lee* was dead even on its facts; the government could not take property without compensation because the owner could always seek compensation in the Court of Claims. "That's some catch, that catch-22."

9. The background to *In re Neagle* can be found in Walker Lewis, "The Supreme Court and a Six-Gun: The Extraordinary Story of *In re Neagle*," *American Bar Association Journal*, vol. 43, p. 415 (May, 1957).

10. *In re Neagle*, 135 U.S. 1, 76 (1890).

11. See Karen J. Greenberg & Joshua Dratel, eds., *The Torture Papers: The Road to Abu Ghraib*, pp. 11, 212, 213, 264, 311–12 (2005). *Neagle* was primarily cited for two propositions: (1) the Executive Branch has inherent powers, beyond those given by statute (the Supreme Court had confirmed that the Attorney General could deputize Neagle as a marshal, though no statute allowed this), and (2) federal employees had broad powers to kill in defense of other persons, and so presumably could torture in that defense as well.

12.   Deborah Blum, "The Chemist's War: The Little-Told Story of How the U.S. Government Poisoned Alcohol During Prohibition with Deadly Consequences," *Slate*, Feb. 19, 2010, online at http://www.slate.com/articles/health_and_science/medical_examiner/2010/02/the_chemists_war.html.

13.   *Ibid.*

14.   *Bivens v. Six Unknown Narcotics Agents,* 403 U.S. 388 (1971).

15.   *White v. Pauly, U.S. Supreme Court,* No. 16–67, Jan. 9, 2017, slip opinion.

16.   28 U.S. Code §2680(a).

17.   26 U.S. Code §2680(h).

Chapter 1

1.   House Judiciary Committee, *Texas City Disaster,* Report No. 1386, 83rd Cong., 2d Sess., p. 1 (1954) [hereinafter "House Judiciary Report"].

2.   Mrs. Dalehite's experiences were recounted in her testimony before the House Judiciary Committee. House Judiciary Committee, *Texas City Disaster: Hearings before a Special Subcommittee of the House Judiciary Committee* (83rd Cong. 1st Sess.), p. 102–07 (1953) [hereinafter "1953 Hearings"]. They are also recounted in a moving book, *City on Fire* by Bill Minutaglio (2003). Mrs. Dalehite died in 1988, having outlived her Captain by forty-one years. She is buried by his side in Evergreen Cemetery, Galveston, Texas.

3.   1953 Hearings, p. 14.

4.   *Hearings on the Texas City Claims Act, before Subcommittee No. 2 of the House Committee on the Judiciary,* 84th Cong., 1st Sess., p. 152–53 (1955) [hereinafter "1955 Hearings"].

5.   1953 Hearings, p. 228.

6.   *Record of Proceedings of Board of Investigation Inquiring into Losses by Fire and Explosion of the French Steamship Grandcamp and U.S. Steamships Highflyer and Wilson B. Keene at Texas City, Texas,* p. 351 [hereinafter "Record of Proceedings"]; House Judiciary Committee Report, p. 10.

7.   Hugh W. Stephens, *The Texas City Disaster,* p. 21 (1997).

8.   1955 Hearings, p. 50.

9.   1953 Hearings, p. 229.

10.   *Ibid.*

11.   *Ibid.*

12.   Hugh W. Stephens, *op. cit.,* pp. 30–31.

13.   Hugh W. Stephens, *op. cit.,* p. 30.

14.   Mr. Luna's recollections are set out in the Record of Proceedings, p. 465 *ff.*

15.   Hugh W. Stephens, *op. cit.,* p. 33.

16.   1955 Hearings, p. 40; Bill Minutaglio, *op. cit.,* p. 119.

17.   Record of Proceedings at 542.

18.   Bill Minutaglio, *op. cit.*, p. 120.

19.   Hugh W. Stephens, *op. cit.*, p. 100.

20.   Author's conversation with Robert Baer, Apr. 22, 2016.

21.   Bill Minutaglio, *op. cit.*, pp. 148, 198.

22.   Hugh W. Stephens, *op. cit.*, p. 101.

23.   Bill Minutaglio, *op. cit.*, p. 187.

24.   Hugh W. Stephens, *op. cit.*, pp. 102–105.

25.   1953 Hearings, p. 57.

26.   1953 Hearings, pp. 57, 134–35. The trial court cited and rejected the argument that the government did not own the ammonium nitrate. *Ibid.* at 255.

27.   The judgment is reproduced in the 1953 hearings, at pp. 247 *ff.* The summary quoted is at p. 248.

28.   346 U.S. 15 (1953).

29.   350 U.S. 61 (1955).

30.   467 U.S. 797 (1984).

31.   486 U.S. 531 (1988).

32.   *Rosenbush v. United States*, 119 F.3d 438 (6th Cir. 1997).

33.   "Deepwater Horizon Oil Spill," Wikipedia, online at http://en.wikipedia.org/wiki/Deepwater_Horizon_oil_spill#Civil_litigation_and_settlements.

34.   *Riley v. United States*, 486 F.3d 1030 (8th Cir. 2007). The Tenth Circuit reached the same result in *Lopez v. United States*, 376 F.3d 1055 (10th Cir. 2004).

35.   The average payment under the September 11th Victim Compensation Fund was $1.8 million. Wikipedia, online at http://en.wikipedia.org/wiki/September_11th_Victim_Compensation_Fund.

36.   1955 Hearings, p. 13.

37.   *Hearings before a Subcommittee of the Committee on the Judiciary on S.1077* (84th Cong., 1st Sess.), p. 41 (1955).

CHAPTER 2

1.   Martha Bardoli Laird, quoted in House Committee on Oversight and Foreign Commerce, Subcommittee on Oversight and Investigations, *"The Forgotten Guinea Pigs": A Report on Health Effects of Low-Level Radiation Sustained as a Result of the Nuclear Weapons Testing Program Conducted by the United States Government*, 96th Cong., 2nd Sess., p. 14 (1980) [hereinafter "House Report"].

2.   Carole Gallagher, *American Ground Zero*, p. 300 (1993); Howard Ball, *Justice Downwind*, p. 45 (1986).

3.   *Hearings on Radioactive Fallout from Nuclear Testing at Nevada Test Site, before a Special Subcommittee of the Senate Appropriations Committee* (105th Cong., 1st Sess.), p. 23 (1998). Online at https://www.gpo.gov/fdsys/pkg/CHRG-105shrg44045/html/CHRG-105shrg44045.htm.

4.   Philip Fradkin, *Fallout: An American Tragedy*, pp. 8–9 (1989).

5.   Sally Whipple Mosher Mooney, *On the Sunnyside of Life*, unpaginated (2012).

6.   *Ibid.*, pp. 7–8, 167.

7.   Glenn Alan Cheney, *They Never Knew: The Victims of Nuclear Testing*, p. 40 (1996).

8.   *Ibid.*

9.   Bill Curry, "Clouds of Death Haunt the Mesas," *Washington Post*, July 2, 1978, online at https://www.washingtonpost.com/archive/politics/1978/07/02/the-clouds-of-death-haunt-the-mesas/904dd6a8-1725-44b2-a9b6-964f134e8b85/?utm_term=.dc2df32d535c.

10.   Carole Gallagher, *op. cit.*, p. 124. It is not clear that Harry was the blast that affected Mrs. Nelson; her husband did not know which test it was, and thought it came in 1955. But the 1955 tests involved bombs set off at three thousand feet or more, rather than Harry's three hundred feet. The greater altitude would have reduced fallout since the fireball was too high to scoop up and irradiate earth.

11.   Glenn Alan Cheney, *op. cit.*, pp. 40, 44–45.

12.   J. C. Jones, *Atmospheric Pollution*, p. 105 (2008), download available at https://books.google.com/books?id=tt64O4JOB3gC&pg=PA105&lpg=PA105&dq=chernobyl+i-.

13.   Arthur B. Schneider, "Ionizing Radiation and Thyroid Cancer," in *Thyroid Cancer*, pp. 27, 47, edited by James A. Fagin (1998).

14.   J. C. Jones, *op. cit.*

15.   Carl J. Johnson, "Cancer Incidence in an Area of Radioactive Fallout Downwind from the Nevada Test Site," in *Journal of the American Medical Ass'n*, vol. 251, p. 230 (1984).

16.   Carol Gallagher, *op. cit.*, p. 129.

17.   J. H. Foley, W. Borges & T. Yamawaki, "Incidence of Leukaemia in Survivors of the Atomic Bomb in Hiroshima and Nagasaki, Japan," in *American Journal of Medicine*, vol. 13, p. 311 (1952); R. D. Lange, W. C. Moloney & T. Yamawaki, "Leukaemia in Atomic Bomb Survivors," *Blood*, vol. 9, p. 574 (1954).

18.   "Atomic Device Firing in 11th Postponement," The [Provo] *Daily Herald*, May 26, 1957, p. 1. A similar announcement was made four months later, when a test was postponed for a day "because winds would have carried

fallout over populated areas." "21st Nuclear Shot Delayed," The [Provo] *Daily Herald*, Sept. 17, 1957, p. 17.

19. AEC handbill dated Jan. 11, 1951, online at http://en.wikipedia.org/wiki/ Nevada_Test_Site#/media/File:NTS_-_Warning_handbill.jpg.

20. "Derides Fear of Radiation," *Ogden Standard-Examiner*, Aug. 19, 1957, p. 1.

21. "We Don't Know Enough," *Salt Lake Tribune*, May 9, 1952, p. 10.

22. "Controls Make Atomic Tests Harmless," *Salt Lake Tribune*, May 29, 1952, p. 6.

23. "Salt Lake City (UP)," The [Provo] *Daily Herald*, May 19, 1953, p. 1.

24. "Utah Clear of Harmful Atom Cloud," *Ogden Standard-Examiner*, May 20, 1953, p. 1.

25. "Radiation in Atomic Tests Held Negligible," [Provo] *Sunday Herald*, May 24, 1953, p. 14.

26. "No Danger in Nevada Nuclear Tests, Utah Residents Assured," The [Provo] *Daily Herald*, Jan. 21, 1955, p. 1.

27. House Report, pp. 4–5.

28. Richard Miller, *Under the Cloud*, p. 183 (1986).

29. *Ibid.*, p. 183.

30. House Report, p. 6.

31. Howard Ball, "Downwind from the Bomb," *New York Times Magazine*, Feb. 9, 1986, online at http://www.nytimes.com/1986/02/09/magazine/downwind -from-the-bomb.html.

32. Glenn Alan Cheney, *op. cit.*, pp. 44–45.

33. House Report, p. 7.

34. House Report pp. 7–8; see also *Hearing before the Senate Judiciary Committee on S. 2454* (99th Cong., 2nd Sess.), p. 187 (1986) (statement of Stewart Udall).

35. House Report, p. 7.

36. Lindsay Mattison & Richard Daly, "Nevada Fallout: Past and Present Hazards," *Bulletin of the Atomic Scientists*, p. 41 (Apr. 1964).

37. Margaret Jones Patterson & Robert H. Russell, *Behind the Lines: Case Studies in Investigative Reporting*, p. 164 (1986).

38. See Howard L. Rowsenberg, *Atomic Soldiers* (1980); Jennifer LaFleur, *America's Atomic Vets*, online at https://www.revealnews.org/article/us-veterans -in-secretive-nuclear-tests-still-fighting-for-recognition/; Harvey Wasserman and Norman Solomon, *Killing Our Own*, online at https://ratical.org/radiation/ KillingOurOwn/index.html.

39. "U.S. Expands Care of Atom Veterans," *New York Times*, Apr. 6, 1983, online at http://www.nytimes.com/1983/04/07/us/us-expands-care-of-atom-veterans.html.

40.   Jeremy Pearce, "Edward Lewis, Nobelist Who Studied Fly DNA, Dies at 86," *New York Times*, July 26, 2004, online at http://www.nytimes.com/2004/07/26/us/edward-lewis-nobelist-who-studied-fly-dna-dies-at-86.html.

41.   Richard L. Miller, *op. cit.*, pp. 361–62.

42.   *Ibid.*, p. 363.

43.   *Ibid.*, p. 364.

44.   Bill Curry, "A-Test Officials Feared Outcry After Health Study," *Washington Post*, Apr. 14, 1979, online at https://www.washingtonpost.com/archive/politics/1979/04/14/a-test-officials-feared-outcry-after-health-study/9c4519f1-e71e-4f6f-83a3-d09de85b06f5/?utm_term=.e38ef554b737.

45.   *Ibid.*

46.   "U.S. Ignored Atomic Test Leukemia Link," *Washington Post*, Jan. 8, 1979, online at https://www.washingtonpost.com/archive/politics/1979/01/08/us-ignored-atomic-test-leukemia-link-phs-ignored-leukemia-link-in-western-a-tests/545f354a-07f2-404b-bb3b-8cedd885f5a9/.

47.   Gordon Eliot White, "U.S. Kept Ignoring Evidence about Fallout's Deadly Effects," *Deseret News*, Oct. 28, 1990, online at http://www.deseretnews.com/article/129362/US-KEPT-IGNORING-EVIDENCE-ABOUT-FALLOUTS-DEADLY-EFFECTS.html.

48.   Margaret Jones Patterson & Robert H. Russell, *op. cit.*, pp. 159–60.

49.   Joseph L. Lyon, *et al.*, "Childhood Leukemias Associated with Fallout from Nuclear Testing," *New England Journal of Medicine*, vol. 300, p. 397 (1979).

50.   Philip L. Fradkin, *op. cit.*, p. 74.

51.   Susan Stramaham, *Downwind Deals*, online at http://aliciapatterson.org/stories/downwind-deals.

52.   Howard Ball, *op. cit.*, p. 153.

53.   *Ibid.*, p. 44.

54.   *Ibid.*

55.   *Allen v. United States*, 588 F. Supp. 247 (D. Utah 1984).

56.   588 F. Supp. at 337-38.

57.   467 U.S. 797 (1984). The facts discussed here are taken from the Supreme Court opinion and also from the ruling of the Ninth Circuit, *Varig Airlines v. United States*, 692 F.2d 1205 (9th Cir. 1982), which the Court reversed.

58.   467 U.S. at 813.

59.   467 U.S. at 820.

60.   *Allen v. United States*, 816 F.2d 1417 (10th Cir. 1987).

61.   The crewman had been given transfusions to remedy anemia caused by the fallout and died of hepatitis contracted from the transfusions.

62.   Mark Schreiber, "Lucky Dragon's Lethal Catch," *Japan Times*, Mar. 18, 2012, online at http://www.japantimes.co.jp/life/2012/03/18/general/lucky-dragons-lethal-catch/#.WDsjR2UzP8s.

CHAPTER 3

1.   Quoted in Alexander Cockburn & Jeffrey St. Clair, *Whiteout: The CIA, Drugs, and the Press*, p. 67 (1998).
2.   "Selected Letters Between the United States Public Health Service, the Macon County Health Department, and the Tuskegee Institute," in *Tuskegee's Truths*, pp. 84–85, edited by Susan M. Reverby (2000) [hereinafter "Selected Letters"].
3.   Jared Diamond, *Guns, Germs, and Steel*, p. 210 (1997).
4.   Thomas Johnson, trans., *The Works of that Famous Chirurgion Ambrose Parey*, p. 727 (1634, reprinted 1968) (spelling modernized).
5.   *Ibid.*, p. 749.
6.   Julie M. Fenster, *Mavericks, Miracles, and Medicine*, p. 136 (2003).
7.   Mark S. Rasnake, *et al.*, "History of U.S. Military Contributions to the Study of Sexually Transmitted Diseases," *Military Medicine*, vol. 170, pp. 61, 63 (2005).
8.   M. Tampa, *et al.*, "Brief History of Syphilis," *Journal of Medicine and Life* (Mar. 15, 2014), online at http://www.ncbi.nlm.nih.gov/pmc/articles/PMC3956094/.
9.   Dr. Richard Arnold, quoted in John Firth, "Syphilis – Its early History and Treatment until Penicillin," *Journal of Military & Veterans' Health*, online at http://jmvh.org/article/syphilis-its-early-history-and-treatment-until-penicillin-and-the-debate-on-its-origins/.
10.   K. J. Williams, "The Introduction of 'chemotherapy' using arsphenamine – the first magic bullet," *Journal of the Royal Society of Medicine*, vol. 102, p. 343 (Aug. 1, 2009), online at https://www.ncbi.nlm.nih.gov/pmc/articles/PMC2726818/.
11.   Dep't of Health, Education and Welfare, "Final Report of the Ad Hoc Tuskegee Syphilis Study Panel," in *Tuskegee's Truths*, edited by Susan M. Reverby, p. 168 (2000).
12.   Marianna Karamanou *et al.*, "Hallmarks in History of Syphilis Therapeutics," *La Infezioni in Medicina*, vol. 4, p. 317 (2013), online at http://www.infezmed.it/media/journal/Vol_21_4_2013_10.pdf.
13.   James H. Jones, *op. cit.*, Selected Letters, p. 75, 77.
14.   *Ibid.*, pp. 77, 86–88.
15.   *Ibid.*, p. 80.
16.   *Ibid.*, p. 75.

17. *Ibid.,* pp. 75–76.

18. *Ibid.,* pp. 78–80.

19. The author's father, living on the Arizona frontier, was bitten by a rattlesnake in the 1930s. He had to survive without medical care because the nearest doctor was sixty miles away, no small distance at the time, and his grandparents, who were raising him, could not afford the treatment. When his grandfather was dying of cancer, the family smuggled morphine up from Mexico, I assume because they could not afford the domestic product.

20. Again, not a minor consideration to a poor sharecropper at the time. The author's great-grandparents rest in the cemetery in St. David, Arizona. Many of the tombstones there consist of cast concrete, mixed from a bag, with names and dates scratched into it, or spelled out by inserted pebbles. The author's great-uncle rests in a cemetery in Buckeye, Arizona; his memorial is a galvanized metal tag with his name stamped on it, fastened to a wooden stake. In much of 1930s rural America, medical care and headstones were not affordable.

21. Fred D. Gray, *The Tuskegee Syphilis Study,* pp. 58–59 (1998).

22. Selected Letters, p. 81.

23. James H. Jones, *Bad Blood: The Tuskegee Syphilis Experiment,* p. 117 (1993).

24. *Ibid.,* p. 119.

25. *Ibid.,* p.123.

26. *Ibid.,* p. 124.

27. *Ibid.,* pp. 127–28.

28. *Ibid.,* p. 128.

29. Selected Letters, pp. 82–83.

30. M. P. Vora, "Cardiovascular Syphilis," *The Medical Bulletin,* vol. 10, p. 444 (Oct. 3, 1942).

31. Memorandum dated Feb. 18, 1938, through Medical Directors, Bureau of Prisons, to Surgeon General. Files of Attorney General Homer Cummings, University of Virginia, collection no. 9973, Box 85.

32. Selected Letters, pp. 84-85.

33. Allen M. Brandt, "Racism and Research: the Case of the Tuskegee Syphilis Study," *Hasting Center Reports,* vol. 8, p. 25 (1978).

34. "Doctor Says He Was Told Not to Treat Men in V.D. Experiment," *New York Times,* Aug. 8, 1972, online at http://www.nytimes.com/1972/08/08/archives/doctor-says-he-was-told-not-to-treat-men-in-vd-experiment.html.

35. Selected Letters, p. 95.

36. John F. Mahoney, R. C. Arnold & Ad Harris, "Penicillin Treatment of Early Syphilis," *American Journal of Public Health,* vol. 33, p. 1387 (1943).

The article states it was presented at an October 14, 1943, meeting of the American Public Health Association. The duration of the study, and the time required to prepare the paper, is unknown. But since it was undertaken on a request from the National Research Council it seems likely there was talk of penicillin's curative powers for quite some time.

37.   Allan M. Brandt, "Racism and Research: The Case of the Tuskegee Syphilis Study," in *Sickness and Health in America*, p. 399, edited by Judith Leavitt & Ronald Numbers (1997).

38.   R. A. Vonderlehr, Taliaferro Clark, O. C. Wenger & J. R. Heller, "Untreated Syphilis in the Male Negro," *Journal of the American Medical Association*, vol. 107, p. 856 (Sept. 12, 1936).

39.   J. R. Heller & P. T. Bruyere, "Untreated Syphilis in the Male Negro: Mortality During 12 Years of Observation," *Journal of Venereal Disease Information*, vol. 27, p. 34 (1946).

40.   Selected Letters, p. 98.

41.   Sydney Olansky, *et al.*, "Twenty Years of Clinical Observation of Untreated Syphilitic and Presumably Nonsyphilitic Groups," *Journal of Chronic Diseases*, p. 177 (Aug. 1956).

42.   Donald H. Rockwell, Anne Roof Yobs & M. Brittain Moore, "The Tuskegee Study of Untreated Syphilis," *Archives of Internal Medicine*, vol. 114, p. 792 (1964).

43.   Selected Letters, p. 104.

44.   *Ibid.*

45.   Dr. Schatz's letter was never published, but the *Wall Street Journal* uncovered it via a Freedom of Information Act request. As a result, he received the Mayo Clinic's Distinguished Alumni Award. He died in 2015 at the age of eighty-three. Sam Roberts, "Irwin Schatz, 83, Rare Critic of Tuskegee Syphilis Study, Is Dead," *New York Times*, Apr. 18, 2015, online at https://www.nytimes.com/2015/04/19/health/irwin-schatz-83-rare-critic-of-tuskegee-study-is-dead.html.

46.   Peter Buxtun, conversation with author, Sept. 29, 2016. See also "Testimony by Peter Buxtun," in *Tuskegee Truths*, pp. 151–54.

47.   Peter Buxtun, conversation with author, Sept. 29, 2016.

48.   James H. Jones, *op. cit.*, p. 199.

49.   "Of Microbes and Mock Attacks: Years Ago, the Military Sprayed Germs on U.S. Cities," *Wall Street Journal*, online at http://www.wsj.com/articles/SB10037032266974960 80; Kevin Louis, "'One of the Largest Human Experiments in History' Was Conducted on Unsuspecting Residents of San Francisco," *Business Insider*, July 9, 2015, online at http://www.businessinsider.com/the-military-tested-bacterial-weapons-in-san-francisco-2015-7.

50.   *Nevin v. United States*, 696 F.2d 1229 (9th Cir. 1983).

51.   Selected Letters, p. 105.

52.   "Human Guinea Pigs / Syphilis Patients Died Untreated," *Washington Star*, July 25, 1972, p. 1.

53.   "Syphilis Victims In U.S. Study Went Untreated For 40 Years," *New York Times*, July 26, 1972, p. 1.

54.   *Final Report of the Ad Hoc Tuskegee Syphilis Study Panel* (1973).

55.   Fred D. Gray, *op. cit.*, pp. 24–25 (1998).

56.   *Ibid.*, pp. 98-99.

CHAPTER 4

1.   Danny O. Coulson & Elaine Shannon, *No Heroes*, pp. 407–8 (1999).

2.   Randy and Sara Weaver, *The Federal Siege at Ruby Ridge*, p. 55 (1998).

3.   *Ibid.*, pp. 14–15 (1998).

4.   *Ibid.*, p. 27.

5.   *Ibid.*

6.   *Ibid.*, p. 30.

7.   United States Department of Justice (USDOJ), *Internal Investigation of Shootings at Ruby Ridge, Idaho, During Arrest of Randy Weaver*, Part 1 (1994), online at http://law2.umkc.edu/faculty/projects/ftrials/weaver/dojruby1.html [hereinafter "USDOJ Report"].

8.   Randy and Sara Weaver, *op. cit.*, p. 30 ("When I sent a copy of the document stating the March 20, 1990 trial date to the media, they confronted the U.S. Marshal's Office in Boise").

9.   *Ibid.*

10.   Randy and Sara Weaver, *op. cit.*, p. 30.

11.   USDOJ Report, Part 2.

12.   *Ibid.*

13.   *Ibid.*

14.   James Bovard, "No Accountability at the FBI," *Wall Street Journal*, Jan. 10, 1995, online at http://jimbovard.com/blog/2012/08/22/20-years-ago-at-ruby-ridge-fbi-sniper-slays-mother-holding-her-baby/.

15.   USDOJ Report, Part 2. With regard to typos, the first two sentences of the psychologist's report are illustrative: "In my best professional judgement, Mr. Randall would be an extreme threat to any police officer's attempt to arrest him. Further, Mr. Randall has indoctrated his family into a belief system that the end of the world is near and that his family must fight the fences for evil that want to take over the world."

16. USDOJ Report, Part 4.

17. USDOJ Report, Part 2.

18. Department of Justice, Office of the Inspector General, *An Assessment of the 1996 Department of Justice Task Force Review of the FBI Laboratory*, July 2014, online at https://oig.justice.gov/reports/2014/e1404.pdf; "FBI Admits to Flawed Forensics Analyses for Cases," National Whistleblower Center, online at http://www.whistleblowers.org/press-room/video-and-audio/1551.

19. Jess Walter, *Ruby Ridge, The Truth & Tragedy of the Randy Weaver Family*, p. 390 (1996).

20. USDOJ Report, Part 3.

21. Timothy Egan, "Idaho Neighbors Resent Police for Pursuing 'Patriot' Fugitive," *Santa Fe New Mexican*, Aug. 27 1992, p. A-3.

22. Associated Press, "Fugitive's Son Killed in Gunfight," (Xenia Ohio) *Daily Gazette*, Aug. 25 1992, p. 2.

23. Associated Press, "Fugitive Keeps Officials at Bay on Mountain," (Arlington Heights, IL) *Daily Herald*, Aug. 23, 1992, p.1.

24. USDOJ Report, Part 4.

25. See generally Danny O. Coulson & Elaine Shannon, *op. cit.*

26. Gary Noesner, *Stalling for Time: My Life as an FBI Hostage Negotiator*, p. 91 (2010).

27. USDOJ Report Part 4.

28. *Idaho v. Horiuchi*, 253 F.3d 359 (9th Cir. 2001) (summarizing testimony of HRT sniper Lon Horiuchi).

29. Danny Coulson & Elaine Shannon, *op. cit.*, p. 400.

30. *Tennessee v. Garner*, 471 U.S. 1 (1985).

31. USDOJ Report, Part 4.

32. USDOJ Report, Part 4. Various versions of the rules can be found, and it seems likely that different people recorded them differently. The version given at Randy Weaver's criminal trial, for instance, transposed No. 1 and No. 2, as given here. George Lardner, Jr. & Richard Lei, "Permissive Rules of Engagement at Issue in Ruby Ridge Shooting," *Washington Post*, July 14, 1995, p. 1.

33. USDOJ Report, Part 4.

34. *Ibid.*

35. *Ibid.*

36. *Ibid.*

37. *Ibid.*

38. Danny O. Coulson & Elaine Shannon, *op. cit.*, pp. 407–8.

39.   We here follow the official narrative, but there is another possibility. Each sniping team consisted of a sniper and a spotter. They were armed with M16s in addition to the sniper's rifle. It is hard to see how a sniper, using a proper rifle, could have failed to kill Weaver, a stationary target, at this close a range. If, on the other hand, the shot were taken with the M16 with no telescope sight, it would certainly be possible to wound but miss the kill zone. Moreover, Sara Weaver described Randy Weaver's wound as small: she put a bandage over the entrance wound, and only much later did they find the exit wound in his underarm. His wound was described as beginning to heal at his surrender eleven days later. That is easier to reconcile with an M16 shot than with a shot from a sniper rifle chambered in 7.62 mm NATO, which is twice as powerful. Sara describes Kevin Harris's arm wound, clearly inflicted by Horiuchi's 7.62 mm, as "as big around as a soup can lid," and his arm as swollen to twice its size. Randy and Sara Weaver, *op. cit.*, p. 56.

40.   *Ibid.*, p. 39.

41.   *Ibid.*, p. 53.

42.   Mil-dots are dots on the crosshairs spaced one mil apart; two hundred yards a mil equals 7.2 inches. On the scope used by the HRT snipers, the dot nearest the intersection of the crosshairs is omitted. The sketch shows the first dot aligned with the stick figure, which would indicate a lead of two mils, or just over 14 inches.

43.   Christopher Witcomb, *Cold Zero: Inside the FBI Hostage Rescue Team*, p. 231 (2001).

44.   Randy and Sara Weaver, *op. cit.*, p. 101.

45.   *Ibid.*, p. 53. Both Randy and Sara Weaver refer to the sniper's shots as very loud and being heard at the same instant that the bullets arrived. Most likely what they heard was the incoming bullet's snap, a manner of sonic boom created by a supersonic projectile. The bullet would have covered two hundred yards in about a quarter of a second, while the sound of the shot being fired would have taken just over twice that long.

46.   Danny Coulson & Elaine Shannon, *op. cit.*, p. 412.

47.   Randy and Sara Weaver, *op. cit.*, p. 57.

48.   *Ibid.*, pp. 58–59.

49.   *Ibid.*, p. 59.

50.   "Friendly Fire may have killed Fugitive's son," *Orlando Sentinel*, Aug. 27, 1992. Online at http://articles.orlandosentinel.com/1992-08-27/news/9208 270874_1_weaver-degan-harris.

51. Danny Coulson & Elaine Shannon, *op. cit.*, p. 417. ("Why hadn't HRT detached it before sending the robot up the hill? Sheer carelessness is all I can figure.")

52. *Ibid.,* p. 417.

53. *Ibid.*

54. *Ibid.,* p. 419.

55. Danny O. Coulson & Elaine Shannon, *op. cit.,* p. 416.

56. *Ibid.,* p. 424.

57. Gerry Spence, *Police State*, pp. 52–53 (2005).

58. Notice of Filing of Special Report, *In Re* Special Proceedings, Misc. No. 09-0198, (D.D.C., Mar. 15, 2012), online at https://www.scribd.com/document/85469006/Schuelke-Report.

59. Sidney Powell, *Licensed to Lie: Exposing Corruption in the Department of Justice*, p. 222 (2014).

60. Danny O. Coulson & Elaine Shannon, *op. cit.,* p. 415.

61. Gary Noesner, *Stalling for Time: My Life as an FBI Hostage Negotiator*, p. 95 (2010).

62. *Opening Statement of Louis J. Freeh, before the Subcommittee on Terrorism, Technology and Government Information, of the Senate Judiciary Committee*, online at: http://fas.org/irp/congress/1995_hr/s951019f.htm#punishment%20administered.

63. Jess Walter, *op. cit.*, pp. 380-81.

64. Howard Fischer, "Tucson Couple's Case to Help Supreme Court Probe Penalties for Data-Concealing Lawyers," *Arizona Star*, Dec. 9, 2016, online at http://tucson.com/news/state-and-regional/tucson-couple-s-case-to-help-supreme-court-probe-penalties/article_7d92a742-3097-5cd2-8b03-566aeac36766.html.

65. Jess Walter, *op. cit.*, p. 391.

66. U.S. Constitution, Art. VI, §2.

67. *In re Neagle*, 135 U.S. 1 (1890).

68. *In re Neagle*, 135 U.S. at 75.

69. Traditionally, federal appellate cases are first decided by a three-judge panel. Further appeal (discretionary with the court) is to the court sitting *en banc*, which in most courts means all the judges of the court. But the Ninth Circuit is so large (nearly thirty active judges) that its rules provide the further appeal to an eleven-judge panel consisting of the chief judge and ten other judges picked at random.

70. *State v. Horiuchi*, 253 F.3d 359 (9th Cir. 2001).

71. *Ibid.*

72. Jess Walter, *op. cit.*, p. 396.

73. Gerry Spence, *op. cit.*, p. 63.

CHAPTER 5

1.   Dean M. Kelly, "Waco: A Massacre and its Aftermath," *First Things*, May 1995, p. 37, online at https://www.firstthings.com/article/1995/05/001-waco -a-massacre-and-its-aftermath.

2.   Waco 911 tapes, Feb. 28, 1993.

3.   Clive Doyle with Catherine Messinger and Matthew D. Witmer, *A Journey to Waco*, p. 91 (2012).

4.   Combat grenades are filled with high explosive, with much more power than black powder. Practice grenades are designed for safety in throwing practice. The practice grenade has a hole in the bottom; some black powder is put into the hole before it is plugged with a cork. When it is thrown and the fuse burns down, the black powder ignites, pushing the cork out with a loud sound. Since the grenade casing does not explode, it can be reused.

5.   While federal law now (and then) allows *possession* of a machine gun if legal requirements are met, a 1986 law prohibits civilian possession of machine guns made after this date. Grenade manufacture requires licensing as a manufacturer of "destructive devices," which is hard to obtain, and the registration of each grenade made.

6.   The search warrant and affidavit can be found online at http://www.jaedworks .com/shoebox/waco.html. I have focused here upon the affidavit's major problem. A fuller explanation of its legal shortcomings and errors can be found in David B, Kopel & Paul H. Blackman, *No More Wacos*, pp. 47–78 (1997).

7.   *Report of the Department of the Treasury on the Bureau of Alcohol, Tobacco and Firearms Investigation of Vernon Wayne Howell, also known as David Koresh*, p. E-3 (1993) [hereinafter "Report of the Department of the Treasury"].

8.   Review of *In the Line of Duty: Ambush at Waco* (1993), online at http://www. imdb.com/title/tt0107205/.

9.   "Information Paper," dated 8 Mar. 1992, Dep't of Defense FOIA release, p. 36163.

10.   *David T. Hardy v. FBI, et al.*, No. 95-883 (D. Ariz.), Declaration of Cheryl Kirkwood, pp. 11–13.

11.   *Hardy v. United States Dep't of Defense, et al.*, No. 99–523 (D. Ariz.), Third Declaration of Scott A. Hodes at 4, appended to Defendant's Notice of Filing of a Supplemental Declaration per Court's Order of Aug. 27, 2001 ("Our review of the written statements confirmed that there exist no known videotapes from the CCTV cameras of the events at Waco on Apr. 19, 1993 . . .").

12.   Dick J. Reavis, *The Ashes of Waco*, p. 148 (1995).

13.   *Ibid.*, pp. 141–42.

14.   The author was present during the civil trials in Waco and examined the surviving door at close range. The tracked vehicle marks lend credence to the story of a hastily removed companion door.

15.   Dick J. Reavis, *op. cit.*, p. 142.

16.   Dick J. Reavis, "Trooper Describes Oddities at Waco," *San Antonio Express-News*, Mar. 8, 2000.

17.   *Report of the Department of the Treasury; Report to the Deputy Attorney General on the Events at Waco, Texas, Feb. 28 to Apr. 19, 1993* (1993).

18.   Mike McNulty died of a heart attack on February 20, 2015, at his home in Loveland, Colorado.

19.   Sarah J. McCarthy, "Pyrotechnics at Waco," *World Net Daily*, Aug. 31, 1999, online at http://www.wnd.com/1999/08/5839/#lU7ZfR066642ZXXd.03 ("Now, with new admissions by the FBI that after six years of denials by Janet Reno and the FBI, pyrotechnic tear gas canisters were used on the final day of the 1993 government standoff with the Branch Davidians at Waco, Texas, mistrust of government will justifiably grow . . .").

20.   Report of the Department of the Treasury, p. 136.

21.   Report of Investigation (Law Enforcement) from Special Agent Davy Aguilera to SAC Houston Field Office, dated Feb. 29, 1993.

22.   See generally David T. Hardy, "The Firearm Owners' Protection Act: A Historical and Legal Perspective," *Cumberland Law Review*, vol. 17, pp. 585, 604–06 (1986); David T. Hardy, ed., *The BATF's War on Civil Liberties* (Second Amendment Foundation, 1979).

23.   Carol Vinzant, "BATF Troop," *Spy Magazine*, Mar. 1994, p. 49.

24.   Carol Vinzant, *op. cit.*, p. 44.

25.   Trial transcript, *United States v. Branch*, No. 93-CR-046 (D. Texas), 1959.

26.   *Ibid.*, p. 2080.

27.   *Ibid.*, p. 1884.

28.   David T. Hardy and Rex Kimball, *This Is Not an Assault*, pp. 81–82 (2001).

29.   Survivor David Thibodeau said that Koresh called out, "What's going on? There are women and children in here." David Thibodeau, *A Place Called Waco*, p. 166 (1999). A few days after the gunfight, a wounded Koresh told negotiators, "I was standing there in the door, they did hear me say, you know, 'Go back, there's women and children here, let's talk about this.'" FBI negotiation transcripts, Mar. 3, 1993, p. 47. The ATF agents who testified at the civil trial all agreed that Koresh left the building and ran toward them while calling out, although not all could understand his words.

30.   David Thibodeau, *op. cit.*, p. 166.

31.   The image can be found online at: http://images.usatoday.com/news/_photos/2003/04/18-waco-inside.jpg.

32.   *United States v. Branch*, No. 93-CR-046 (W.D. Texas), trial transcript, p. 1744.

33.   *Ibid.*, pp. 1745–47.

34.   *Ibid.*, p. 2689.

35.   *Ibid.*, p. 2331.

36.   Wendel E. Frost, *ATF Sierra One Waco*, pp. 59, 61 (2009).

37.   A sniper firing at just over two hundred yards is unlikely to inflict a survivable wound, and none of the survivors of the fire had previous gunshot injuries.

38.   Data taken from the autopsy of David Koresh.

39.   Book of Revelation, 7:4, 14:1–3.

40.   *James D. Tabor & Eugene v. Gallagher, Why Waco?*, pp. 11–15 (1995).

41.   *Ibid.*, p. 15.

42.   *Ibid.*, pp. 15–16.

43.   *Ibid.*, p. 20.

44.   FBI negotiation transcripts, online at http://www.serendipity.li/waco/tapes.html.

45.   Christopher Whitcomb, *Cold Zero* (2001).

46.   *Ibid.*, pp. 293, 306.

47.   Tabor & Gallagher, *op. cit.*, pp.18–19.

48.   Christopher Whitcomb, *op. cit.*, p. 302.

49.   *Ibid.*, p. 307.

50.   *Activities of Federal Law Enforcement Agents Toward the Branch Davidians: Joint Hearings before the Subcommittee on Crime, House Judiciary Committee, and the Subcommittee on Nat'l Security, House Committee on Government Reform and Oversight* (104th Cong., 1st Sess.), Pt. 3 at 112.

51.   *Ibid.*, Pt. 3, p. 113.

52.   *Ibid.*, Pt. 2, p. 346.

53.   Dow Chemical Inc., Material Hazard Safety Sheet.

54.   Richard Stewart, "Paint Remover Hazard," *Journal of the American Medical Association,* vol. 235, p. 398 (1976).

55.   *Brown v. United States*, No. H-95-587 (W.D. Tex.), Declaration of Eric Larson.

56.   Failure Analysis Associates, *Final Assault on Mount Carmel*, p. 7 (July 21, 1995).

57.   William Lowry, *et al.*, "Studies of Toxic Gas Production During Actual Residential Fires in the Dallas Area," *Journal of Forensic Sciences*, vol. 30, pp. 59, 63 (1985).

58.   *Isabel G. Andrade v. Phillip J. Chojnacki*, No. W-96-CA-139 (W.D. Tex.), Memorandum opinion dated July 1, 1999, p. 63.

59.   *Castillo v. United States*, 530 U.S. 120 (2000).

60. House Report, pp. 306–14, 322–29.

61. *Ibid.*, pp. 315–21, 330–36.

62. *Ibid.*

63. John C. Danforth, *Final Report to the Deputy Attorney General Concerning the 1993 Confrontation at the Mt. Carmel Complex, Waco, Texas* (2000), online at https://en.wikisource.org/wiki/Final_report_to_the_Deputy_Attorney_General_concerning_the_1993_confrontation_at_the_Mt._Carmel_Complex,_Waco_Texas. (The author is proud of a passage on p. 99 of the report, where the independent counsel states, with regard to accusations of USDOJ perjury, "The Hardy situation is the most troubling.")

64. Robert Bryce, "Killing the Messenger: John C. Danforth's Indictment of Whistleblower Bill Johnston may lead to a Nasty Courtroom Showdown," *The Austin Chronicle*, Nov. 17, 2000, online at http://www.austinchronicle.com/news/2000-11-17/79443.

65. Affidavit of Richardo Ojeda, filed in *State of Oklahoma v. Terry Nichols*, District Court of Oklahoma County, No. CF-99-1845, dated May 21, 2001.

66. John C. Danforth, *op. cit.*, p. 98 (Nov. 8, 2000).

67. Gary Cartwright, "The Case of the Persecuted Prosecutor," *Texas Monthly*, Aug. 2001, online at http://www.texasmonthly.com/politics/the-case-of-the-persecuted-prosecutor.

CHAPTER 6

1. Glenmore S. Trenear-Harvey, *Historical Dictionary of Intelligence Failures*, p. 148 (2015).

2. National Commission on Terrorist Attacks upon the United States, *The 9/11 Commission Report*, p. 271 (2003) [hereinafter "9/11 Commission Report"].

3. Richard Miniter, *Losing Bin Laden*, pp. 29–30 (2003).

4. *Ibid.*, pp. 51–52.

5. Thus becoming the first Jarhead noncom to become a head of state. See James C. McKinley, "How a U.S. Marine Became Leader of Somalia," *New York Times*, Aug. 12, 1996, online at http://www.nytimes.com/1996/08/12/world/how-a-us-marine-became-leader-of-somalia.html.

6. Rich Lowry, *Legacy; Paying the Price for the Clinton Years*, p. 300 (2003); Susan Page, "Why Clinton failed to stop bin Laden," *USA Today*, Nov. 12, 2001, online at http://usatoday30.usatoday.com/news/attack/2001/11/12/clinton-usatcov.htm#more. The two sources give somewhat different translations.

7. "President Clinton's remarks," CNN, June 25, 1996, online at http://www.cnn.com/WORLD/9606/25/clinton.remarks.

8.   Louis J. Freeh, "Khobar Towers," *Wall Street Journal*, June 23, 2006, online at http://www.wsj.com/articles/SB115102702568788331.

9.   Rich Lowry, *op. cit.*, pp. 309–10 (2003).

10.   Louis J. Freeh, *My FBI: Bringing Down the Mafia, Investigating Bill Clinton, and Fighting the War on Terror*, p. 30 (2005).

11.   Associated Press, "Bombings in East Africa," *New York Times*, Aug. 8, 1998. Online at http://www.nytimes.com/1998/08/08/world/bombings-in-east-africa-clinton-pledges-a-hunt-for-those-responsible.html.

12.   BBC News, *World: Americas, Clinton Statement in Full*, Aug. 26, 1998. Online at http://news.bbc.co.uk/2/hi/americas/155412.stm.

13.   Rich Lowry, *op. cit.*, p. 318.

14.   "Breaking News, President Clinton Vows to Hold USS Cole attackers accountable," CNN transcripts, Oct. 12, 2000, online at http://www.cnn.com/TRANSCRIPTS/0010/12/bn.44.html.

15.   9/11 Commission Report, p. 191.

16.   Gerald Posner, *Why America Slept*, p. 101 (2003).

17.   Barton Gellman, "U.S. was Foiled Multiple Times in Efforts to Capture bin Laden or Have Him Killed," *Washington Post*, Oct. 3, 2001, online at http://www.washingtonpost.com/wp-dyn/content/article/2006/06/09/AR2006060900911.html.

18.   Gerald Posner, *op. cit.*, p. 103.

19.   Barton Gellman, *op. cit.*

20.   Richard Miniter, *op. cit.*, p. 102.

21.   Alexandra Poolos, "Afghanistan: The Taliban's Rise to Power," *Radio Free Europe*, Sept. 18, 2001, online at http://www.rferl.org/a/1097442.html.

22.   George Tenet, *op. cit.*, pp. 104–05.

23.   Richard Miniter, *op. cit.*, p. 168.

24.   Technically, it would be double hearsay, each component of which must qualify for admission into evidence. Bin Laden saying he did it would be admissible in his prosecution, within the rule's exception for statements of a party opponent. But the witness's claim that he heard someone else describe bin Laden's confession would not be admissible.

25.   Richard Miniter, *op. cit.*, p. 198.

26.   *Ibid.*, pp. 198–99.

27.   See Grant J. Lilly, "In the Crosshairs: Lifting the Ban on Assassination," *American Diplomacy* (June 2006), online at http://www.unc.edu/depts/diplomat/item/2006/0406/lill/lilly_crosshairs.html.

28.   Richard A. Clarke, *Against All Enemies*, p. 204 (2004).

29.   *Ibid.*, pp. 145, 204 (2004).

30.   Richard Miniter, *op. cit.*, p. 87.

31.   George Tenet, *At the Center of the Storm*, pp. 30–31 (2007).

32.   9/11 Commission Report, p. 260.

33.   National Security Presidential Directive 1, online at https://fas.org/irp/off-docs/nspd/nspd-1.pdf.

34.   Online at https://fas.org/irp/offdocs/nspd/nspd-1.pdf.

35.   Richard Clarke, *op. cit.*, pp. 231–32.

36.   *Ibid.*, p. 237. It should be noted that FBI Director Louis Freeh contends that Clarke, whom he describes as "the self-appointed Paul Revere of 9/11," was quite a minor player in counterterrorism: "Here's what I remember about Dick Clarke: almost nothing of any significance." Louis J. Freeh, *My FBI: Bringing Down the Mafia, Investigating Bill Clinton, and Fighting the War on Terror*, p. 297 (2005). CIA Director George Tenet, on the other hand, reports dealing with Clarke on many occasions. George Tenet, *op. cit.*, pp. 131, 143–45, 151, 200 (2007).

37.   Robert H. Churchill, *To Shake Their Guns in the Tyrant's Face* (2012).

38.   Online at http://www.constitution.org/y2k/megiddo.pdf.

39.   For those too young to remember and fellow Mac users for whom it was irrelevant—the Y2K bug resulted from operating systems that stored year dates as two-digit strings, so that 1999 was stored as 99. There were various fears as to what would happen on January 1, 2000, when the two-digit date string would become 00. The operating systems might crash entirely, or they might start dating files as 1900 rather than 2000. But by 2000 enough operating systems had been upgraded to where very little actually happened.

40.   General Accounting Office, *Combatting Terrorism: Need for Comprehensive Threat and Risk Assessments of Chemical and Biological Attacks*, Sept. 1999, online at http://www.investigativeproject.org/documents/testimony/167.pdf

41.   Office of the Inspector General, *A Review of the FBI's Counterterrorism Program: Threat Assessment, Strategic Planning, and Resource Management*, report no. 02-38, Sept. 2002, online at https://oig.justice.gov/reports/FBI/a0238.htm.

42.   Richard Blair, "FBI's 'Phoenix' Memo Unmasked," *Fortune.com*, Oct. 12, 2011, online at http://fortune.com/2011/10/12/fbis-phoenix-memo-unmasked.

43.   Office of the Inspector General, *A Review of the FBI's Handling of Intelligence Prior to the September 11 Attacks*, Nov. 2004, online at https://oig.justice.gov/special/0506/chapter3.htm.

44.   9/11 Commission Report, p. 273.

45.   George Tenet, *op. cit.*, pp. 201–2.

46.   "Coleen Rowley's Memo to FBI Director Robert Mueller," *TIME*, June 3, 2002, online at https://web.archive.org/web/20020602115353/http://www.time.com/time/covers/1101020603/memo.html.

47.   *Ibid.*

48.   *Ibid.*

49.   Margaret Talbot, "The Way We Live Now," *New York Times Magazine*, Sept. 28, 2003, online at http://www.ala.org/Template.cfm?Section=ifissues&-Template=/ContentManagement/ContentDisplay.cfm&ContentID=21662.

50.   Bob Egelko, "FBI Checking Out Americans' Reading Habits," *SF Gate*, June 23, 2002, online at http://www.sfgate.com/politics/article/FBI-checking-out-Americans-reading-habits-2826830.php.

51.   Technically, the sound to sound-plus-noise ratio.

52.   Brian Wingfield, "Dress Code May Hinder Their Work, Air Marshals Say," *New York Times*, July 17, 2004, online at http://www.nytimes.com/2004/07/17/us/dress-code-may-hinder-their-work-air-marshals-say.html.

53.   *Ibid.*

54.   "U.S. Air Marshals Dodge 'Suit Nazis,'" *Washington Times*, Dec. 23, 2004, online at http://www.washingtontimes.com/news/2004/dec/23/20041223-104021-4191r/.

55.   See 49 U.S. Code §44921.

56.   "Faulty rules blamed for gun's firing," *Washington Times*, Mar. 28, 2008, online at http://www.washingtontimes.com/news/2008/mar/28/faulty-rules-blamed-for-guns-firing/.

57.   Michael Ross and John M. Broder, "Aspin Rejects Calls for His Resignation," *Los Angeles Times*, Oct. 8, 1993, online at http://articles.latimes.com/1993-10-08/news/mn-43575_1_secretary-aspin; "Aspin Defends Refusal of Armor for Somalia," *NWI.com*, Oct. 8, 1993, online at http://www.nwi-times.com/uncategorized/aspin-defends-refusal-of-armor-for-somalia/article_b158f774-9413-5ec4-80e9-12beec647aa4.html.

58.   The downing of the helicopters was unrelated to a lack of American armor, but the fact that the rescue column took fourteen hours to reach the trapped soldiers, some of whom died of wounds while waiting, certainly was. The American commander had to locate and recruit Pakistani and Malaysian units that were equipped with armor, albeit of the Vietnam era.

CHAPTER 7

1.   Online at http://abcnews.go.com/Politics/story?id=6960824&page=1.

2.   Mark Landler, "Clinton Says U.S. Feeds Mexico Drug Trade," *New York Times*, Mar. 25, 2009, online at http://www.nytimes.com/2009/03/26/world/americas/26mexico.html?_r=0.

3.   John Dodson, *The Unarmed Truth*, p. 3 (2013).

4. The description of the firefight and of Agent Terry's death is taken from the Declarations of Timothy Keller, William Castano, and Gabriel Fragoza, *United States v. Manuel Osorio-Arellanes*, No. CR 11-150-TUC-DCB (D. Ariz).

5. Mike Detty, *Guns Across the Border: The Inside Story*, pp. 2–3 (2013). See also Office of the Inspector General, Dep't of Justice, *A Review of ATF's Operation Fast and Furious and Related Matters*, p. 31 (Nov. 2012), online at https://oig. justice.gov/reports/2012/s1209.pdf [hereinafter, "OIG Report"].

6. Mike Detty, *op. cit.*, pp. 24–25, OIG Report pp. 36–37.

7. OIG Report, p. 66.

8. *Hinsley v. Standing Rock Child Protective Services*, 516 F.3d 668 (8th Cir. 2008).

9. OIG Report, p. 50.

10. *Ibid.*, p. 50.

11. *Ibid*, pp. 68–69.

12. Mike Detty, *op. cit.*, p. 248.

13. *Ibid.*, p. 259.

14. Congressional Research Service, *The Bureau of Alcohol, Tobacco, Firearms and Explosives (ATF): Budget and Operations for FY2008, FY2009, and FY2010*, online at https://www.everycrsreport.com/reports/RL34514.html.

15. OIG Report, pp. 72–73.

16. John Dodson, *The Unarmed Truth: My Fight to Blow the Whistle and Expose Fast and Furious*, pp. 42–43 (2013).

17. See generally David A. Keene, *Shall Not Be Infringed: The New Assaults on Your Second Amendment* (2016).

18. Stephen Dinan, "Obama Blames U.S. Guns in Mexico," *Washington Times*, Apr. 17, 2009, online at http://www.washingtontimes.com/news/2009/apr/17/obama-blames-us-guns-in-mexico.

19. Dennis Wagner, "Burke of Fast and Furious Had Anti-Gun History," *Arizona Republic*, Jan. 28, 2012, online at http://archive.azcentral.com/arizonarepublic/news/articles/2012/01/27/20120127dennis-burke-fast-furious-scandal-career.html.

20. Document obtained from the Clinton Presidential Library. The assault weapons ban was part of the 1994 Crime Act, referenced in the memo.

21. Undated fax from Department of the Treasury, Office of Policy Development, to Dennis Burke, obtained from the Clinton Presidential Library.

22. OIG Report, p. 110.

23. Online at http://oversight.house.gov/wp-content/uploads/2012/10/10-29-12-Exhibits-for-Fast-and-Furious-The-Anatomy-of-a-Failed-Operation-Part-II-of-III-Report.pdf.

24.   OIG Report, p. 128.

25.   *Ibid.*, p. 115.

26.   *Ibid.*, p. 119.

27.   *Ibid.*, pp. 120–21.

28.   *Ibid.*, pp. 128–29.

29.   Sharyl Atkinsson, "Documents: ATF used 'Fast and Furious' to make the case for gun regulation*s*," *CBS Evening News*, Dec. 7, 2011, online at http://www.cbsnews.com/news/documents-atf-used-fast-and-furious-to-make-the-case-for-gun-regulations.

30.   *Ibid.* See also OIG Report, p. 181.

31.   Sharyl Atkinsson, *Fast and Furious*, p. 57 (2012).

32.   OIG Report, p. 182.

33.   Katie Pavlich, *Fast and Furious: Barack Obama's Bloodiest Scandal and its Shameless Cover-up*, p. 46 (2012).

34.   John Dodson, *op. cit.*, p. 74.

35.   *Ibid.*, p. 49.

36.   *Ibid.*, pp. 49–50.

37.   *Ibid.*, pp. 56–57.

38.   Joint Staff Report, *The Department of Justice's Operation Fast and Furious: Accounts of ATF Agents*, p. 43, online at http://www.washingtonpost.com/wp-srv/nation/documents/atf-fast-and-furious-4.html [hereinafter, "Joint Report"].

39.   *Ibid.*, p. 28.

40.   *Ibid.*, p. 36.

41.   *Ibid.*, pp. 37–38.

42.   *Ibid.*, p. 23.

43.   *Ibid.*, p. 24.

44.   *Hearings before the House Committee on Oversight and Gov't Reform, Operation Fast and Furious: The Other Side of the Border* (112th Cong., 1st Sess.) p. 65 (July 26, 2011).

45.   Newell became Assistant Special Agent in Charge of the Phoenix Office in 2006. After establishment of the Denver Field Division late the following year, Colorado, Montana, Wyoming, and Utah were given to Denver. "ATF Opens New Field Division in Denver," Dec. 10, pp. 2–7, online at http://www.prnewswire.com/news-releases/atf-opens-new-field-division-in-denver-58654957.html.

46.   Statement of William Newell before the U.S. House of Representatives Committee on Oversight and Government Reform, July 26, 2011, online at https://oversight.house.gov/wp-content/uploads/2012/01/7-26-11_Newell_FF_Testimony.pdf.

47. Dennis Wagner, "Burke of Fast and Furious Had an Antigun History," *Arizona Republic,* Jan. 28, 2012, online at http://archive.azcentral.com/arizonarepublic/news/articles/2012/01/27/20120127dennis-burke-fast-furious-scandal-career.html.

48. J. J. Hensley, "Feds Link Arizona Buyers to Drug Cartels' Guns, *Arizona Republic*, Sept. 18, 2010, online at http://archive.azcentral.com/arizonarepublic/news/articles/2010/09/18/20100918gunbust0918.html.

49. Joint Staff Report, Part. 2 (Oct. 29, 2012), pp. 92, 96. Online at https://oversight.house.gov/wp-content/uploads/2012/10/10-29-12-Fast-and-Furious-The-Anatomy-of-a-Failed-Operation-Part-II-of-III-Report.pdf.

50. Joint Report, p. 36.

51. Joint Report, p. 38.

52. Sari Horwitz & James Grimaldi, "U.S. Gun Dealers with the Most Firearms Traced over the Past Four Years," *Washington Post*, Dec. 13, 2010.

53. James Grimaldi & Sara Horwitz, "As Mexico Drug Violence Runs Rampant, U.S. Guns Tied to Crime South of Border," *Washington Post*, Dec. 15, 2010.

54. *Ibid.*

55. John Dodson, *op. cit.*, p. 158.

56. Mike Vanderboegh, online at http://sipseystreetirregulars.blogspot.com/2010/12/border-patrol-agent-killed-with-atf.html.

57. John Dobson, *op. cit.*, p. 167.

58. *Ibid.*, p. 172.

59. Online at https://www.scribd.com/doc/47909152/ATF1-1.

60. Online at https://web.archive.org/web/20110508031440/http://grassley.senate.gov/about/upload/Judiciary-ATF-02-04-11-letter-from-DOJ-deny-allegations.pdf.

61. Peter Yost, "Justice Dept. Details How It Got Statements Wrong," *Associated Press*, Dec. 2, 2011, online at https://www.yahoo.com/news/justice-dept-details-got-statements-wrong-215322145.html?ref=gs.

62. Ryan J. Reilly, "Ex U.S. Attorney Called Grassley's Staff 'Stooges for the Gun Lobby' for Fast and Furious Probe," *Talking Points Memo*, Dec. 2, 2011, online at http://talkingpointsmemo.com/muckraker/ex-u-s-attorney-called-grassley-s-staff-stooges-for-the-gun-lobby-for-fast-and-furious-probe.

63. John Dodson, *op. cit.,* p. 189.

64. "ATF Fires Fast and Furious Whistleblower Agent Vince Cefalu." *Polisite*, online at http://www.politisite.com/2011/06/27/atf-fires-fast-and-furious-whistle-blower-agent-vince-cefalu.

65. Elisabeth Meinecke, "The DoJ Corruption that Led to Fast and Furious," *Townhall*, Jan. 30, 2012, online at http://townhall.com/tipsheet/elisabeth-meinecke/2012/01/30/diary_of_an_atf_whistleblower_and_the_corruption _that_led_to_fast_and_furious.

66. Interview of Kenneth Melson, p. 39, online at http://oversight.house.gov/ wp-content/uploads/2012/10/10-29-12-Exhibits-for-Fast-and-Furious-The-Anatomy-of-a-Failed-Operation-Part-II-of-III-Report.pdf.

67. Sari Horwitz, "Operation Fast and Furious: Gunrunning Sting Gone Wrong," *Washington Post*, July 26, 2011, online at https://www.washingtonpost.com/ investigations/us-anti-gunrunning-effort-turns-fatally-wrong/2011/07/14/ gIQAH5d6YI_story.html.

68. *Ibid.*

69. Richard Serrano, "Justice Department Trying to Shield Officials in Guns Scandal, ATF Chief Says," *The Daily Press*, July 19, 2011, online at http:// www.dailypress.com/la-na-guns-scandal-20110719-story.html.

70. Dennis Wagner, "House Memo: Entire Fast and Furious Mission Was a Failure," *USA Today*, Feb. 10, 2012, online at http://usatoday30.usatoday.com/ news/nation/story/2012-02-10/fast-furious/53037494/1; Richard Serrano, "Gun-smuggling Cartel Figures Possibly Were Paid FBI Informants," *Daily Press*, July 17, 2011, online at http://www.dailypress.com/la-na-cartel-guns -20110717-story.html.

71. John Dodson, *op. cit.*, p. 58.

72. *Hearings before the House Committee On Oversight and Gov't Reform, Operation Fast and Furious: The Other Side of the Border* (112th Cong., 1st Sess.) pp. 167–68 (July 26, 2011).

73. Judicial Watch, *Justice Department Documents Reveal Widespread use of Fast and Furious Weapons by Major Mexican Drug Cartels*, May 25, 2016, online at https://www.judicialwatch.org/press-room/press-releases/judicial-watch-justice-department-documents-reveal-widespread-use-fast-furious-weapons-major-mexican-drug-cartels-linked-least-69-killings.

74. Katie Pavlich, *op. cit.*, p. 126. These are all minimum figures, reflecting crimes after which the gun was recovered and traced. Crimes in which a Fast and Furious gun was used but the criminal left with it in his possession cannot be known.

75. Charlie Savage, "House Finds Holder in Contempt over Inquiry on Guns," *New York Times*, June 28, 2012, online at http://www.nytimes. com/2012/06/29/us/politics/fast-and-furious-holder-contempt-citation-battle.html?pagewanted=all&_r=0.

76.   Mary Michel, "Fast and Furious Cover-up Rewarded," *American Thinker*, Mar. 24, 2015, online at http://www.americanthinker.com/articles/2015/03/fast_and_furious_coverup_rewarded_in_appointment_of_new_atf_director.html.

77.   John Dobson, *op. cit.*, p. 280. This could happen because federal pay grades ("GS" for General Schedule levels) have much overlap. Each has ten "steps," which are climbed one per year at the outset, rising to one per two or three years at the higher steps. Thus, currently the base pay (i.e., without locality adjustments, which can be considerable) for a GS 14 step 1 is $88,136, and a GS 13 step 7 is $89,500.

78.   *Ibid.*

79.   Katie Pavlich, *op. cit.*, p. 117.

80.   Katie Pavlich, "After Inappropriate Firing, ATF Settles Lawsuit from Agent and Whistleblower Vince Cefalu," *Townhall*, Oct. 7, 2014, online at http://townhall.com/tipsheet/katiepavlich/2014/10/07/after-inappropriate-firing-atf-settle-lawsuit-with-agent-vince-cefalu-n1901826.

81.   "Univision Exposes Fast and Furious' Rising Body Count," *Investors' Business Daily*, Oct. 1, 2012, online at http://www.investors.com/politics/editorials/univision-reveals-fast-and-furious-murders/ (reporting estimates of 100 to 300 deaths resulting from Fast and Furious).

CHAPTER 8

1.   Joseph Mallia & Maggie Mulvihill, "Minister Dies as Cops Raid Wrong Apartment," online at http://www.druglibrary.org/think/~jnr/botched.htm.

2.   "Mistaken Drug Raid on Venice Mayor," *St. Louis Post-Dispatch*, June 5, 1992, p. 12.

3.   Some would term him, and not without reason, a Fascist. See Peter Moskos, "RIP Daryl Gates," *Cop in the Hood*, Apr. 16, 2010, online at http://www.copinthehood.com/2010/04/rip-daryl-gates.html.

4.   Donald Ostrow, "Casual Drug Users Should Be Shot, Gates Says," *Los Angeles Times*, Sept. 6, 1990, online at http://articles.latimes.com/1990-09-06/news/mn-983_1_casual-drug-users.

5.   Canning Kennedy, "Daryl Gates: The Thin Blue Line Between Personal and Structural Racism," *Colorlines*, online at http://www.colorlines.com/articles/daryl-gates-thin-blue-line-between-personal-and-structural-racism.

6.   Peter B. Kraska & Louis J. Cubellis, "Militarizing Mayberry and Beyond: Making Sense of American Paramilitary Policing," *Justice Quarterly*, vol. 14, p. 607 (1997), online at http://cjmasters.eku.edu/sites/cjmasters.eku.edu/files/mayberry.pdf.

7.   John Fund, "The United States of SWAT," *Mediachecker*, Apr. 18, 2014, online at https://mediachecker.wordpress.com/2014/04/18/the-united-states-of-swat.

8.   *Ibid.*

9.   See "Ex-Marine Shot by SWAT has Local Roots," *Nogales International*, May 12, 2001, online at http://www.nogalesinternational.com/news/ex-marine-shot-by-swat-has-local-roots/article_ad1df515-5c1a-5c65-a0da-ac-4ba356447b.html; "23 Seconds: Documents Show the May 5 SWAT Raid Moved Quickly," *KGUN TV*, June 10, 2011, online at http://www.webcitation.org/5zuTCDuuW; Fernada Echavarri, "SWAT Team Fired 71 Shots in Raid," *Arizona Daily Star*, May 11, 2011, online at http://tucson.com/news/local/crime/article_d7d979d4-f4fb-5603-af76-0bef206f8301.html; Tim Steller, "Let's Learn Something from Guerena Killing," *Arizona Daily Star*, Sept. 29, 2013, online at http://tucson.com/news/local/column/steller-let-s-learn-something-from-guerena-killing/article_d2079a62-f68c-5bdc-8b84-6e6eb60d7e87.html.

10.   Associated Press, "Police to Release Details of Fatal Drug Raid," *Santa Cruz* [CA] *Sentinel*, Jan. 28, 1993, p. 6; "Officer, Retiree Killed in Bogus Raid," *Sacramento Bee*, Jan. 26, 1994, online at http://www.druglibrary.org/think/~jnr/botched.htm.

11.   Joseph Mallia & Maggie Mulvihill, "Minister Dies as Cops Raid Wrong Apartment," online at http://www.druglibrary.org/think/~jnr/botched.htm; "Boston Oks $1 Million in Raid Death," *Chicago Tribune*, Apr. 25, 1996, online at http://articles.chicagotribune.com/1996-04-25/news/9604250226_1_police-commissioner-paul-evans-police-officer-informer; "Police Mistakes Cited in Death of Boston Man," *New York Times*, May 16, 1994, online at http://www.nytimes.com/1994/05/16/us/police-mistakes-cited-in-death-of-boston-man.html.

12.   Cheye M. Calvo, "Berwyn Heights Mayor Cheye Calvo Recalls Errant SWAT Raid," *Washington Post*, Sept. 20, 2009, online at http://www.washingtonpost.com/wp-dyn/content/article/2009/09/17/AR2009091701680.html. See also Radley Balko, *Rise of the Warrior Cop* (2014).

13.   "Shoot First, Ask Later," *Washington Post*, Aug. 7, 2008, online at http://www.washingtonpost.com/wp-dyn/content/article/2008/08/06/AR2008080602795.html.

14.   Kate Abbey-Lambertz, "Lawsuit Alleges Police Cover-Up in Fatal Shooting," *The Huffington Post*, Apr. 2, 2015, online at http://www.huffingtonpost.com/2015/04/02/aiyana-stanley-jones-lawsuit-conspiracy_n_6993756.html.

15.   Radley Balko, *op. cit.*, pp. 171, 249.

16. Eyder Peralta, "Arizona Sheriff Uses a Tank and Steven Seagal to Arrest a Cockfighting Suspect," *National Public Radio*, online at http://www.npr.org/sections/thetwo-way/2011/03/23/134803230/arizona-sheriff-uses-a-tank-to-arrest-cockfighting-suspect; Richard Ruelas and J. J. Hensley, "MCSO, Actor Seagal Sued over 2011 Arrest," *Arizona Republic*, Mar. 7, 2012, online at http://archive.azcentral.com/community/phoenix/articles/20120301mcso-seagal-sued-arrest.html.

17. Jim Fisher, "Did Veterans Affairs Police Kill Dialysis Patient Jonathan Montano?," *Jim Fisher True Crime*, June 23, 2015, online at http://jimfishertruecrime.blogspot.com/2014/05/did-veteran-affairs-police-kill.html.

18. Jim Armstrong, "FBI Uses Chainsaw in Raid on Wrong Fitchburg Apartment," *CBS Boston*, Jan. 31, 2012, online at http://boston.cbslocal.com/2012/01/31/fbi-uses-chainsaw-in-raid-on-wrong-fitchburg-apartment.

19. Taylor Wofford, "Former Cop Indicted in Maiming of Toddler in Botched SWAT Raid," *Newsweek*, July 28, 2015, online at http://www.newsweek.com/former-cop-indicted-maiming-toddler-botched-swat-raid-357570.

20. George Joseph, "New SWAT Documents Give Snapshot of the Ugly Militarization of U.S. Police," *The Intercept*, July 7, 2015, online at https://theintercept.com/2015/07/07/new-swat-documents-give-snapshot-ugly-militarization-u-s-police.

21. ACLU, *War Comes Home: The Excessive Militarization of American Policing*, online at https://www.aclu.org/sites/default/files/assets/jus14-warcomeshome-report-web-rel1.pdf.

22. Radley Balko, *op. cit*, p. 175.

23. Peter B. Kraska and Victor E. Kappeler, "Militarizing American Police: The Rise and Normalization of Paramilitary Units," *Social Problems*, vol. 44, p. 9 (1997).

24. *Ibid.*, p. 10.

25. Radley Balko, *op. cit*, p. 308.

26. Tom Coburn and Adam Andrzejewski, "Why Does the IRS Need Guns?" *Wall Street Journal*, June 17, 2016, online at http://www.wsj.com/articles/why-does-the-irs-need-guns-1466117176.

27. Candice Bernd, "USDA and Submachine Guns," *Truth-out*, June 7, 2014, online at http://www.truth-out.org/news/item/24186-usda-and-submachine-guns-latest-example-of-mission-creep-as-federal-policing-expands.

28. Radley Balko, *op. cit*, p. 243.

29. Jonathan S. Landay, "Police Tap High-Tech Tools of Military to Fight Crime," *Christian Science Monitor*, Apr. 2, 1997, online at http://www.csmonitor.com/1997/0402/040297.us.us.2.html.

30. Dwight D. Eisenhower, Farewell Speech, *Papers of the Presidents, Dwight D. Eisenhower*, pp. 1035–40 (1960).

31. P.L. 104–201, 110 Stat. 2639, codified as 10 U.S.C. §2576a.

32. Congressional Research Service, *The "1033 Program," Department of Defense Support to Law Enforcement*, Aug. 28, 2012, p. 3. Online at https://www.fas.org/sgp/crs/natsec/R43701.pdf.

33. *Ibid.*

34. Aaron Poynton, "Military and Civilian Resources," *Dom Prep Journal*, Sept. 2014, vol. 10, p. 24, online at http://www.webcitation.org/6XKhUGKS2?url=http%3A%2F%2Fwww.domesticpreparedness.com%2Fpub%2Fdocs%2FDPJSeptember14.pdf.

35. Arezou Rezvani, "MRAPs and Bayonets: What We Know About the Pentagon's 1033 Program," *National Public Radio*, Sept. 2, 2014, online at http://www.npr.org/2014/09/02/342494225/mraps-and-bayonets-what-we-know-about-the-pentagons-1033-program.

36. Radley Balko, *op. cit*, p. 240.

37. Robert Bottum, "Even Small Towns Are Loading up on Grenade Launchers," *The Federalist*, Dec. 19, 2014, online at http://thefederalist.com/2014/12/19/even-small-towns-are-loading-up-on-grenade-launchers.

38. Totals are taken from the interactive map at http://www.nytimes.com/interactive/2014/08/15/us/surplus-military-equipment-map.html.

39. Radley Balko, "Obama Moves to Demilitarize America's Police," *Washington Post*, May 18, 2015, online at https://www.washingtonpost.com/news/the-watch/wp/2015/05/18/obama-moves-to-demilitarize-americas-police.

40. Andrew Becker & G. W. Schulz, "Local Police Stockpile High-Tech, Combat-Ready Gear," *Center for Investigative Reporting*, Dec. 21, 2011, online at http://cironline.org/reports/local-police-stockpile-high-tech-combat-ready-gear-2913.

41. Dan Bauman, "Campus Police Acquire Military Weapons," *Chronicle of Higher Education*, Sept. 21, 2014, online at http://www.nytimes.com/2014/09/22/world/americas/campus-police-acquire-military-weapons.html.

42. Molly Knefel, "What Obama's New Military-Equipment Rules Mean for K-12 School Police," *Rolling Stone*, May 29, 2015, online at http://www.rollingstone.com/politics/news/what-obamas-new-military-equipment-rules-mean-for-k-12-school-police-20150529.

43. This factor was brought home by my experience in a Waco-related Freedom of Information Act lawsuit. The BATF, FBI, and the Department of Justice all lied repeatedly and outrageously to the court in order to conceal documents. The military just sent me the documents to which I was entitled.

CHAPTER 9

1. VA Office of Inspector General, *Veteran's Health Administration, Review of Alleged Patient Deaths, Patient Wait Times, and Scheduling Practices at the Phoenix VA Health Care System,* online at https://osc.gov/PublicFiles/ FY2016/16-41-DI-14-2839-DI-14-2975/16-41-DI-14-2839%20and%20 DI-14-2975%20Agency%20Report.pdf.

2. "Shinseki's statement on VA problems," *USA Today,* May 30, 2014, online at https://www.usatoday.com/story/news/nation/2014/05/30/shinseki-statement-veterans-affairs-problems/9763139.

3. Luke Rosiak, "VA Paid $871M in Medical Malpractice Deals in Past Decade," *Daily Caller,* Dec. 17, 2015, online at http://dailycaller.com/2015/12/17/ va-has-paid-230m-in-medical-malpractice-settlements.

4. Luke Rosiak, "Feds Return Nurse's Aide Accused of Manslaughter to Work," *The Libertarian Republic,* Dec. 11, 2015, online at http://thelibertarianrepublic.com/feds-return-nurses-aide-accused-of-manslaughter-to-work.

5. "Whistleblower describes encounter with new Phoenix VA Medical Center Director in 2012," *AZcentral,* online at http://www.azcentral.com/videos/ news/politics/investigations/2014/05/02/8595901.

6. "Triage" comes from military medicine, where it referred to the division of incoming wounded into three classes: those who will recover without further treatment, those who will die despite whatever treatment is available, and those who will recover with further treatment but may die without it. The last class gets the priority for treatment.

7. Office of Special Counsel, letter to the President, Sept. 17, 2015. Online at https://osc.gov/publicfiles/fy2015/15-40%20di-14-2754/15-40-di-14-2754 %20letter%20to%20the%20president.pdf.

8. Dennis Wagner, "Second VA doctor blows whistle on patient-care failures," *AZcentral,* May 1, 2014, online at http://www.azcentral.com/story/ news/investigations/2014/05/02/second-va-doctor-blows-whistle-patient-care-failures/8595863.

9. Dennis Wagner, "The Doctor Who Launched the VA Scandal," online at http://www.azcentral.com/story/news/arizona/investigations/2014/05/31/ va-scandal-whistleblower-sam-foote/9830057.

10. Merritt Hawkins, *2014 Survey, Physician Appointment Wait Times and Medicaid and Medicare Acceptance Rates,* online at https://www.merritt hawkins.com/uploadedfiles/merritthawkings/surveys/mha2014waitsurvpdf.pdf.

11. VA Office of the Inspector General, *Review of Alleged Patient Deaths, Patient Wait Times, and Scheduling Practices at the Phoenix VA Health Care System,* p. iii (Aug. 26, 2014).

12.   *Ibid.*

13.   VA Office of the Inspector General, *Access to Urology Service Phoenix VA Health Care System*, p. 4 (Oct. 15, 2015).

14.   *Ibid.*, pp. 11–13.

15.   Office of Special Counsel, letter to the President, Sept. 17, 2015, online at https://osc.gov/publicfiles/fy2015/15-40%20di-14-2754/15-40-di-14-2754%20letter%20to%20the%20president.pdf.

16.   VA Office of Inspector General, *Interim Report: Review of Alleged Shredding of Claims-Related Evidence at the VA Regional Office Los Angeles, California*, Aug. 17, 2015.

17.   VA Office of Inspector General, *Veterans Crisis Line Caller Response and Quality Assurance Concerns Canandaigua, New York*, Feb. 11, 2016.

18.   Edwin Mora, "VA Hospitals Potentially Exposed 2,609 Veterans to Infections," *CNS News*, Sept. 28, 2010, online at http://www.cnsnews.com/news/article/va-hospitals-potentially-exposed-2609-veterans-infections-such-hiv-and-hepatitis.

19.   "Anatomy of a Calamity," *Denver Post*, Aug. 9, 2015, online at http://extras.denverpost.com/aurora-va-hospital.

20.   U.S. Government Accountability Office, *VA's Actions to Address Cost Increases and Schedule Delays at Major Medical-Facility Projects*, p. 5 (2016), online at https://www.documentcloud.org/documents/2193893-gao-report-january-2015.html.

21.   "It's Not Just Phoenix," *The American Legion's Burn Pit*, online at http://burnpit.us/2014/05/its-not-just-phoenix.

22.   "VA Hospital May Have Infected 1,800 Veterans with HIV," *CNN*, July 1, 2010, online at http://www.cnn.com/2010/US/06/30/va.hospital.hiv.

23.   Travis J. Tritten, "House Considers Bill to Reclaim Implicated VA Managers' Bonuses," *Stars and Stripes*, Jan. 13, 2015, online at http://www.stripes.com/news/us/house-considers-bill-to-reclaim-implicated-va-managers-bonuses-1.323744.

24.   Mark Flatten, "Veterans Affairs Moves to fire Retiring Hospital Director," *Washington Examiner*, Sept. 26, 2014, online at http://www.washington-examiner.com/veterans-affairs-moves-to-fire-retiring-hospital-director/article/2554015.

25.   Bill Theobald, "More Bonuses for VA Employees Despite Ongoing Problems at the Agency," *USA Today*, Oct. 28, 2016, online at http://www.usa-today.com/story/news/politics/2016/10/28/more-bonuses-va-employees-despite-ongoing-problems-agency/92837218.

26.   Government Accounting Office, *VA Health Care: Actions Needed to Improve Administration of the Provider Performance Pay and Award Systems*, pp.

12–13, 27 (2013), online at http://docplayer.net/6458291-Va-health-care-actions-needed-to-improve-administration-of-the-provider-performance-pay-and-award-systems-report-to-congressional-requesters.html.

27. Office of Special Counsel, letter to the President, Sept. 17, 2015, online at https://osc.gov/publicfiles/fy2015/15-40%20di-14-2754/15-40-di-14-2754%20letter%20to%20the%20president.pdf.

28. Luisa Yanez, "Nurse Is Implicated in VA Patient's Death," *[Miami] Sun-Sentinel*, May 8, 1999, online at http://articles.sun-sentinel.com/1999-05-08/news/9905070751_1_blood-medical-assistance-nurse.

29. Jonah Bennett, "Most Recent Phoenix VA Whistleblower Suffers Retaliation after Filing Claim," *Daily Caller*, Apr. 20, 2015, online at http://dailycaller.com/2015/05/20/most-recent-phoenix-va-whistleblower-suffers-retaliation-after-filing-claim.

30. Tom Richards, "VA officials used medical records to smear Whistleblowers," *Watchdog*, Sept. 22, 2015, online at http://watchdog.org/239323/va-smear-campaign/.

31. Office of Special Counsel, letter to the President, Sept. 17, 2015, online at https://osc.gov/publicfiles/fy2015/15-40%20di-14-2754/15-40-di-14-2754%20letter%20to%20the%20president.pdf.

32. Tom Richards, "VA officials used medical records to smear Whistleblowers," *Watchdog*, Sept. 22, 2015, online at http://watchdog.org/239323/va-smear-campaign.

33. Luke Rosiak, "Senate Caves to All of Union's Demands on Veterans Affairs Firing Bill," *Daily Caller*, May 3, 2016, online at http://dailycaller.com/2016/05/03/senate-caves-to-all-of-unions-demands-on-veterans-affairs-firing-bill.

34. Nicole Ogrysko, "DoJ Says Key VA Choice Provision for SES Appeals Is Unconstitutional," *Federal News Radio*, June 3, 2016, online at http://federalnewsradio.com/workforce-rightsgovernance/2016/06/doj-says-key-va-choice-provision-ses-appeals-unconstitutional.

35. Online at https://en.wikipedia.org/wiki/Old_soldiers%27_home. The conqueror's perks arose from a nineteenth-century custom. Traditionally, an army that captured a resisting city would subject it to a "sack," during which conquering forces drank all available wine while engaging in rape, murder, looting, and arson. By the nineteenth century, this was frowned upon (the last major sack occurred when Wellington's army got out of control at the siege of Badajoz in 1812). It was, however, felt that the conquerors should at least be compensated for having waived their rights to a sack, and so conquered towns would negotiate and pay an agreed-upon price for this. By custom, one-third of the price went to the victorious commander, so that by the end of the Mexican War General Scott had quite a bit of ready cash.

36. See Office of Personnel Management, *Healthcare & Insurance*, online at https://www.opm.gov/healthcare-insurance/healthcare/plan-information/plans/.

37. Online at https://www.opm.gov/healthcare-insurance/healthcare/plan-in-formation/plan-codes/2017/brochures/71-005.pdf.

CONCLUSION

1. 346 U.S. 15, 50.

2. *Discretionary Function Exemption of the Federal Tort Claims Act and the Radiation Exposure Compensation Act: Hearings before the Subcommittee on Administrative Law and Governmental Relations of the House Judiciary Committee*, 91 (1989).

3. U.S. Department of State, "Departmental History," online at https://history.state.gov/departmenthistory.

4. Henry Barrett Learned, "The Attorney General and the Cabinet," *Political Science Quarterly*, vol. 24, p. 444 (1909).

5. "Federal Employees by State," *Governing*, online at http://www.governing.com/gov-data/federal-employees-workforce-numbers-by-state.html; "Automotive Spotlight," online at https://www.selectusa.gov/automotive-industry-united-states.

6. Chris Edwards, "Federal Workers Earning More Than $100,000," *Cato*, Feb. 5, 2016, online at https://www.cato.org/blog/federal-workers-earning-more-100000.

7. "List of Highest-Income Counties in the United States," Wikipedia, online at https://en.wikipedia.org/wiki/List_of_highest-income_counties_in_the_United_States. The median family incomes for the four Washington suburb counties range from $117,876 to $100,474. Marin and Santa Clara Counties, California, come in at $90,535 and $91,425.

8. Carol Hardy Vincent, Laura Hanson, and Jerome Bjelopera, "Federal Land Ownership: Overview and Data," Congressional Research Service, Dec. 29, 2014, online at http://fas.org/sgp/crs/misc/R42346.pdf.

9. *Dugard v. United States*, 835 F.3d 915 (9th Cir. 2016).

10. *Myslakowski v. United States*, 806 F.2d 94 (6th Cir. 1986), reversing *Galanos v. United States*, 608 F. Supp. 360 (E.D. Mich. 1985).

11. *Wysinger v. United States*, 784 F.2d 1252 (5th Cir. 1986).

12. *LM, Guardian v. United States*, 344 F.3d 695 (7th Cir. 2003).

13. Jonathan R. Bruno, "Immunity for 'Discretionary' Functions: A Proposal to Amend the Federal Tort Claims Act," *Harvard Journ. on Legislation*, vol. 49, pp. 411, 412 (2012).

14. *United States v. Gaubert*, 499 U.S. 315, 324–25 (1991).

15.   *Kiehn v. United States*, 984 F.2d 1100 (10th Cir. 1993).

16.   *Childers v. United States*, 40 F.3d 973 (9th Cir. 1995).

17.   *Petzneck v. United States*, 575 F. Supp. 698 (D. Neb. 1983).

18.   *Kennesaw Irrigation District v. United States*, 880 F.2d 1018 (9th Cir. 1989).

19.   *Spillway Marina v. United States*, 445 F.2d 876 (10th Cir. 1971).

20.   Walter Gellhorn & Louis Lauer, "Federal Liability for Personal and Property Damages," *N.Y. Univ. Law Review*, vol. 29, p. 1325 (1954).

21.   *Smith v. Jones-Manville Corp.*, 795 F.2d 301 (3d Cir. 1986).

22.   28 U.S.C. §2679. The statute was a response to *Westfall v. Erwin*, 484 U.S. 292 (1988), where the Supreme Court held that a federal supervisor's actions (allowing a toxic chemical to be stored where it could harm another federal employee) was not protected because the actions were not within the supervisor's discretion. Congress apparently found this too appalling.

23.   *Garcia v. United States*, 23 F.3d 609 (5th Cir. 1994).

24.   *McHugh v. University of Vermont*, 966 F.2d 67 (1992).

25.   *Tom Lowery v. United States*, No. 15-4972-DDC-KGS, online at https://ecf.ksd.uscourts.gov/cgi-bin/show_public_doc?2015cv4972-9.

26.   *United States v. Olsen*, 737 F.3d 625 (9th Cir. 2013) (Kozinski, J., dissenting).

27.   Rule 6(e), Federal Rules of Criminal Procedure.

28.   353 U.S. 657 (1957).

29.   18 U.S. Code §3500.

30.   18 U.S. Code §3500(a).

31.   Comment, "Criminal Discovery at and Before the Preliminary Examination," *Santa Clara Lawyer*, vol. 15, p. 665 (1975).

32.   Laural L. Hooper, Jennifer E. Marsh, and Brian Yeh, "Treatment of *Brady v. Maryland* Material in United States District and State Courts' Rules, Orders, and Policies, Report to the Advisory Committee on Criminal Rules of the Judicial Conference of the United States," (2004), online at http://www.fjc.gov/public/pdf.nsf/lookup/BradyMat.pdf/$file/BradyMat.pdf.

33.   *TVA v. Hill*, 437 U.S. 153 (1978).

34.   An obscure endangered plant found in Maine. In the course of representing U.S. Fish and Wildlife Service, the author occasionally heard it discussed.

35.   A majority of courts apply the "hard look" standard to assessing agency compliance with the National Environmental Protection Act. See *Sierra Club v. U.S. Forest Service*, 46 F.3d 835 (8th Cir. 1995); *Hughes River Watershed Conservancy v. Glicksman*, 81 F.3d 437 (4th Cir. 1996); *Ocean Advocates v. U.S. Army Corps of Engineers*, 402 F.3d 846 (9th Cir. 2005).

ACKNOWLEDGMENTS

My thanks go, first, to my agent, Pamela Leigh, who introduced me to Skyhorse, and to Donna Weisner, who put in many hours editing the manuscript before it was submitted. I also owe much to my editor at Skyhorse, Olga Greco, who likewise put in much effort (largely on persuading me to clarify the obscure). For assistance on the Randy Weaver affair, I thank my friend Jim Norell. On the Waco chapter, many people have helped over the years. Some of them are no longer with us: Mike McNulty, Gordon Novel, Carlos Ghigliotti. Others, I am happy to say, remain: in particular Dan Gifford, Barbara Grant, and Carol Moore. On Fast and Furious, we all are indebted to David Codrea and the late Mike Vanderboegh.

INDEX

A

Abdullah, Crown Prince, 118

Adams, Dave, 132

Aidid, Hussein, 117

Aidid, Mohamed, 116

Air Marshals

    arming, 132–33

    dress codes, 133

Allen, Irene, 38

Allen v. United States, 39–41

al-Qaeda, 118, 126–27

Alt, Larry, 148

ammonium nitrate, 10–14

Arnold, Phillip, 104–05

Arpaio, Joe, 167

Aryan Nations, 63, 64

assassination ban, 123–24

Atomic Energy Commission, 27, 30–32, 33

atomic testing

    human cost, 26–29

    sheep losses, 32–33

    cover-ups, 33–35

    lawsuits, 38–42

B

Baer, Robert, 17

Bain, Sarah, 87

Balko, Radley, 168

Baumgartner, Henry, 10

Brady requirement, 196

    violations, 113

Berger, Sandy, 118–21

Berkowitz v. United States, 21–22

Bivens civil rights lawsuits, 5

Blum, Prof. Deborah, 5

Border Patrol, BORTAC operations, 135–36

Boston Massacre, 2

Bowler, Willard, 39

Brandon, Thomas, 162

British Petroleum explosion, 22–23

Brown, Michael, 171

Brown, Dr. William, 56

Bureau of Alcohol, Tobacco, Firearms and Explosives

    at Ruby Ridge, 63–64

    at Waco, 87–91, 96–103

    in Operation Fast and Furious, 137–40

Breuer, Lanny, 140

Butrico, Frank, 27–28, 34, 39

Burger, Warren, 23

Burke, Dennis, 142–44, 151–55, 157–58, 161–62

Bush, George H. W., 119

Bush, George W., 125–26

Buxtun, Peter, 55–58

Byrne grants for drug enforcement, 170

C

Calvo, Cheye, 165

Capone, Al, 45, 51

Cavanaugh, Jim, 87

Cefalu, Vince, 159, 162

Chernobyl reactor disaster, 28

Chojnacki, Phillip, 112

Churchill, Prof. Robert H., 127

Clarke, Richard, 125–27

Clark, Dr. Taliaferro, 48, 49–50, 53

CleanUpATF.org, 154

Clinton, Bill, 116–120, 123

Clinton, Hillary, 135, 146

Codrea, David, 154–55, 241

Cooper, Larry, 66, 67, 80

Coulson, Danny, 61, 69, 73, 77, 79–80, 81, 82

CS "tear gas," 108

Cutler, Dr. John, 56

Cuyler, Christopher, 90

D

Daigo Fukuryu Maru ship, 41

Dalehite, Elizabeth, 9, 10

Dalehite, Captain Henry, 9, 10

Dalehite v. United States, 18–21

Danforth, John, 112–13

Davidian Church
    beliefs, 87–88
    members killed, 111
    members imprisoned, 112

Declaration of Independence, 1, 3, 201

Deitrick, Col. Carroll, 14

Degan, William, 66, 68, 70, 79, 80

Department of Justice, 18, 19, 39, 40, 62, 64, 78–80, 83–85, 113, 128, 136, 160, 194

Detty, Mike, 137, 138, 139

Dibble, Dr. Eugene, 47, 48, 52

Dirty Harry atomic test, 26–28

discretionary function exception. *See* Federal Tort Claims Act

Dodson, John, 135, 147–152, 158, 161, 162

Doyle, Clive, 88, 107

Doyle, Sherri, 88

Dunning, Dr. Gordon, 34–35, 36

E

Ehrlich, Dr. Paul, 46

Embassy bombings in Kenya and Tanzania, 119

Erwa, General Elfatih, 122

Evans, Ronald, 65–66

F

FBI
    at Ruby Ridge, 69–78
    at Waco, 91–96
    and terrorism, 128
    concealed evidence in "zero files," 113
    laboratory scandal, 66

Federal Tort Claims Act
    origin, 6
    discretionary function exception, 6–7, 20–23, 40–41, 58–59, 189–90, 191
    at Waco, 109
    success rate in court, 189
    encourages dangerous conduct, 187–88
    intentional tort exception, 193

Field, Justice Stephen, 4, 83

flash-bang grenades, 166, 168

Foote, Dr. Sam, 177–78

Freedom of Information Act, 95, 102

Freeh, Louis, 118–19

Fund, John, 164

Fukushima nuclear reactor, 28

G

Garrido, Phillip, 187
Gates, Daryl, 164
Gazecki, Bill, 95
George III, 1, 2, 201
Gerson, Stuart, 185
Ghigliotti, Carlos, 241
Gifford, Dan, 95, 241
Gillett, George, 154, 158–59
Glenn, Gene, 70
Gofman, Dr. John, 25
Gowdy, Rep. Trey, 150
Grandcamp, ship, 15–16, 18
Grant, Barbara, 241
Grassley, Sen. Chuck, 155, 156, 159–60
Gray, Fred D., 58–59
Griffin, Richard, 175
Gritz, James "Bo," 77–78
growth of federal employment, 186–87
grand jury abuse, 196–97
Guerena, Jose, 164–65

H

Haralson, Dale, 38
Harper, Dr. John, 56
Harris, Kevin, 62, 67–72, 75–79, 81
Heller, Jean, 58
Heller, Dr. J. R., 53
Heller, Dr. John, 43
Hellman, Sharon, 176, 183–84
Herbert, Dexter, 166
Hezbollah, 118
High Flyer, ship, 17
Hiroshima, 30
Holder, Attorney General Eric, 135, 141, 152, 162
Holifield, Rep. Chester E., 25
Hoover, William, 141

Horiuchi, Lon
    shoots at Weavers, 74–75
    testifies, 80
    is prosecuted, 82, 85
Ron Howen, 78, 80–81

I

In re Neagle, 83
Indian Towing v. United States, 21
Intolerable Acts, 2
Iodine-131, 28, 35, 36
Issa, Rep. Darrell, 159–60

J

Jackson, Elmer, 27
Jackson, Justice Robert H., 185
Jahn, Ray, 106
Jamar, Jeff, 110–11
James, Dr. Reginald, 52
Jencks Act, 197
Jencks v. United States, 197
Johnston, Bill, 113
Jones, Aiyana Stanley, 166
Judgment Fund, 82, 176

K

Kennedy, Judge T. M., 19–20
Khobar Towers bombing, 117–18
Kipling, Rudyard, 9
Knapp, Harold, 36
Kootenai Indian War, 62
Koresh, David, 87, 88, 90, 92, 93.
    calls 911 during gun fight, 102
    wounded, 103
    calls BATF Agent Cavanaugh
        during gun fight, 103
    tells negotiators is ready to come
        out, 105

L

Laird, Martha, 25
Larson, Dr. Eric, 109
Lee, Robert E., 3
Leigh, Pamela, 241
Lewis, Edward B., 36
Llovera, Jesus Sanchez, 167
Luna, Julio, 16
Lynch, Sheriff's Lieutenant Larry, 103
Lynch, Loretta, 183–84
Lyon, Dr. Joseph L., 25, 37–38

M

Mannering, Agatha, 27
MacAllister, Hope, 162
Matthews, Ellie, 78
Marshall, Chief Justice John, 3
Martin, Wayne, 102–03
McNulty, Mike, 95–96, 113, 241
Meinecke, Elisabeth, 159
Melson, Kenneth, 156, 160
methylene chloride, 108–09
Millar, Dr. J. D., 58
Miniter, Richard, 124–25
Mitchell, Dr. Katherine, 176–77
Mogadishu (Somalia), 116–17
Monsanto Corporation, 18
Moore, Carol, 241
Moore, Dr. Joseph, 48
Mount Carmel, 87, 88, 90–91
Moussaoui, Zacarias, 116
      arrested, 120–21
      FBI declines to search, 130
Murphy, Mark, 166
Myslakowski v. United States, 187

N

Nagasaki, 30
National Firearms Act, 63

National Intelligence Estimate, 122–23
National Security Council, 126
Neagle, David, 4
Nelson, Oleta, 27
Neumann, Keith, 166
Neosalvarsan, 46, 48, 51
Nevin, David, 78
Nevin, Edward, 57
Newell, William, 143, 144, 145, 150,
      151, 153–54, 155
Noesner, Gary, 69, 81–82
Norell, Jim, 241
Northern Front, 124–25
Novel, Gordon, 241

O

Obama, Barack, 141
Operation Fast and Furious, 141–162
Operation Wide Receiver, 138, 141

P

Pare, Ambroise, 44
Parks, Rosa, 58
Patriot Act, 132
Pendleton, Prof. Robert C., 35
penicillin, 47
Peterson, Chuck, 78
Pollard, Charles, 58
Posner, Gerald, 121
Project Megiddo, 116, 128
Potts, Larry, 70, 77, 79, 82
Powell, Sidney, 81
private bills, 6

R

Ramirez, Manuel Medina, 165
Reno, Janet, 105, 106, 112, 113
Revelation, Book of, 103–05
Roderick, Arthur, 67

Rodriguez, Robert, 90
Rogers, Dick, 69–71
    at Ruby Ridge, 82–82
    at Waco, 109–111
Rolince, Mike, 120
Rosenwald Foundation, 47
Rowley, Coleen, 130–31
Ruby Ridge *see also* Weaver family
    BATF involvement, 63–64
rules of engagement changed, 70–71
    Sammy Weaver killed, 67
    Vicki Weaver killed, 75–76
    Department of Justice report, 71
    civil suit, 82

S
Salvarsan, 46, 49
Salisbury, Morse, 34
Sarabyn, Charles, 112
Schatz, Dr. Irwin, 55
Scott, General Winfield, 184
Scottsdale Gun Club, 146
Seagal, Steven, 187
Sedan atomic test, 35
Shinseki, General Eric, 175, 184
Sepulveda, Alberto, 167
Sexton, Gregory, 71
sovereign immunity, 2–3
Spence, Gerry, 78, 85
Spence, Kent, 78
Stalin, Josef, 29
Stevens, Sen. Ted, 80
Supremacy Clause, 83–84
SWAT teams
    origin of term, 163
    spread of concept, 164, 168–69,
        173–74
    federal use, 169
    minor agencies creating, 170

federal grants for creation, 173
    accidental shootings, 166–67
syphilis
    origin, 43
    stages, 44
    symptoms, 45

T
Tabor, James, 104–05
Terry, David, 4
Terry, Brian, 136, 152, 161
Texas City explosion
    causes, 11–14
    death toll, 16–17
    litigation, 18–21
    private bill, 23
Thibodeau, David, 100
Thompsett, Dr. Richard, 33
Thonetheva, Wanis, 167

U
USS *Cole* bombing, 120–21
U.S. Postal Service
    sells unsafe jeeps, 187
    "Lester the Molester," 189
United States v. Lee, 3–4
United States v. Varig Airlines, 21, 37, 40
Udall, Stewart, 38–39
Utah cancer registry, 37

V
Vanderboegh, Mike, 154–55, 241
Veterans Administration hospital system
    origins, 184
    malpractice payments, 176
    punishment of whistleblowers,
        182–83
    bonuses, 181–82
Vinzant, Carol, 99

Vonderlehr, Dr. R. A., 49, 50, 51, 52, 53, 54

Voth, David, 143, 144, 146, 148–50, 152

"giddy" over guns at Mexican crime scenes, 162

W

Waco

Feb. 28 fire fight, 90–91, 18–102

machine gun claims, 100–101

radio van tapes, 101–02

conflict between Hostage Rescue Team and negotiators, 105–06

Apr. 19 fire, 106–07

vanishing evidence, 93–94

Waco: The Rules of Engagement documentary, 95

Weaver family. *See also* Ruby Ridge

Elisheba Weaver, 75, 76

Randy Weaver, 61–82

Rachel Weaver, 75

Sammy Weaver, 61, killed, 67

Sara Weaver, 74, 75

Vicki Weaver, 61, 62, 74, killed 75, 76, 79

Weisner, Donna, 241

Weiss, Dr. Edward, 36–37

Weich, Ronald, 156–57

Wenger, Dr. O. C., 51, 54

Westfall Act, 193

Wheeler, Sharon, 89

Whipple, Keith, 26–27

Whipple, Kent, 27

Whistleblower Protection Act, 155

Whitcomb, Christopher, 105–06

White, Gordon Eliot, 37

Whitehurst, Frederic, 66

Williams, Rev. Accelyne, 165

Wilkinson, Monte, 152

Williams, Kenneth, 129

Wolff, Dr. Arthur, 33

Y

Y2K computer bug, 128

Yobs, Dr. Anne, 55